No limit to what YOU can do!

Sky's the limit

2de

A2/B1

Sous la direction de

Séraphine Lansonneur
Agrégée
Professeure et formatrice (75)

et

Anne Wilkinson
Agrégée
Professeure (49)

Myriam Amrous
Agrégée
Professeure (93)

Sarah Bisson
Agrégée
Professeure et formatrice (75)

Damienne FitzPatrick
Certifiée
Professeure (49)

Hélène Koch
Agrégée
Professeure et formatrice (75)

avec la contribution de

Vincent Burgatt
(banque d'exercices de grammaire)
Certifié
Professeur (75)

bordas
éditeur

Les auteurs tiennent à remercier chaleureusement Kelly Usseglio-Viretta pour sa contribution.

L'éditeur tient à remercier chaleureusement les enseignants consultés lors d'études réalisées en cours de conception de Sky's the limit 2de*. Leurs contributions ont permis d'enrichir le concept, pour une meilleure adéquation aux besoins et usages des professeurs et des élèves de lycée. Nous remercions tout particulièrement : Mme E. Alain (75), Mme P. Duval (75), Mme C. Landès (75), Mme D. Mitchell (93), Mme O. Prebay (75), Mme L. Puch (91), Mme C. Salpétrier (78).*

L'éditeur tient à remercier chaleureusement Évelyne et Joëlle pour leur efficacité et leur bonne humeur et Octave, toujours disponible, volontaire et prêt à partager ses goûts de lycéen.

CECR

En **LVA**, les élèves de **Seconde** confortent leur niveau **B1** du Cadre européen commun de référence pour les langues vivantes (**CECR**, 2001) pour atteindre le niveau **B2** à la fin de la **Terminale**.

En **LVB**, les élèves de **Seconde** consolident et complètent leur niveau **A2** pour atteindre le niveau **B1** à la fin de la **Terminale**.

Un **volume complémentaire du CECR avec de nouveaux descripteurs** a été publié en 2018.

Des **grilles pour l'auto-évaluation, incluant l'interaction à l'écrit et la médiation**, sont disponibles p. 177-182 de ce volume, consultable et téléchargeable à l'adresse suivante :
https://rm.coe.int/cecr-volume-complementaire-avec-de-nouveaux-descripteurs/16807875d5

Vous trouverez les pdf des **grilles des niveaux A1 à B2,** ainsi que du **nouveau programme de Seconde,** paru au BOS n° 1 du 22/1/2019, **sur le site** lycee.editions-bordas.fr.

Réception	Interaction	Production	Médiation
Écouter	Interaction orale	Production orale	Médiation de textes
Lire	Interaction écrite et en ligne	Production écrite	Médiation de concepts
			Médiation de la communication

Édition : Josiane Attucci-Jan
Responsable d'édition : Céline Ullas assistée de Virginie Lassarre puis Amandine Chappet
Directrice éditoriale : Véronique Gilles de la Londe
Directeur artistique : Pierre Taillemite
Droits étrangers : Aurore Kauffmann
Iconographie : Sophie Suberbère et ponctuellement Annie-Claure Auliard
Concept graphique : David Bart
Réalisation intérieure : Évelyne Boyard et Joëlle Parreau
Relecture : Gilles Chauvin
Fabrication : Françoise Leroy
Gravure : Irilys
Réalisation sonore : Les studios de la Seine
Direction d'acteurs : Adrien Hermans

ISBN 978-2-04-733584-0

FlashPAGE

L'art de vivre ensemble, thématique du **nouveau programme de Seconde** applicable à la rentrée 2019, se décline selon **huit axes** :

- Vivre entre générations
- Les univers professionnels, le monde du travail
- Le village, le quartier, la ville
- Représentation de soi et rapport à autrui
- Sports et société
- La création et le rapport aux arts
- Sauver la planète, penser les futurs possibles
- Le passé dans le présent

Le programme stipule qu'il faut aborder « au moins **six de ces huit axes dans l'année**, selon un ordre choisi par l'enseignant, **chacun d'eux étant envisagé à travers une à trois séquences** portant sur des problématiques qui y sont reliées ».

Pour chacun de ces axes, Sky's the limit 2de propose deux séquences.

Les langues vivantes font partie du **tronc commun** et à ce titre font l'objet de **trois épreuves communes en cours d'année en classes de Première et de Terminale comptant pour le baccalauréat.**

Sky's the limit 2de y prépare en douceur.

- 1re **épreuve** (2e trimestre de Première) : **Compréhension de l'oral** et **Expression écrite**
- 2e **épreuve** (3e trimestre de Première) : **Compréhension de l'écrit** et **Expression écrite**
- 3e **épreuve** (2e trimestre de Terminale) : **Compréhension de l'oral**, **Compréhension de l'écrit** et **Expression écrite** + **Expression orale**

→ Voir détails p. 5

Le nouveau programme de 2de avec le tableau des descripteurs des activités langagières est mis à disposition sur notre site compagnon lycee.editions-bordas.fr.

Sommaire des pages de début

Réussir en anglais avec Sky's the limit

16 séquences pour découvrir différentes facettes du monde anglophone

AU CHOIX

◆ **11 séquences avec 2 doubles-pages de leçon**

Rappel de l'axe

Actions à réaliser en bleu

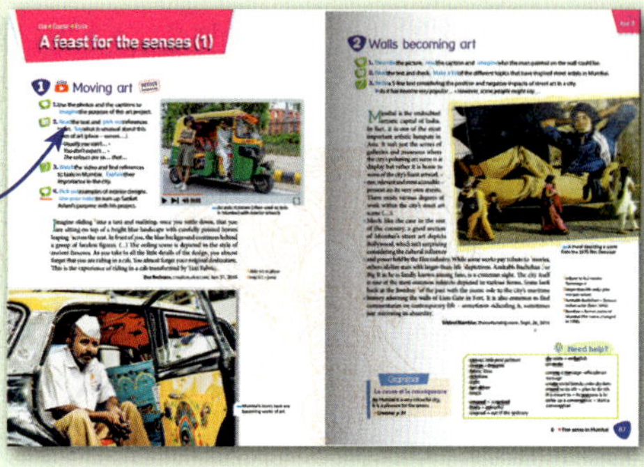

Dossier documentaire

Ici, par exemple, activité de médiation

Préparation au projet de fin de séquence

◆ **5 Séquence + avec 4 doubles-pages de leçon dont 1 double-page Différenciation** pour accompagner tous vos élèves

38 *Worksheets* disponibles dans le manuel numérique et sur le site enseignant

2 à 3 *topics*

1er temps : chaque élève travaille sur l'un des *topics*

2e temps : mise en commun des connaissances en groupe

Étude de la langue en contexte pour améliorer la compréhension et l'expression

AUTONOMIE

◆ **Le lexique**

> Dans chaque ouverture de séquence, BASICS pour réactiver le lexique vu au collège WORKSHEET

> 1 page ou 1 double-page *Words*

Activités numériques autocorrectives pour rebrasser le lexique

Carte mentale du lexique : essentiel de la séquence à écrire et écouter

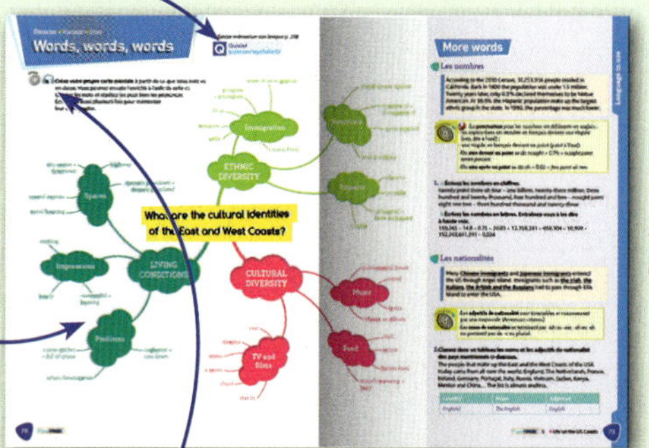

Enregistrement de tous les mots pour bien les prononcer

◆ **La grammaire et la phonologie**

> 1 à 3 faits de langue

> 1 point de phonologie

> Repères grammaticaux et phonologiques

Rappel de la règle

Comparaison français-anglais

Nombreux exercices d'entraînement

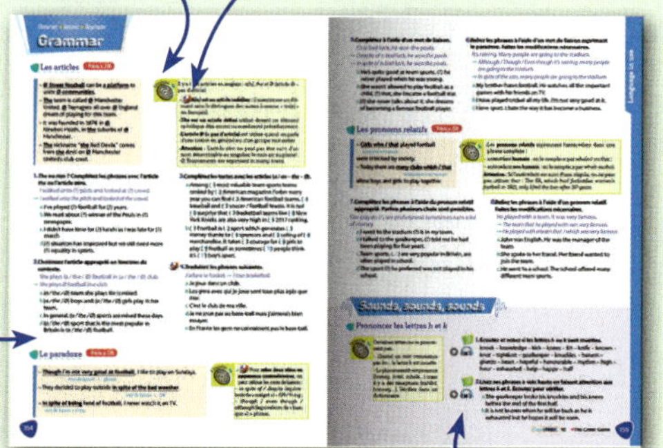

Exercices d'entraînement avec MP3 pour la phonologie

→ **Une banque d'exercices de grammaire interactifs autocorrectifs est accessible via le manuel numérique**

Une approche par projet pour réinvestir les acquis

◆ Correspondance entre la stratégie et le projet pour une mise en œuvre immédiate

AUTONOMIE

16 pages de stratégie pour favoriser l'autonomie (liste, cf p. 12)

Ici, par exemple, expression écrite en interaction

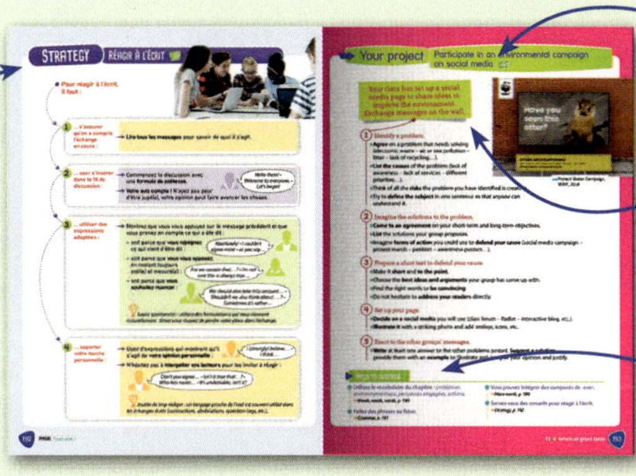

Ici, par exemple, expression écrite en interaction

Projet pour réinvestir les compétences et les connaissances acquises dans la séquence

Rappel des outils pour réussir le projet

Entraînement en douceur aux deux premières épreuves communes en cours d'année de 1re

AUTONOMIE

Vers le BAC

◆ Entraînement ❶
Compréhension de l'oral (cf p. 64)

◆ Entraînement ❷
Compréhension de l'oral et expression écrite (cf p. 128)

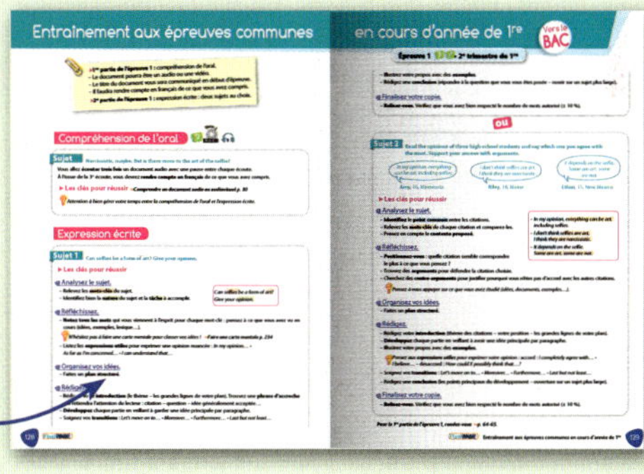

Conseils

◆ Entraînement ❸
Compréhension de l'écrit et expression écrite (cf p. 180)

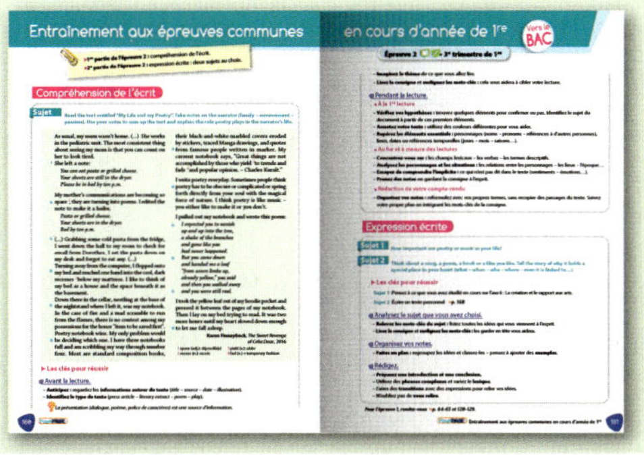

Sommaire

L'art de vivre ensemble

– Au moins **6 axes** et **1 à 3 séquence(s) par axe** dans l'année
– **Varier les thématiques** et préserver la **motivation** de vos élèves
– Avoir la possibilité d'**approfondir**

Avec Sky's the limit, c'est possible :
☑ Un **choix** de **16 séquences** déclinées selon les **8 axes** du nouveau programme ; **2 séquences** par axe.
☑ Une **variété de documents authentiques** et **accessibles.**
☑ **11 séquences** déjà riches et complètes pour travailler efficacement
☑ **5** « Séquences + » pour aller plus loin :
+ de documents,
+ une double page Différenciation,
+ de points grammaticaux et de lexique en contexte.
☑ **38** *Worksheets* (1 *Worksheet* BASICS et 2 ou 3 *Worksheets* Différenciation par séquence)

Axe 1 Vivre entre générations

1 Hanging out

How can shared spaces bring people together?

2 Between generations in South Africa

Can generations learn from one another?

Axe 2 Les univers professionnels, le monde du travail

3 Transition Year Ireland

How can school help us to discover career possibilities?

4 Finding your way

How can personal implication give you ideas for your future?

Axe 3 Le village, le quartier, la ville

5 Life on the US Coasts Séquence +

What are the cultural identities of the East and West Coasts?

6 Five senses in Mumbai

How can the five senses contribute to discovering a city?

Axe 4 Représentation de soi et rapport à autrui

7 Our fashion matters Séquence +

What do our clothes say about us and our society?

8 Self(ie)-portraits Séquence +

How are portraits, self-portraits and selfies related?

Compréhension de l'oral · Expression orale en continu · Expression orale en interaction · Compréhension de l'écrit · Expression écrite · Expression écrite en interaction · Pairwork · Groupwork · Médiation de textes, de concepts, de la communication

vidéo · Classe / Piste 1 · 1 = MP3

Sommaire

Compréhension de l'oral · Expression orale en continu · Expression orale en interaction · Compréhension de l'écrit · Expression écrite · Expression écrite en interaction · Pairwork · Groupwork · Médiation de textes, de concepts, de la communication

vidéo · Classe / Piste 1 · = MP3

Liste des vidéos dans le manuel numérique et sur le site enseignant

Outils pour enrichir son lexique et améliorer sa prononciation

- Tous les mots des cartes mentales sont enregistrés. Écoutez-les pour mieux les prononcer.
- Entraînez-vous à la prononciation et l'accentuation grâce aux MP3 des *Sounds*.
- Entraînez-vous aux épreuves communes en cours d'année de 1re : épreuve 1, compréhension de l'oral.

Vers le BAC

Liste des MP3 disponibles

Les MP3 sont consultables et téléchargeables gratuitement
avec l'application FlashPAGE
et sur le site **lycee.editions-bordas.fr**,
et accessibles sur le manuel numérique.

Outils pour réussir et gagner en autonomie en 2de

Dans le manuel

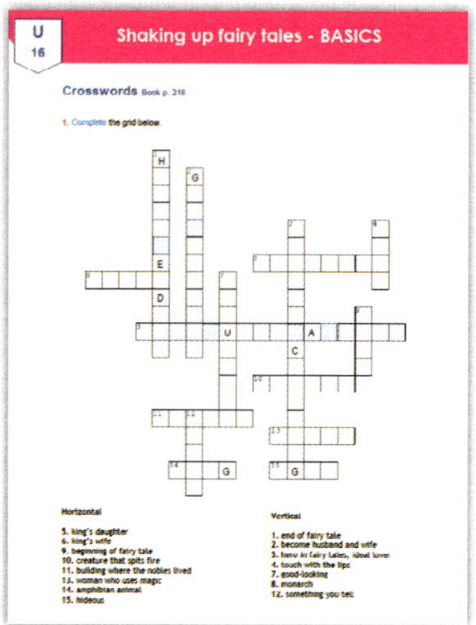

▶ **Renvois vers les mots croisés pour rebrasser le lexique vu au collège** WORKSHEET
(ressources PDF FlashPAGE et lycee.editions-bordas.fr)

▶ **Stratégie en contexte au sein de chaque unité**

Stratégie de réception

Stratégie de production

Stratégie d'interaction

Stratégie de médiation Médiation

▶ **Outils pour réussir**

Stratégie transversale

Repères et banque d'exercices

En numérique

▶ **Activités *Quizlet* pour réviser le lexique de la séquence**

▶ **Banque d'exercices grammaticaux autocorrectifs**

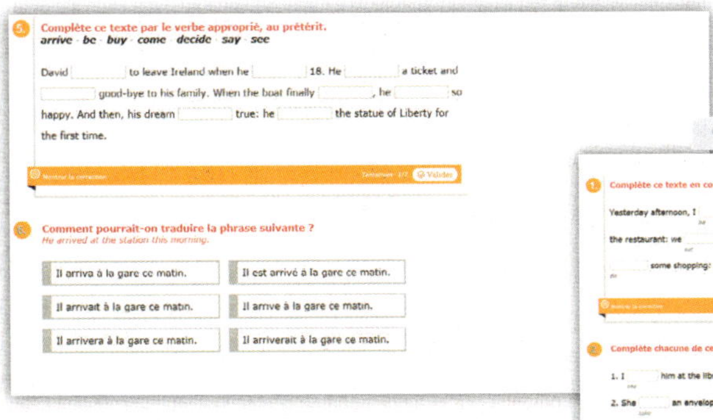

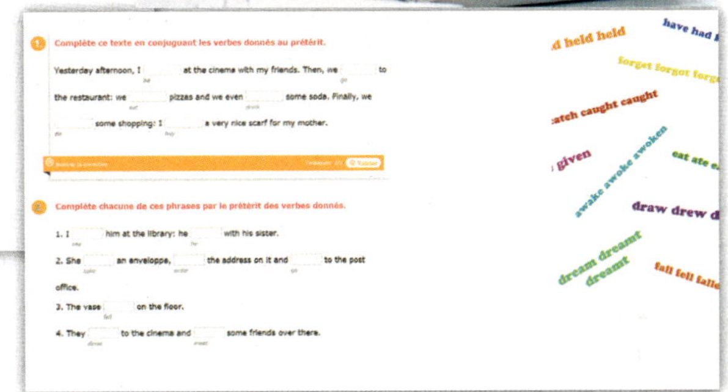

Outils pour se préparer aux épreuves de 1re BAC

▶ **En anglais**

Entraînement en douceur aux deux premières épreuves communes en classe de 1re comptant pour le baccalauréat

- Entraînement 1 – Compréhension de l'oral – *64-65*
- Entraînement 2 – Compréhension de l'oral et expression écrite – *128-129*
- Entraînement 3 – Compréhension de l'écrit et expression écrite – *180-181*

▶ **Dans toutes les matières**

Tuto : Tutoriels vidéo pour l'oral

Disponibles avec FlashPAGE, sur lycee.editions-bordas.fr et dans le manuel numérique

- **Tuto** : Prendre la parole en public
- **Tuto** : Se présenter
- **Tuto** : Faire un exposé
- **Tuto** : Débattre
- **Tuto** : Mener une interview
- **Tuto** : Lire un texte littéraire
- **Tuto** : L'épreuve orale de français : l'explication de texte
- **Tuto** : L'épreuve orale de français : l'entretien

Chaque vidéo propose des conseils et des exercices (à faire par les élèves, seul(e) ou à deux, ou en groupe), avec pour chacune une fiche mémo et une grille d'évaluation en pdf.

English is everywhere

The quiz

1 Quel est le point commun entre les Bahamas, le Liberia et Singapour ?

a. Il y fait beau toute l'année.
b. La mer n'est jamais loin.
c. La langue officielle est l'anglais.

2 De combien de pays dans le monde l'anglais est-il la langue officielle ?

a. 25
b. 40
c. 75

3 Pour combien de personnes dans le monde l'anglais est-il la première langue ?

a. 525 millions
b. 375 millions
c. 215 millions

4 On dit *chips* aux États-Unis mais *crisps* en Grande-Bretagne. Saurez-vous dire d'où viennent les mots…

a. *sweater* et *jumper* ?
b. *flat* et *apartment* ?
c. *lift* et *elevator* ?
d. *candy* et *sweets* ?

Réponses : 1. Les trois sont vraies ! **2. c.** 75 **3. b.** 375 millions **4.** *Sweater* (US) / *jumper* (GB) – *flat* (GB) / *apartment* (US) – *lift* (GB) / *elevator* (US) – *candy* (US) / *sweets* (GB)

Parfois, vous avez l'impression de parler comme un Anglais et pourtant c'est du ***broken English*** !

Par exemple, si vous vouliez décrire cet acteur, vous pourriez être tenté(e) de dire ***He's wearing a smoking and baskets***.

Voici ce que visualiserait un anglophone : Robert Downey Junior avec un nuage de fumée et des paniers aux pieds.

Et voici la phrase correcte…
He's wearing a tuxedo with sneakers.

Saurez-vous faire la différence ?

Les mots suivants, utilisés en français, ont-ils le même sens en anglais ?

1. gloss
2. parking
3. flyer
4. best-seller
5. baby-foot
6. disc-jockey
7. coach
8. brushing
9. vintage
10. camping-car

Réponses : 1. oui **2.** on dira *parking lot* (US) ou *car park* (UK) **3.** oui **4.** oui **5.** non, on dit *table football* ou *foosball* (qui lui-même vient de l'allemand !) **6.** oui **7.** oui **8.** non, on dit *blow dry* **9.** oui **10.** non, on dit *motor home*

Dive in!

English is... all day long!

Au petit-déjeuner,

vous êtes plutôt *pancakes, muffins, doughnuts, corn flakes* ou *cookies* ?

Time 2 go!

Allez, en route pour le lycée, bus ou tramway aujourd'hui ? Et qu'allez-vous écouter comme musique sur le chemin ? À moins que vous ne profitiez du trajet pour regarder un épisode de votre série préférée sur votre smartphone ?

On vous l'a dit, l'anglais est partout, tout le temps, et c'est une langue en constante évolution, de nouveaux mots sont ajoutés au dictionnaire régulièrement pour coller à l'actualité : en 2018 ***binge-watching*** (le fait de regarder tous les épisodes d'une série sans s'arrêter) et ***hangry*** (mot valise *hungry* + *angry* = être de mauvaise humeur parce qu'on a faim) faisaient partie des ajouts. Pour découvrir les mots les plus récents, tapez : New – words – Oxford – dictionary – (+ année en cours) dans votre moteur de recherche.

Ou plutôt un jogging, un T-shirt et des baskets ?

Qu'allez-vous mettre aujourd'hui ?

Aujourd'hui ce sera un top, un jean et des boots ?

D'ailleurs, est-ce que ces mots existent en anglais ?

Réponses : *top, jeans, boots, tracksuit bottoms / track pants*
*T-shirt, **sneakers** / **trainers***

How can I improve my English?

... ou comment progresser en anglais sans (presque) s'en rendre compte

Continuez à faire ce que vous aimez... en VO !

Internet vous permet d'avoir un accès illimité à des contenus en anglais sur tous les sujets.

Que vous aimiez le sport, la cuisine, le jeu vidéo ou la mode, il y a mille et une vidéos sur ces sujets. **Explorez !**

Ouvrez vos oreilles

Écoutez le plus d'anglais possible : des paroles de vos chansons préférées, aux films et séries en VO, c'est une façon d'apprendre sans même s'en apercevoir !

Jouez !

Jouer en ligne permet d'enrichir son lexique. Si vous êtes fan de *gaming*, faites-vous plaisir, paramétrez les dialogues en anglais et échangez avec des joueurs du monde entier.

Lisez !

Oui, mais quoi ?

- Commencez par des textes courts (nouvelles, *fan fiction*, articles de magazine, de blog…) ;
- des *comics*, des *graphic novels* ;
- des magazines en ligne ;
- votre saga préférée.

Demandez conseil à votre professeur ou allez faire un tour au CDI…

Vous verrez, ça deviendra de plus en plus facile et vous progresserez à la vitesse de l'éclair !

Restez connecté(e) !

- **Linguee**
- **WordReference**
- **BBC Learning English**
- **Cambridge Dictionary (UK)**
- **Merriam-Webster Dictionary (US)**

De nombreuses applications gratuites ou des sites internet permettent de progresser en anglais tout en s'amusant.

Il existe aussi des dictionnaires qui donnent des traductions mais aussi des définitions, des exemples d'emploi en contexte, des expressions courantes pour toujours trouver les mots justes.

Communiquez !

Même sans aller dans un pays anglophone, on peut parler anglais.

Organisez un après-midi jeux de société en anglais (celui qui parle français a un gage !) ou un ***English challenge*** (français interdit pendant une heure) avec vos amis.

Si vous voulez trouver un correspondant, allez faire un tour sur ePals (**epals.com**) ou sur le Mixxer (**language-exchanges.org**).

English really *is* everywhere!
Commencez dès aujourd'hui. Plus vous pratiquerez en anglais régulièrement, plus vous progresserez ! Go, go, go!

Sky's the limit

LET'S GO TO HAWAII!

Speaking

Examine the photos, factfile, pie chart and map (➡ *the inside back cover*). Use what you have understood to **record** a 1-minute presentation about Hawaii.

Factfile about the Island State

Hawaii is the 50th and most recent State of the USA.

- **Capital:** Honolulu
- **Location:** North Pacific Ocean
- **Distance from California:** over 3,600 km
- **Official languages:** Hawaiian and English
- **Main industries:** tourism, military defense, agriculture (sugar cane, pineapples, flowers...)

Ethnicity in Hawaii 2019

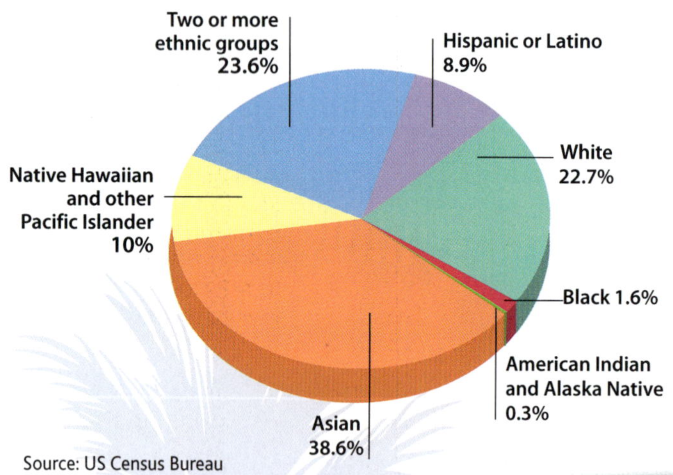

Source: US Census Bureau

Stairway to Heaven, Haiku Stairs, Oahu, Hawaii, USA

Listening

Classe 1 Piste 1

1. **Listen** to the recording. **Pick out** references to places and numbers.
2. **Focus on** stressed words linked to geographical features and activities.
3. **Use** your notes as a basis to **sum up** in English or in French what you have understood.

Reading

1. Read the text and introduce it (nature – subject – main characters – place).

2. Focus on the main characters. Pick out information about each of them (name – probable age – occupation – personality).

3. Use what you have understood to write a short description of the characters. Quote the text to justify elements of your description.

4. Pick out references to places, time and distances. Use them to explain what is particular about family life for the people in the text.

"Is today Steamer[1] Day?"

"No." (…) "Could be another week, anyway, before he comes."

"Oh, no, Mama." They'd received a letter from Papa exactly five weeks ago, mailed in Samoa, informing them he'd be leaving for home in a month; and Rachel knew for a fact that the crossing took no more than a week. "Two thousand, two hundred and ninety miles from Samoa to Honolulu," she announced proudly.

Her mother regarded her skeptically. "You know how big is a mile?"

Rachel thought a moment, her round chubby face sober[2] in reflection, then stretched her arms as wide as she could. (…)

Honolulu harbour was a forest of ships' masts[3] huddled[4] within encircling coral reefs, a narrow channel threading through the reefs and out to open sea. (…)

As the *Mariposa* eased into its berth[5] beside a mountain of black coal, Rachel caught sight of a sailor (…) He was a stocky Hawaiian in his young thirties, his thick muscled arms tanned by the blistering of even lower latitudes. "Papa!" she yelled waving. (…)

Henry Kalama, a happy grin on his broad friendly face, hefted his suitcase as though he were about to throw it. "Ey! Little girl! Catch!"

Rachel giggled[6]. Henry ran up and Dorothy gave him a reproachful look: "Good-for-nothing rascal[7], where you been in the last eight months?" And she kissed him with a ferocity that quite belied her words.

"Papa!" Rachel was jumping up and down, and now Henry scooped her up in his big arms. "Ey! There she is. There's my baby!" He kissed her on the cheek and Rachel wrapped her arms around his thick neck. "I missed you little girl," he said in a tone so gentle it made Dorothy want to cry. Then he looked at his wife with exaggerated afterthought, "Oh, you too."

Alan Brennert, *The Hawaii Novels: Moloka'i and Honolulu*, 2015

1. steamer (n.) = a steam boat
2. sober (adj.) = serious
3. mast (n.): *mât*
4. huddled (adj.): *rassemblé*
5. ease into its berth (exp.): *accoster en douceur*
6. giggle (v.) = laugh
7. rascal (n.): *vaurien*

Writing

You are thinking of visiting Hawaii. Write an email to the Hawaiian tourist office to ask for information to prepare you for your stay (history – location – travel options – places to see – things to do). (10 lines)

► *Dear Sir/Madam, … • I am writing to enquire about… • I've researched Hawaii and… • What I'd really love to discover is… • Could you tell me more about… • Many thanks for your advice • Yours faithfully.*

Axe 1 : Vivre

entre générations

Axe 1 : Vivre entre générations

1 Hanging out

Your project

Present ideas for a shared space in your school and listen to those of your classmates, *p. 31*
- Come up with a shared space project for a sport or activity, *p. 25*

Keys to success

- **Strategy: comprendre un document audio ou audiovisuel**, *p. 30*
- **Mind map:** shared spaces, activities, reactions, *p. 28*
- **Grammar:** auxiliaires modaux (sens 1), *p. 29*
- **Sounds:** lettres *ou*, *p. 29*

How can shared spaces bring people together?

Different generations enjoying a game of chess, Union Square, NYC

1 Basics

List all the words that come to mind when you think about how you can spend your free time (places – people – activities).

WORKSHEET 2

2 Discover

Classe 1 Piste 2

Listen and **pick out** stressed words. Divide them into categories (people – feelings – places – interests / activities). **Compare** the speakers and say which one you relate to the most.

Game 3 Play

Guessing game: Write down the places where you like to spend your free time. Share them with the class.
See if you can **guess** who hangs out where.

Lire • Écouter • Échanger

Sharing spaces

1 An intergenerational passion

1. Describe the place and the people you see in the photo (environment – ages – clothes – activities).
2. Read the text and pick out information about the place you see in the picture (name – location – frequentation – reputation). Link what you have found to the photo.
   ▶ *As you can see in the photo… • This place is famous for… • People from different generations…*
3. Focus on the people (names – ages – roles – feelings) and compare the significance of this place in their lives.
4. Médiation — Use what you have understood to explain the popularity of this place.
   ▶ *People of all ages can… • People don't have to… • It prevents young people from…*

In the five boroughs[1], over 500 outdoor basketball courts remain places for IRL[2] connection.

The Cage is nothing more than a square of asphalt beside the West Fourth Street subway stop, but it is a place of worship[3] and coolness and budding[4] dreams.

On a Friday in June, the excitement of Kenny Graham's summer league is in full swing. Passersby cling to the chain-link fence. One man is camped out on the sidewalk with a beach chair. Abe Weinstein (…) sits in his usual seat, front row center, sucking a pink lollipop and wearing the T-shirt from his 40th wedding anniversary. The announcer, who goes by Worthy, commentates each play into a megaphone: "Here's the next NBA player versus the young one!" Adrenaline is running high because it's an unwritten rule you have to be good to play on this court. Really good. Otherwise, you'll embarrass yourself. (…)

After the game, Kareem Welch hangs around as people slap[5] his back in congratulations. He's 17 and had a good day: 46 points and 18 rebounds. One day, he hopes to play for the Knicks, even though they're not so great. "If I didn't have basketball, I don't know what I'd be doing," he says. In his neighborhood, he's seen people go to jail and do drugs. He looks up at the trees before he speaks. "I choose to do better," he says.

Basketball players in New York will tell you the Cage is where the party's at, and on a temperate summer evening, no doubt they're right.

Britta Lokting, ny.curbed.com, Jul. 20, 2018

Andre Wagner, The Cage, one of New York's outdoor basketball courts, 2018

1. borough (n.): *arrondissement*
2. IRL = in real life
3. worship (n.): *culte*
4. budding (adj.): *naissant*
5. slap (v.) = hit with hand

Grammar

Les auxiliaires modaux (sens 1)

Players **must be** talented if they want to play.
modal + BV

➡ *Grammar p. 29*

2 Giving teens a place

Classe 1 – Pistes 3-4

1. **Look** at the photo and **comment on** the situation. **Guess** the content of the recording.
2. **Listen** to the 1st part of the recording and check. **Note down** stressed and repeated words then **classify** them (people – places – conflict).
3. **Listen** to the 2nd part of the recording. **Focus on** references to Jacques Gilbert (occupation – link to skaters – feelings). **Use** what you have understood to describe the problem.
4. **Note down** stressed words and organise your notes (idea – objectives – people concerned).

Durango Police Department works actively to improving relationships between police officers and residents of all ages.

3 Where can teens go?

1. **React** to the signs and the information box. **Guess** the motivations behind the signs.
   ► *Some people think teens mustn't… • The local residents are afraid of…*
2. Groupwork **Imagine** a neighbourhood meeting between the people who put up the signs and the young people who photographed the signs. **Share out** the roles and **act out** the scene.
   ► *We think young people should… • You can't just ban… • We should work together to…*

1. loitering (n.) = hanging out
2. no trespassing (exp.): *défense d'entrer*

The **Yes Loitering** project is a teen project working on places to hang out in New York. As part of their research, the team walked around the block where they met in the Bronx, and documented all the signs they saw that discouraged teens from hanging out.

Need help?

- boredom [ˈbɔːdəm]: *ennui*
- encounter: *rencontre*
- meeting point
- outdoors ≠ indoors
- allowed = authorised
- forbidden = prohibited
- inclusive ≠ excluding
- intergenerational
- ban = forbid
- discourage ≠ encourage
- gather = meet up
- loiter: *traîner*
- relate to = identify with

Prepare your project

Groupwork Come up with a shared space project in your city (sport / activity – place – people – objectives – activities – impacts). Vote for the most convincing project.

Écouter • Lire • Parler

Old and new spaces to hang out

1 vidéo The mall: a dying American tradition? DOSSIER documentaire

1. Use the captions to describe and comment on the two pictures. Imagine what the video is about.
   ▶ *The first picture shows… whereas the second… • They look… • Contrary to… • Maybe… • I guess…*

2. Watch the video without the sound and take notes on what you see (places – activities – people – styles).

3. Watch with the sound and note down what you understand. Focus on numbers and say what they refer to.

4. Read the posts and pick out words and expressions used to describe the shopping mall. Find other ways of hanging out that are mentioned. Compare with your own experience.
   ▶ *Young people still like … • Although I hang out with my friends…*

5. Use what you have understood from the different documents to explain the role of shopping malls in the USA over the years. (Médiation)

Michael Galinsky, *Malls across America*, 1989

Rolling Acres Mall, Ohio.
It has been a dead mall since it closed in 2008.

For decades the mall was the cool place to hang out for millions of American teenagers. But have times changed?

Jack January 8, 2019 · 8:32 am
I think the mall has become a less popular place for teenagers to hang out. We have more access to social media and contact with each other than when malls were popular.

Graham January 8, 2019 · 8:40 am
Wait, what? Malls are great! What happened??

Hailey January 8, 2019 · 10:08 am
I guess it depends. Me and my friends sometimes hang out at the mall, it's practical when the weather is bad, and we just walk around talking to each other and go for a coffee. Other times we just stay at home and chat online.

2 Hanging out online

1. **Scan** the text for information about Kevin (age – occupation – origins – style).

2. **Find** references to the iGeneration (definition – characteristics – contact with technology).

3. **Pick out** references to previous generations and **use** them to **say** what has changed.
   ▶ *Compared with previous generations… • iGens are far less likely to…*

4. **Find** the probable reasons behind the ways teens hang out today.

Pairwork

5. **List** the pros and cons of hanging out online and hanging out in real life.

1. curmudgeon (n.): *grincheux*

Kevin and I sit down at two desks just outside his third period class at a high school in northern San Diego. He is 17 years old and Asian American, with spiky[1] black hair, fashionable glasses, and a wan[2] smile. (…) "I feel like we don't party as much. People stay in more often. My generation lost interest in socializing in person – they don't have physical get-togethers, they just text together, and they can just stay at home."

Kevin is onto something. For example, iGen teens – those who were born in 1995 and later, grew up with cell phones, had an Instagram page before they started high school, and do not remember a time before the Internet – spend less time at parties than any previous generation. (…)

Why are parties less popular? Kevin has an explanation for that: "People party because they're bored – they want something to do. Now we have Netflix – you can watch series nonstop. There's so many things to do on the web." He might be right – with so much entertainment at home, why party? Teens also have other ways to connect and communicate, including the social media websites they spend so much time on. (…) The number of teens who get together with their friends every day has been cut in half in just fifteen years, with especially steep declines recently.

This might be the most definitive evidence that iGen'ers spend less time interacting with their peers[3] face-to-face than any previous generation – it's not just parties or craziness but merely getting together with friends, spending time hanging out.

Jean M. Twenge, wired.com, 2017

1. spiky (adj.): *en épi*
2. wan (adj.) = sad
3. peer (n.): *pair*

Need help?

- consumer society
- economic boom
- generation gap
- accessible ≠ inaccessible
- convenient = practical
- trendy = in fashion
- go shopping
- mingle = mix with people
- socialize ['səʊʃəlaɪz] = meet friends
- spend (money): *dépenser*
- spend (time): *passer (du temps)*
- stroll: *flâner*
- face-to-face
- get-together = gathering
- waste time: *perdre son temps*

Did you know?

According to a 2017 report, it is probable that one out of every four malls in the U.S. will have closed down by 2022.

Mémoriser • Prononcer • Écrire

Words, words, words

➡ *Faire une carte mentale p. 234*
➡ *Mémoriser et enrichir son lexique p. 235*

Quizlet
quizlet.com/skysthelimit2e

Classe 1 Pistes 5-7 1 3

Créez votre propre carte mentale à partir de ce que vous avez vu en classe. Vous pourrez ensuite l'enrichir à l'aide de celle-ci. Écoutez les mots et répétez-les pour bien les prononcer. Écrivez-les aussi plusieurs fois pour mémoriser leur orthographe.

More words

Do et make

– I'm not doing anything.
– You're making too much noise.
– What do you do in your free time?
– I've made a lot of friends at the skatepark.

L'essentiel
• ***Do*** et ***make*** signifient tous les deux « faire » en français.
• ***Do*** signifie « faire » dans le sens accomplir une activité (sans toujours la préciser) : *What are you going to do later?*
• Le plus souvent, ***make*** exprime l'idée de fabriquer, de produire, avec un résultat concret : *They made a skatepark for the skaters.*

1. Complétez les phrases avec *do* ou *make*, puis vérifiez dans un dictionnaire.

I will (*do / make*) a decision this weekend.
→ *I will make a decision this weekend.*

a. They will (*do / make*) their homework this evening.
b. You should (*do / make*) an effort to come to an agreement.
c. What do you (*do / make*) in your free time?
d. The school could (*do / make*) a place for us to hang out together.
e. We can (*do / make*) a suggestion if we like.

2. Traduisez les phrases.

a. Je vais faire un gâteau pour ce soir.
b. Qu'allez-vous faire ?
c. Tu peux faire une liste avec tes idées.
d. Il va faire un discours.

Observer • Retenir • Appliquer

Grammar

Les auxiliaires modaux (sens 1) Repères, p. 253

- Players **must be** talented if they want to play.
- Teens **can't hang** out here.
- You **may go** out until 9 p.m.
- You **should go** out more often.
- They **should have organised** a neighbourhood meeting.

L'essentiel

- Les **auxiliaires modaux de sens 1** expriment la capacité (*can, could*), l'obligation (*must*), l'interdiction (*mustn't / can't*), l'absence d'obligation (*needn't*), la permission (*may, can, might, could*).
- *Should* + BV sert à donner un conseil alors que *should* + *have* + participe passé exprime un reproche.
- Les modaux ont des équivalents (*must* → *have to / can* → *be able to* ou *be allowed to*, etc.).

Attention : Un modal est toujours suivi d'une base verbale. Deux modaux ne se suivent jamais !

1. Remettez les mots dans l'ordre.

harder. – could – She – tried – have

→ *She could have tried harder.*

a. remember – He – he – the last time – to the mall. – went – can't

b. have – was going out. – her parents – should – she – She – told

c. mustn't – a ball. – to bring – You – forget

d. must – before – I – nighttime. – leave

e. hang out. – create – You – to – should – a new place

2. Complétez les phrases avec un modal approprié.

I've been practising and now I (?) skate very well.

→ *I've been practising and now I can skate very well.*

a. Skating is forbidden here! You (?) skate where you see the sign telling you not to.

b. It's my property but I don't mind: you (?) skate in my driveway if you like.

c. I wanted to come! You (?) have told me you were all going to the mall.

3. Reformulez avec un modal.

They are allowed to hang out here.

→ *They may hang out here.*

a. I advise you to spend more face-to-face time with your friends.

b. They have to remember to include everyone.

c. I give you permission to go out with your friends.

d. He is able to play basketball better than anyone.

e. I think you were wrong to skate in that driveway yesterday.

f. They are forbidden to go to the mall by themselves.

4. Traduisez les phrases suivantes.

a. Ils devraient sortir voir leurs amis.

b. Nous ne pouvons pas rester ici.

c. Elle aurait dû venir avec nous.

d. Tu ne dois pas rentrer trop tard.

e. Vous n'êtes pas obligés d'acheter quelque chose.

Sounds, sounds, sounds

Lettres *ou* Repères, p. 245

L'essentiel

Les lettres ***ou*** peuvent être prononcées de plusieurs façons : [uː] (*group*), [aʊ] (*sound*), [əʊ] (*shoulder*), [ɔː] (*brought*), [ʊ] (*could*) et [ʌ] (*country*). Vous pouvez utiliser un dictionnaire en ligne pour écouter et vérifier (dictionary.cambridge.org).

Classe / 4 – Piste 8

1. Écoutez et regroupez les mots en fonction de la prononciation des lettres *ou*.

out – your – loud – proud – should – tough – though – through – encourage – court – young

Classe / 5 – Piste 9

2. Écoutez puis répétez les phrases en vous concentrant sur les lettres soulignées.

a. A gr<u>ou</u>p of friends c<u>ou</u>ld hang <u>ou</u>t here, it's big en<u>ou</u>gh.

b. A c<u>ou</u>ple of y<u>ou</u>ng kids were so l<u>ou</u>d the neighb<u>ou</u>rs th<u>ou</u>ght they were fighting.

c. It takes c<u>ou</u>rage to hang out <u>ou</u>tside when it's freezing.

STRATEGY COMPRENDRE UN DOCUMENT AUDIO OU AUDIOVISUEL

Pour comprendre un document audio ou audiovisuel, il faut :

AVANT L'ÉCOUTE

1 ... anticiper :

- Regardez les **éléments périphériques** (titre – sous-titre – légende – image – date) pour **imaginer** le sujet du document.
- **Notez** les mots et les expressions qui vous viennent à l'esprit.
- Si le document est **daté** et / ou l'**aire géographique** est précisée, pensez aux particularités de l'époque et du lieu (personnages célèbres – contexte).

PENDANT L'ÉCOUTE

2 ... s'appuyer sur les éléments non verbaux :

- À la 1re écoute, **vérifiez** si vos **hypothèses** étaient correctes.

  Acceptez de ne pas tout comprendre.
- Comptez le **nombre de voix**, identifiez l'**âge**, le **genre** et le **type de document** (interview – reportage – discours...).
- Faites attention aux **bruits** de fond, qui peuvent indiquer le lieu et l'environnement (extérieur / intérieur), ainsi qu'au **ton**, à la **vitesse** et à l'**intonation des voix**.
- **Vidéo :** Appuyez-vous d'abord sur **ce que vous voyez** pour accéder au sens (personnes – lieux – expressions – couleurs).

  Visionnez sans le son pour vous consacrer aux éléments visuels.

3 ... prendre des notes :

- S'il y a plusieurs interlocuteurs, un tableau avec des colonnes peut aider à **faire le tri des informations**.
- **Vidéo :** Faites **deux colonnes** pour établir le lien entre ce que vous voyez et ce que vous entendez lors de la prise de notes.
- Lors des **2e et 3e écoutes**, notez les **mots accentués**, porteurs de sens et les **mots répétés**.

APRÈS CHAQUE ÉCOUTE

4 ... établir des liens :

- Partez de vos notes pour **reconstituer le message**.
- **Réorganisez-les** sans vouloir faire du mot à mot. Cherchez une **logique** : quel est le contexte ? qui a parlé ? quel est le sujet ? quel est l'objectif du message ?
- Servez-vous de ce que **vous savez** et de ce que **vous avez compris** pour **faire des liens logiques** : quels mots / éléments **vont ensemble** ? quelles **interprétations** sont possibles ?

  Faites confiance à votre bon sens pour interpréter.

Your project — Present and listen to ideas for a shared space

Present ideas for a shared space to hang out in your school and listen to those of your classmates.

Young people hanging out at Lincoln Centre, New York

1 Do the background work for your shared space.

- Decide **who it is for**: students from one year – all years – teachers – people with a specific interest.
- **Investigate**, **measure** and **photograph** or **draw** underused **places** in your school that could serve your purpose.
- **Detail the material** you would need to make this space viable.

2 Outline the main aspects of your shared space.

- What are people **able to do** in this space?
- What **equipment** would be available and why?
- How many people would **have access** and when?

3 Justify why this shared space is necessary.

- Explain the **impacts** of this space (bringing people together – learning new skills…).
- Bring to light the lack of a similar shared space in your school.
- Reassure about the **time** and **financial aspects** of the project.

4 Prepare your audio document.

- **Organise** your **ideas** in a logical manner.
- Write the main ideas to **present your project**. Keep it simple and make sure that your sentences are adapted to an oral recording.
- **Practise** before you record and try not to read but to speak using your notes.

5 Record your presentation.

- **Make** an audio version of your presentation. **Listen to** your recording and do it again if necessary before putting it on the class blog or on Padlet.
- Choose one or more **photos** / **drawings** to **illustrate** your recording.
- **Listen to** the presentations of your classmates and **take notes**.
- The class will **vote** for the **most convincing project**.

Keys to success

- **Utilisez le vocabulaire du chapitre :** espaces partagés, activités, réactions.
  ➥ *Words, words, words, p. 28*
- **Utilisez *do* et *make*.**
  ➥ *More words, p. 28*
- **Utilisez les auxiliaires modaux (sens 1).**
  ➥ *Grammar, p. 29*
- **Servez-vous des conseils pour améliorer votre prononciation.**
  ➥ *Strategy, p. 126*
- **Servez-vous des conseils pour comprendre un document audio.**
  ➥ *Strategy, p. 30*

Axe 1 : Vivre entre générations

2 Between generations in South Africa

1 Basics

Write a list of all the words that come to mind when you think of South Africa.

WORKSHEET 3

2 vidéo Discover

Watch teenagers talking about their parents and about life in South Africa during and after apartheid. **Pick out** information and **compare** the two generations.

▶ *Parents used to suffer from…* • *Their children…*

Game 3 Play

The odd ones out game: Discover a list of personalities and guess who is South African. The group with the most correct answers wins.

Your project

Pairwork **Make and present a slideshow about generations in South Africa,** *p. 41*

Pairwork – Make a presentation about a South-African activist from each generation, *p. 37*

Keys to success

- **Strategy: faire un diaporama,** *p. 40*
- **Mind map:** common history, transmission, commitment, *p. 38*
- **Grammar:** voix passive, *p. 39*
- **Sounds:** diphtongues, *p. 39*

Young people in front of a mural showing former President Nelson Mandela (1918-2013)

Can generations learn from one another?

Écouter • Lire • Écrire

The legacy

Did you know?

Apartheid was introduced in 1948 and lasted until 1994. The word "apartheid" comes from the Afrikaans (language that comes from the Dutch spoken by white settlers in South Africa) word meaning "separation".

1 vidéo Understanding their parents' story DOSSIER documentaire

1. Watch the video without the sound and list everything you can remember (people – places – objects). Relate them to the pictures.

2. Watch again with the sound on. Pick out stressed words and classify them (dates – events – life under apartheid) to make a timeline of the history of apartheid.
▶ *In 1948, black and white people were… • Black people were removed from…*

Médiation **3.** Sum up what the laws under apartheid imposed and how people tried to oppose them.

From 1948 to 1994, laws under apartheid imposed a separation in public facilities. Signs were both in English and in Afrikaans.

In 1960, a peaceful protest organised in the city of Sharpeville was repressed by the police. Today it is known as the Sharpeville massacre. 69 people died and 180 were injured (= *blessés*).

In the 70s, over 60,000 black people were forcibly removed from this inner-city near Cape Town to Bantustans (homelands especially created for black people far from the cities).

CULTURE QUEST

Discover more about Nelson Mandela's life to understand why he's still a hero today.

Keywords: Nelson Mandela – prison years – art and culture.

2 Accepting the legacy

1. **Look** at the photo and read the caption. **Imagine** what Barack Obama says about Nelson Mandela.
2. **Read** paragraphs 1 & 2 and **pick out** the keywords that define Mandela's legacy.
3. Use your notes to **explain** why Mandela defended these values.
4. **Read** the rest of the text. **Focus** on Obama's quote and **imagine** what the two different visions of humanity's future might be.
   ▶ *Instead of fighting / being divided people should… • If we all try to promote…*
5. Médiation — **Read** the last paragraph. **Pick out** verbs and use them to **write** a paragraph on how the young generation could continue Mandela's legacy.

Barack Obama giving a speech to mark the 100th anniversary of the birth of Nelson Mandela, 2018

Just last month, the world celebrated what would have been Nelson Mandela's 100th birthday. And in the spirit of the celebration, one had to simply ask themselves what they are doing to continue his legacy and what he stood for.

Mandela's legacy symbolises a beam of hope for a completely new South Africa; a country that exemplifies equality for all people, education for all children, and promotes peace, justice, and freedom for all. (…)

As former president of the United States Barack Obama said in his speech at the 2018 Nelson Mandela annual lecture in Johannesburg, "we now stand at a crossroads – a moment in time at which two very different visions of humanity's future compete for the hearts and the minds of citizens around the world. Two different stories, two different narratives about who we are and who we should be. How should we respond?"

Obama's question is pertinent, not only as an individual, but for society as a whole. There is hope because we have the foundation Mandela laid for us. Now, we can continue his legacy by acknowledging[1] both narratives: what our grandparents did to fight against apartheid, to learn from their mistakes and their successes, and to start writing a story of our own.

We need to create a new vision for ourselves that encapsulates what we truly want to eradicate, and what we want to improve on as a country, and actively find ways to achieve it.

Humelo Siphe Williams, globalcitizen.org, August 21, 2018

1. acknowledge (v.) – admit

Need help?

- apartheid [əˈpɑːthaɪt]
- demonstration = protest
- freedom = liberty
- law [lɔː]: *loi*
- legacy = heritage
- notice board: *panneau*
- passport
- public facilities = public buildings
- township = segregated area
- discriminated against
- segregated = separated
- ban = forbid
- pass on = transmit
- promote
- take over: *prendre le relais*

Grammar

La voix passive

During apartheid, black and white people **were separated** in public places.
be (au prétérit) + part. passé

➥ *Grammar p. 39*

New fights, new voices

1 Student activism over the years

DOSSIER documentaire

1. **Look** at the pictures and **read** the captions to **guess** what these two generations have in common.
2. **Read** the text and check. **Focus on** information about the Soweto uprising (problems – aims – reactions).
3. **Read** again and **pick out** information about the young generation's movement.
4. **List** the common points and the differences between the two generations. (Médiation)
   ▶ *Both generations were committed to... • Unlike their parents... • Today's students are not as...*

The Soweto uprising led by black students, 1976

#FeesMustFall, a student-led protest movement that lasted one year, starting in October 2015

As South Africa marks the 42nd anniversary of the 1976 Soweto student uprisings[1] the spotlight returns on the condition of today's youth and their counterparts of the time. (...) Among the more pronounced threads[2] that bind[3] these two generations of young people can be found in the sphere of education. On the one hand, the 1976 Soweto student uprisings tragically ended with hundreds of young people killed by the apartheid government when they protested the imposition of Afrikaans as a medium of instruction. On the other hand, today's youth is equally vibrant and exhibits fearless activism for universal access to quality education and transformation of the national curriculum[4] to future-proof their livelihoods[5].

(...) The #FeesMustFall marches led by vibrant youth across the country and disruptions[6] in tertiary institutions perceived to take a snail's pace[7] approach to transformation shows the parallels between the youth of the two generations. Both generations demonstrated a burning desire to push the boundaries[8], ask the uncomfortable questions and not sacrifice at the altar[9] of preserving peace, the need for real, meaningful transformation. (...)

In conclusion, while the youth of 1976 fought with their lives for freedom and the creation of a democratic state, today's youth activism should be strengthened as it tackles poverty, inequality and unemployment. It is heartening to note that the clear majority of South Africa's youth are not passive but are champions of their own development as active members of society.

Musa Ndlangamandla, tyi.co.za, June 15, 2018

1. uprising (n.) = revolt
2. thread (n.): *fil*
3. bind (v.): *lier*
4. national curriculum (n.): *programme d'enseignement*
5. future-proof their livelihood (exp.): *sécuriser leur avenir*
6. disruption (n.): *perturbation*
7. snail's pace (exp.) = very slow
8. boundary (n.) = limit
9. altar (n.): *autel*

2 Creating a dialogue between generations

Classe 1 Piste 10

1. Look at the picture and read the caption. Guess what the play is about.

2. Listen and pick out stressed words. Use them to explain what the students hope to accomplish with the play.

3. Listen again and find references to education and history. List what the students would like to discuss with the older generation.

Pairwork

4. Choose an issue your generation is dealing with. Agree on how and why you would like it to be staged.

CULTURE QUEST

Discover the trailer of the play.
Keywords: *The Fall* – Royal Court Theater – trailer.

The Fall, 2018, a play inspired by 2015 student movements in Cape Town

Prepare your project

Find information about South-African activists from two different generations. Make a 2-minute presentation to the class. Choose one from each generation:
- **during apartheid:** Steve Biko – Miriam Makeba – Desmond Tutu – Nadine Gordimer;
- **after apartheid:** Zulaikha Patel – Imraan Christian – Mbuyiseni Ndlozi – Sanele Junior Xaba.

Need help?

- activism = action for a cause
- tuition [tʃuːˈɪʃən] fees
- role model
- bold = courageous
- committed = involved
- convincing
- determined
- act
- inherit
- stage: *mettre en scène*
- stand up against = oppose actively
- stand up for = defend
- support
- tackle = deal with
- bridge the gap: *réduire le fossé*
- lack of understanding
- spark a dialogue: *susciter un dialogue*

Words, words, words

➥ *Faire une carte mentale p. 234*
➥ *Mémoriser et enrichir son lexique p. 235*

Quizlet
quizlet.com/skysthelimit2e

Classe 1 — Pistes 11-13 — 6 8

Créez votre propre carte mentale à partir de ce que vous avez vu en classe. Vous pourrez ensuite l'enrichir à l'aide de celle-ci. Écoutez les mots et répétez-les pour bien les prononcer. Écrivez-les aussi plusieurs fois pour mémoriser leur orthographe.

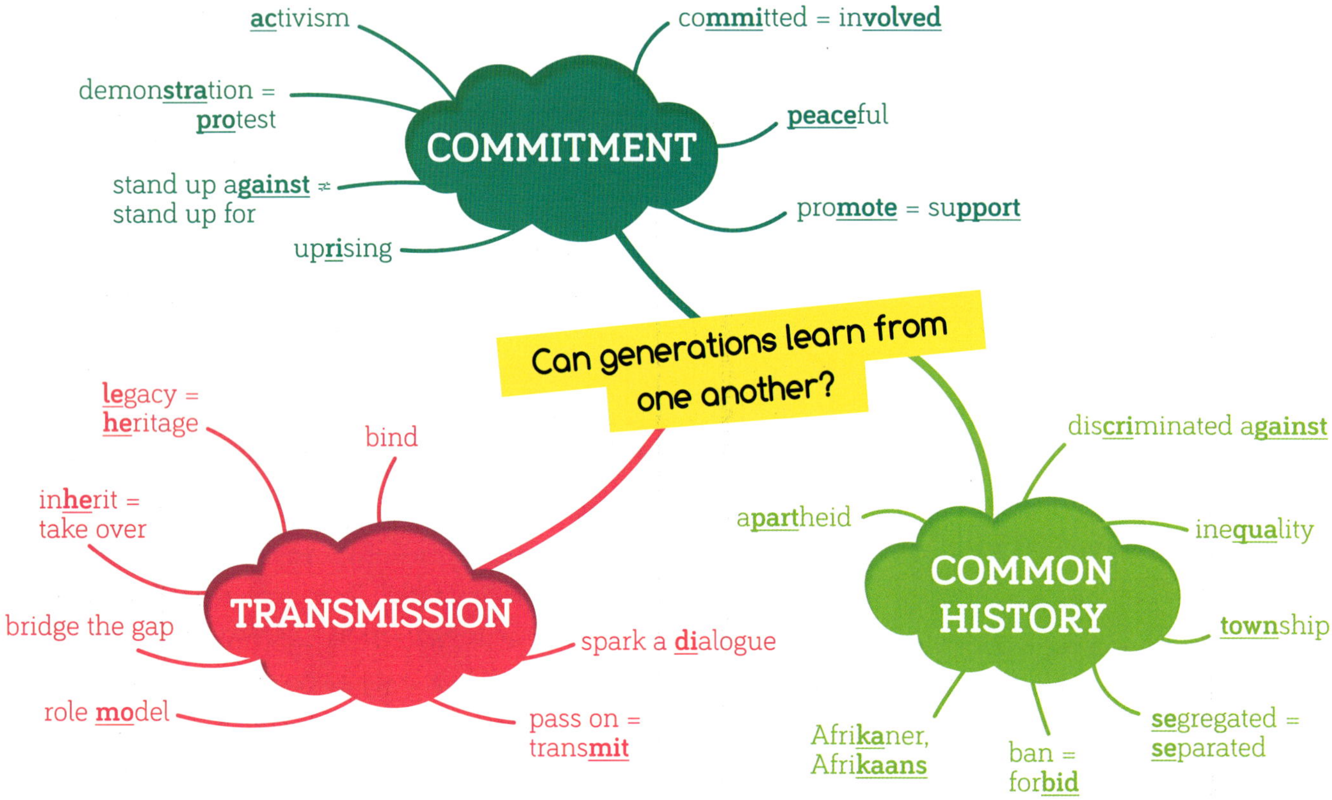

More words

L'ajout d'informations

Repères, p. 263

Under apartheid, black and white people were not allowed to go to the same schools, **not to mention** take the same public transport. **Moreover**, interracial marriages were banned. **On top of that**, black people were removed from their property and segregated in slums. **Last but not least**, they couldn't vote.

L'essentiel

Certains **mots de liaison** servent à ajouter des informations : *not to mention, what's more, moreover, furthermore, on top of that, last but not least.*

1. Parmi ces mots de liaison, utilisez ceux qui permettent de relier les phrases.

moreover – furthermore – last but not least – as well as – what's more – on top of that

Nelson Mandela fought against apartheid all his life. He tried to resist all kinds of injustice. He never gave up the idea of bringing people together. He didn't express any hard feelings against his oppressors.

Grammar

La voix passive

Repères, p. 254

- During apartheid, black and white people **were separated** in public places.
- Mandela **was sentenced** to life imprisonment.
- He **will be remembered** by future generations.
- South Africa **is being reinvented** by its youth.
- The horrors of apartheid **have** not **been forgotten**.

L'essentiel

• **La voix passive** se forme avec l'auxiliaire *be*, qui porte la marque du temps de la phrase, et le participe passé du verbe. ➥ *Verbes irréguliers p. 264*

• On l'utilise quand on s'intéresse, non pas à celui qui fait l'action (l'agent), mais à la personne ou l'objet qui subit l'action. Cet élément devient alors sujet du verbe.

Attention : L'agent est souvent omis. On ne le mentionne que s'il a une importance particulière. Il est alors introduit par la préposition *by*.

1. Dites quelle est la voix employée (passive ou active).

69 people were killed during the Sharpeville massacre. → *voix passive*

a. Hundreds of people were arrested after the protest.

b. Children are told the story of Nelson Mandela.

c. The history of apartheid should be taught in school.

d. The young generations are continuing the fight.

e. Barack Obama will deliver a speech for the celebrations.

2. Réécrivez ces phrases à la voix passive.

The older generation heard the students' message.
→ *The students' message was heard by the older generation.*

a. The jury awarded Nelson Mandela the Nobel Peace Prize. → *Nelson Mandela…*

b. The young generation has tackled many different issues. → *Many different issues…*

c. Barack Obama honours the memory of Mandela. → *The memory of Mandela…*

d. South Africans will elect their new president in 2019. → *The new president…*

e. Young people must spark a dialogue with the older generation. → *A dialogue…*

3. Réécrivez ces phrases à la voix passive en omettant l'agent.

People advised us to visit the apartheid museum.
→ *We were advised to visit the apartheid museum.*

a. The government will not allow the demonstration.

b. People celebrated Mandela's 100th anniversary.

c. They should voice their concerns using social media.

d. People will never forget apartheid.

e. Somebody told me what the students' protest was about.

Sounds, sounds, sounds

Les diphtongues

Repères, p. 245

L'essentiel

• **La diphtongue** est composée de deux sons voyelles qui s'enchaînent en une seule syllabe.

• Pour un même son, l'orthographe peut être différente (*pane* / *pain*). Pour une même orthographe, les sons peuvent être différents (*low* [əʊ] / *cow* [aʊ]).

Classe 9 – Piste 14

1. Écoutez puis classez dans le tableau les mots de la liste en fonction du son de la syllabe soulignée.

grey – child – now – boat – voice – open – find – mouse – Spain – joy

[əʊ] road	[aɪ] kind	[aʊ] how	[eɪ] plane	[ɔɪ] boy

Classe 10 – Piste 15

2. Écoutez puis entraînez-vous à lire ces phrases à voix haute en veillant à bien prononcer les diphtongues.

a. I know that the protest wasn't violent.

b. The South African activists were engaged in negotiations.

c. How did they voice their concern?

d. People enjoyed this play about the dialogue between generations.

STRATEGY FAIRE UN DIAPORAMA

Pour faire un diaporama, il faut :

1 ... sélectionner les images et les autres documents :
- Choisissez des **photos qui vous inspirent**.
- Assurez-vous que les **photos** illustrent bien votre propos.
- Pensez à **légender vos images** (titre – auteur – date).
- Vous pouvez chercher des **citations** ou des **extraits** pour enrichir votre présentation.

2 ... organiser vos informations écrites :
- Faites **un plan pour ordonner les différentes informations**.
- Mettez uniquement en évidence les **titres** ou les **mots-clés**.
- Vous pouvez ajouter **des textes courts** (chanson – citations – extrait littéraire...).

3 ... soigner la mise en page :
- **Faites** des diapositives dont la **mise en page est aérée** pour faciliter la lecture.
- **Vérifiez la cohérence graphique** de votre diaporama (police et taille de caractères – mise en forme des titres – couleurs).
- Vous pouvez avoir recours aux **animations** pour l'apparition des titres et des images.

4 ... faire une présentation dynamique :
- Maintenez un **contact visuel** avec la classe et **ne tournez pas le dos** à vos camarades.
- **Pensez à poser des questions** à la classe.

Habituez-vous à la manipulation du matériel, répétez avant votre passage devant la classe.

Your project | Make and present a slideshow

Pairwork Pairwork

Make and present a slideshow about generations in South Africa.

Nelson Mandela dances with schoolchildren before the first democratic election in 1994.

1 Choose a topic.

- In pairs, **agree on a topic** that you will relate to South Africa.
- It can be sport (rugby – football…), dance (pantsula…), art (paintings – literature – music…), politics, famous people, etc.

2 Find pictures to illustrate your topic.

- **Select pictures** that show aspects of South Africa **before and after the end of apartheid.**
- **Compare** your pictures: **similarities** and **differences** between the two generations.
- Make sure **your pictures** are **captivating**, that the quality is good and that you can source your documents.

3 Select the written information that will appear on your slideshow.

- **Display** titles, quotations and relevant **keywords** only.
- Write a **caption** for each picture.

4 Make sure your presentation is dynamic.

- **Don't reveal** your written information straight away.
- Ask your classmates to **guess what the situation** could be, **when** or **where** it is taking place, what the differences may be.

5 Work as a team.

- **Listen to each other** during the presentation.
- **Divide your speaking time** but make sure you can come to your classmate's help if needed.

Keys to success

- **Utilisez le vocabulaire du chapitre :** histoire commune, transmission, engagement.
  ➥ *Words, words, words, p. 38*
- **Intégrez des mots de liaison lorsque vous ajoutez des informations.**
  ➥ *More words, p. 38*
- **Utilisez la voix passive.**
  ➥ *Grammar, p. 39*
- **Servez-vous des conseils pour faire un diaporama.**
  ➥ *Strategy, p. 40*

Axe 2 :
Les univers professionnels,

le monde du travail

3 Transition Year Ireland, *p. 44*

How can school help us to discover career possibilities?

4 Finding your way, *p. 54*

How can personal implication give you ideas for your future?

Vers le BAC **Entraînement à l'épreuve 1** *p. 64*

Axe 2 : Les univers professionnels, le monde du travail

Transition Year Ireland

How can school help us to discover career possibilities?

Your project

Groupwork **Hold a round table about Transition Year,** *p. 53*

– Design your own ideal personal curriculum for a Transition Year, *p. 47*

– Imagine a year without tests. Share your opinion and justify, *p. 49*

Keys to success

- **Strategy: arriver à un accord**, *p. 52*
- **Mind map:** education, careers, opinions, *p. 50*
- **Grammar:** question-tags, *p. 51*
- **Sounds:** intonation des question-tags, *p. 51*

Transition Year can help students choose their ideal career. Clockwise: Maighread Barron, farmer, Naoise Jo Farrell, fashion designer, Ciaran O'Sullivan, hairdresser, Mike Tweedie, renowned chef.

1 Basics

List all the words that come to mind when you think about education and career choices (subjects – studies – jobs). WORKSHEET 4

2 Discover

Classe / Piste 16

Listen to some young Irish people discuss how they chose their career. Note down stressed words and classify them (education – jobs – reasons for choices – feelings and opinions). **Use** your notes to compare the two speakers.

▶ *Unlike Aisling, Padraic knew… • Both of them are… • In Padraic's case, choosing…*

3 Play

Game

What's that job? Draw a job on the board without writing any words. Answer your classmates' yes or no questions.

Écouter • Lire • Échanger

Preparing for the future

Did you know?

Schools design their own **Transition Year**. In 2018, of Ireland's 714 state secondary schools, 661 have students enrolled in TY.

1 Transition Year (TY)

Classe 1 Piste 17

1. **Listen** and **pick out** references to Transition Year (activities – employment – advantages). Use your notes to **sum up** what you have understood about this year in school.
   ▶ *One of the things students can do is… • Apparently they have the opportunity to…*

2. **Examine** the table and **divide** the subjects and modules into three groups: you have already studied – you have never studied – you would like to study.

3. **Use** the documents to **explain** TY in your own words. (Médiation)
   ▶ *Transition Year is part of… • Basically, students can… • The curriculum is divided into… • Overall…*

TRANSITION YEAR (TY)

Senior cycle is made up of **Transition Year** (often optional) and two full years that end with the Leaving Certificate[1].
In TY there are some obligatory subjects and modules (different lengths) and others that the students choose from to complete their timetable. Each school makes its own curriculum[2]. Students are not evaluated with tests, but complete projects to validate their year.

Subjects (all year round)	Modules (half year)
Irish, English, Maths, Religion, French or German, Career Guidance, Technology, Physical Education…	Mini-Company, Media Studies, School Magazine, Accounting, Work Experience and Vocational Preparation, Art, Cookery, Public Speaking, Film Studies, Business Studies, Driving Licence…

1. Leaving Certificate (n.): *le baccalauréat irlandais* 2. Curriculum (n.): *programme*

2 Discovering the world of work

vidéo

1. **Watch** the video and note down the stressed words. Organise them into the following categories: professional fields – advantages of work experience.

2. **Watch** again. **Focus** on references to time. **Use** what you have understood to **describe** the different forms work experience can take.

3. **List** the various places the students plan to do their work experience. **Organise** them into professional fields.

4. **Pick** three places where you would like to do work experience and **compare** your choices. (Pairwork)
   ▶ *I wouldn't mind trying… • Unlike X, I'd never want to… • If I could, I'd…*

3 vidéo A lawyer or a doctor? DOSSIER documentaire

1. **Watch** the video, **focusing** on what you see. **List** everything you notice related to law.

2. **Watch** again. **Note down** references to numbers and the legal world.

3. **Read** the text and **pick out** numbers and dates. Use them to **introduce** the programme.

4. **Focus** on references to people, places and the world of medicine. **Pick out** reactions to the programme. **Describe** the role the programme may play in students' lives.

5. Groupwork — Would you like to apply to one of these programmes? **Write** a paragraph to **explain** your choice. **Read** your classmates' paragraphs and see if anyone feels the same as you do.

Barristers of law with Transition Year student during a mock trial at Green Street Courthouse, Dublin

There isn't a sound in the large auditorium as Prof Fergal Malone slits open[1] a woman's abdomen at the start of a Caesarean birth that is being filmed for the benefit of 200 teenagers.

The video link relaying the delivery of a baby girl in the Rotunda Hospital to participants in Ireland's "My Health Transition Year Programme" is certainly testing whether or not they have the stomach for surgery. (…)

Not surprisingly, places on this taster of the world of medicine are highly coveted[2], with about 500 schools registering last October for a lottery to select the 200 that could send one pupil each. (…)

"It's brilliant – I am definitely learning a lot," says Patrick on a break between sessions. "I am learning what I would prefer to do" – and currently he's leaning towards physiotherapy. (…)

Grace really wants to study medicine and this RCSI[3] programme is helping her to see what she might like to specialise in. (…)

Sarah McHale (16) from Co Galway is torn between[4] medicine and music in college – "my two babies", she smiles. But the former is definitely becoming more of an option, she says, due to what she's experiencing at the RCSI, not to mention her new-found "addiction" to *Grey's Anatomy*.

Sheila Wayman, *The Irish Times*, March 5, 2018

1. slit open (v.) = cut 2. covet (v.): *convoiter*
3. RCSI = Royal College of Surgeons (= *chirurgiens*) in Ireland
4. be torn between (exp.): *être partagé(e) entre*

Find out more about what it's like to discover medicine in Transition Year.
Keywords: video – RCSI Waterford – Transition Year – Mini Med programme.

Need help?

- career guidance: *orientation*
- curriculum: *programme*
- driving licence: *permis de conduire*
- lawyer
- legal studies
- medicine
- subject: *matière*
- surgeon: *chirurgien*
- work placement: *stage*
- optional ≠ compulsory
- vocational = professional
- break the law
- give evidence: *témoigner*

Prepare your project

Pairwork — Design your own ideal personal curriculum for a TY and then compare with your classmate's one.

▶ *I'd really like to… • Both of us chose… • I'd love to try out…*

Does Transition Year work?

1 Parents' perspectives

DOSSIER documentaire

Classe 1 Piste 18

1. **Describe** the cartoon and **say** what it suggests.
2. **Read** the two texts. **Pick out** numbers and say what they refer to.
3. **Find** the potential impacts of TY and **classify** them (positive – negative).
4. **List** the conditions necessary for a successful TY. **Add** two suggestions of your own.
5. **Listen** to Edwin Landzaad talk about TY. **Use** your findings to add other conditions to the list.
6. Use what you have understood so far to **discuss** the pros and cons of TY according to parents. **Share** your opinion. (Mediation)
   ▶ *On the one hand… on the other (hand)… • I disagree with…*

Nearly 80 per cent of pupils surveyed by the Irish Second-Level Students' Union (ISSU) found TY to be a worthwhile experience, according to a 2014 report, *Transition Year: Exploring the Student Experience.* But what about parents, who are one step removed from what's going on?

Undoubtedly some find it hard to adjust to the effect a dramatic change in school routine can have on their children.

(…)

"I just can't wait for it to be over – a total waste of time," says one mother (…). She wouldn't be the first to think the year's freedom is a dangerous breeding ground for[1] bad habits and excess socialising.

But, of course, the beauty of the TY experience is that freedom – a chance for young people and teachers alike to forget about "learning for the test" and concentrate on learning for life. However, whether this excellent concept works in reality depends on various factors, ranging from the quality of the programmes in schools and success in securing worthwhile work experiences, to the attitudes and personalities of individual children.

Sheila Wayman, *The Irish Times,* March 5, 2018

1. breeding ground for (exp.): *terrain propice à*

To all intents and purposes, this is a year devoted to personal growth, bonding and tasting new skills. (…) But does the year actually deliver anything genuinely worthwhile or meaningful? (…)

There is no good reason why school-going children should require work experience to list on their curriculum vitae (CV)." (…)

There is no doubt that the TY is a major additional cost burden[1] to already hard-pressed parents trying to negotiate their way through the so-called free school system. Contributions range from €300 to well in excess of €1,000, with ongoing additional costs arising throughout the year."

Ita O'Kelly, *Irish Independent,* August 27, 2018

1. burden (n.): *poids*

2 A student's point of view

1. **Read** Pros of TY. **List** the advantages of TY according to this student.

2. **Read** Cons of TY and **list** the disadvantages of TY.
Sum up Brian's advice to future TY students.

Pairwork

3. Use your lists of advantages and disadvantages to **agree on** a ranking (= *classement*) of them from the best aspect to the worst.

Grammar

Les *question-tags*

– Transition Year concerns more and more students, doesn't it?
aux. + *not* + sujet

➥ *Grammar p. 51*

PROS vs CONS

Work experience: This is an extremely valuable part of TY as it shows young people the reality of the working world. It also can really help a student decide what they want, or do not want to do in college[1] and adult life. (…)

Get to know new people: (…) TY really does help you expand your circle of friends through working with them on projects, staying in a room with them on overnight trips and being mixed into new classes with them. (…)

Project work: A lot of the work in Transition Year is project-based. Teachers are not hounding[2] you every class to hand up work (…). This is very good preparation for college and the adult working life.

Extra year in school: If you are the kind of person who really just hates school and can't wait to get out into the real world, then you won't want to willingly choose to spend another year in the place you're dying to get out of. (…)

Get lazy: In TY you receive little to no homework every night and rarely get tests in class. There are no monthly tests, Christmas or summer exams. The opposite can be said for fifth year. Teachers will pile on the homework and a student coming from TY will really be thrown in the deep end[3]. (…)

Forget things: You know when you go back to school after the summer holidays and it feels like everything has just slowly leaked out[4] over the course of the three months? Try that after a year of not doing particularly exerting[5] classwork, no homework, no study and exams.

So to conclude, there are many pros and cons of doing Transition Year. Overall I feel it all comes down to each individual person and how they are suited to it, and how the school runs the programme. If you do choose to do TY, the advice I would give is to get involved in everything that comes your way and don't let yourself fall behind on work (it will come back to bite you). In the end it will be what you make of it.

Brian Manning (student), spunout.ie, July 30, 2018

1. college = university 2. hound (v.): *harceler*
3. be thrown in the deep end (exp.): *être jeté(e) dans le grand bain*
4. leak out (v.): *s'échapper* 5. exerting (adj.) = tiring

Need help?

- advantages ≠ disadvantages
- investment
- affordable = financially accessible
- rewarding = enriching
- self-sufficient: *autonome*
- bond = create links
- fall behind: *prendre du retard*
- outweigh = predominate
- worry about: *s'inquiéter pour*
- all things considered: *tout compte fait*
- pick up bad habits
- project-based learning
- waste one's time: *perdre son temps*

Prepare your project

Groupwork

Imagine a year without tests. Share your opinion and justify.
▶ *I'm convinced that… • I'd find it really difficult to… • What I'd find positive is…*

Mémoriser • Prononcer • Écrire

Words, words, words

➥ *Faire une carte mentale p. 234*
➥ *Mémoriser et enrichir son lexique p. 235*

Quizlet quizlet.com/skysthelimit2e

Classe / Pistes 19-21 — 11 13

Créez votre propre carte mentale à partir de ce que vous avez vu en classe. Vous pourrez ensuite l'enrichir à l'aide de celle-ci. Écoutez les mots et répétez-les pour bien les prononcer. Écrivez-les aussi plusieurs fois pour mémoriser leur orthographe.

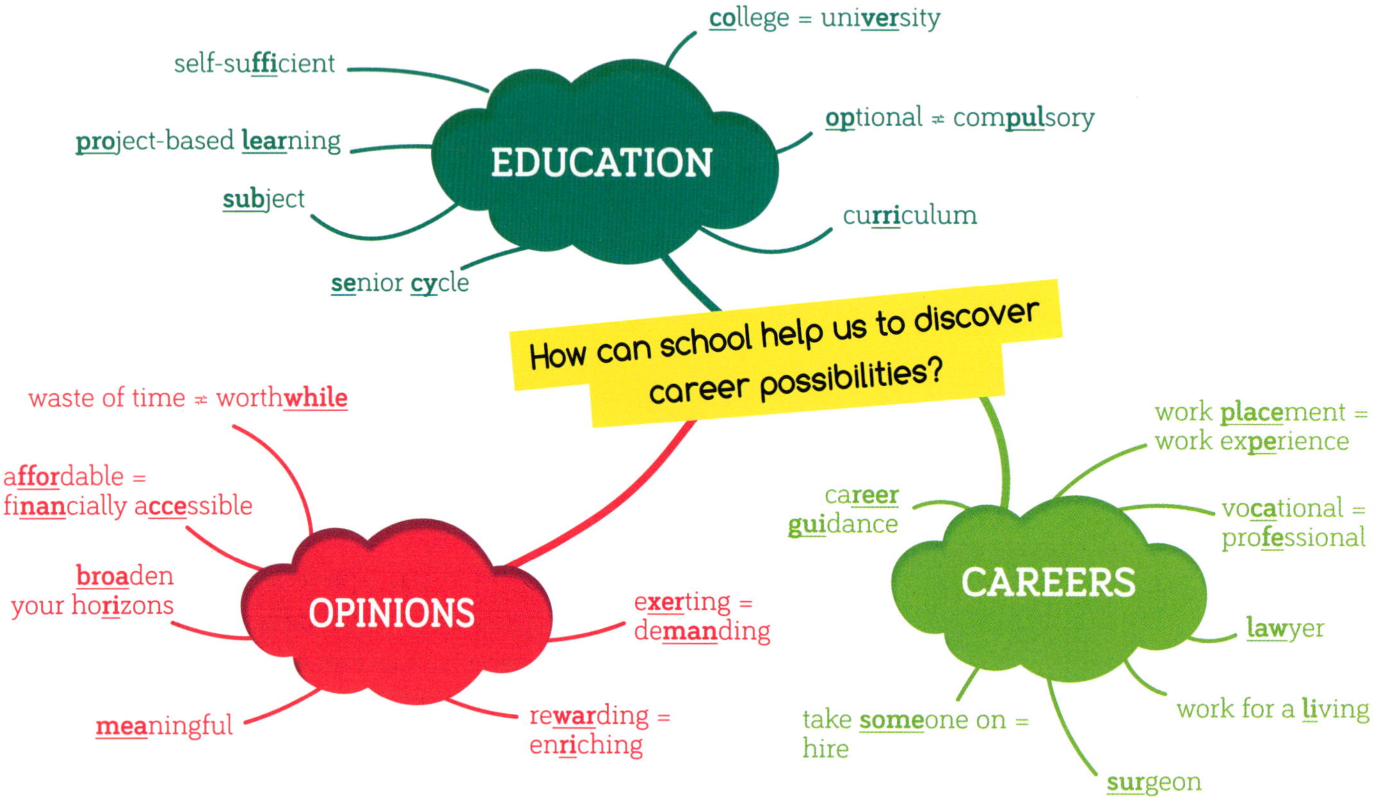

More words

L'accord et le désaccord Repères, p. 263

- I agree with you up to a point.
- You're not serious, are you?
- Surely you have to admit that you might be wrong.
- It cannot be denied that you make a very valid point.

L'essentiel

- Il faut varier vos choix lexicaux pour exprimer l'accord ou le désaccord et nuancer votre propos.

Attention : *Agree* est un verbe, donc on dit *I agree* (sujet + V) / *I don't agree* (sujet + *don't* + BV), alors qu'en français on utilise la construction « être + d'accord ».

1. Divisez les expressions suivantes en trois groupes : *I agree – I partly agree – I disagree.*

You're not serious, are you? – Surely you have to admit that it's far from being the case. – You can say that again! – I agree with you up to a point but it's a complex issue. – Actually, I'd say the exact opposite is true. – Although I see what you mean, I'm not sure it's as simple as that.

2. Écrivez les réponses de B à partir des indices.

A. I think a TY is a waste of time. (B. > I disagree.)
→ B. *You have to admit that it's far from being the case.*

a. A. Everyone should do work experience in secondary school. (B. > I partly agree.)

b. A. All schools should have a TY. (B. > I disagree.)

c. A. There are too many tests in school. (B. > I disagree.)

d. A. Learning about the insides of the legal system must be fascinating. (B. > I agree.)

Observer • Retenir • Appliquer

Grammar

Les *question-tags* Repères, p. 260

– **Transition Year concerns** more and more students, **doesn't it?**
– **They won't** have exams this year, **will they?**
– **She's** studying law, **isn't she?**
– **Let's** sign up for the course, **shall we?**

L'essentiel

- Le ***question-tag*** sert à confirmer une information. Séparé du reste de la phrase par une virgule, il prend la structure d'une question (auxiliaire + (*not*) + sujet).
- Généralement, si la première partie de la phrase est positive, le *tag* est négatif et inversement.

Attention : Avec *let's*, on emploie toujours *shall we?* pour le *tag*.

1. Complétez les phrases en choisissant parmi les *tags* ci-dessous.
aren't they? – won't he? – shall we? – did he? – doesn't she?
They told him to apply for the course, …
→ *They told him to apply for the course, didn't they?*
a. He'll talk about his experience with the group, …
b. Mary wants to become a lawyer, …
c. The teachers are learning new skills too, …
d. John didn't do any exams last year, …
e. Let's apply for the course, …

2. Terminez les phrases avec un *question-tag*.
They will go to Dublin for the course, …
→ *They will go to Dublin for the course, won't they?*
a. He spent a year abroad, …
b. I'll be allowed to go too, …
c. We can sign up next week, …
d. They won't accept you if you don't apply, …
e. She's looking for the orientation teacher, …
f. You've forgotten what we came here for, …

3. Traduisez les phrases suivantes.
Ils ne peuvent pas venir avec nous, n'est-ce pas ?
→ *They can't come with us, can they?*
a. Tu ne connais pas le professeur de français, si ?
b. L'avocate viendra parler de son métier, non ?
c. Elle a participé à la formation (= *training*) la semaine dernière, non ?
d. Il ne voulait pas faire une année de transition, n'est-ce pas ?
e. Vous voulez faire un stage, n'est-ce pas ?

Sounds, sounds, sounds

L'intonation des *question-tags* Repères, p. 247

L'essentiel

L'**intonation des *question-tags*** varie en fonction de l'intention de celui qui parle.

- Si la personne qui parle n'est pas sûre d'elle et attend une réponse précise, **l'intonation monte**.
- Si la personne qui parle est sûre d'elle et n'attend pas de réponse particulière, **l'intonation descend**.

Classe / Piste 22 — 14

1. Écoutez et dites si l'intonation des phrases monte ou descend.

Classe / Piste 23 — 15

2. Servez-vous de l'indice entre parenthèses pour décider si l'intonation des phrases doit monter ou descendre. Écoutez pour vérifier, puis entraînez-vous à haute voix.
a. They wanted to go away for an overnight trip, didn't they? (*Ce n'est pas sûr.*)
b. The judge will decide who is guilty and who is innocent, won't she? (*C'est sûr.*)
c. They aren't going to show the operation to the students, are they? (*Ce n'est pas sûr.*)
d. Yes, they are, it's incredible, isn't it? (*C'est sûr.*)

STRATEGY
Arriver à un accord

Groupwork

Pour arriver à un accord, il faut :

1 ... préparer vos arguments :

→ **Faites une liste de vos arguments** et, pour chacun d'eux, trouvez des **justifications** et des **exemples**.

2 ... imaginer les arguments des autres participants :

→ N'attendez pas l'échange pour découvrir les arguments des autres : mettez-vous à leur place et **faites une liste des points qu'ils pourraient soulever**.

→ Cherchez des **contre-arguments**.

3 ... définir le compromis parfait :

→ Tout le monde ne partagera pas votre avis. **Identifiez ce qui est idéal** et ce qui est **inacceptable** pour vous, puis déterminez à quel point vous êtes prêt(e) à **faire des concessions**.

4 ... être convaincant(e) :

→ **Adaptez le vocabulaire** et **le ton** au sujet.

→ **Soignez votre communication :** regardez les participants dans les yeux, incluez-les avec les *question-tags* par exemple.

5 ... écouter attentivement et rester flexible :

→ Vous pouvez **changer d'avis** si un argument vous paraît convaincant.

→ Si vous n'êtes pas d'accord, **défendez votre position** de façon nuancée.

Si vous faites un compromis, demandez que chacun en fasse un.

Tuto : Débattre : disponible avec FlashPAGE, sur **lycee.editions-bordas.fr** et dans le manuel numérique

Your project | Take part in a round table

Groupwork

Hold a round table to agree on whether and how Transition Year should be introduced in your school.

1 Prepare the organisation of the round table.

- **Distribute tasks among the debaters:** someone to present the subject, a note-taker, someone to write on the board, a time-keeper and a chairperson to head the meeting. **Agree on** the rules of the round table.

2 Present the subject.

- Have the chairperson **open the meeting**. Ask the first speaker to **present the subject** to be discussed. Include a clear definition and description of Transition Year in the presentation.

3 Share opinions.

- All the participants **give their opinion** on the subject and **justify**. You may choose to **take a first vote** (for – against – undecided) to see your starting point in the discussion.

4 Discuss a curriculum.

- **Exchange** on the different subjects and projects that you would like to include if your school decided to introduce a Transition Year. **Agree on** what would be **obligatory**, what would be **optional**, the hours per week… **Draw** a table of the curriculum on the board for clarity.

5 Close the round table with a vote.

- **Present the curriculum** decided by your round table to the class and **vote for the best curriculum** of the different round tables.

Keys to success

- **Utilisez le vocabulaire du chapitre :** éducation, carrières, opinions.
  ➥ *Words, words, words, p. 50*
- **Variez les expressions pour dire l'accord ou le désaccord.**
  ➥ *More words, p. 50*
- **Servez-vous des *question-tags*.**
  ➥ *Grammar, p. 51*
- **Utilisez la bonne intonation avec les *question-tags*.**
  ➥ *Sounds, sounds, sounds, p. 51*
- **Servez-vous des conseils pour arriver à un accord.**
  ➥ *Strategy, p. 52*
- **Servez-vous des conseils pour travailler en groupe.**
  ➥ *Strategy, p. 237*

Axe 2 : Les univers professionnels, le monde du travail

4 Finding your way

How can personal implication give you ideas for your future?

Your project

Create and present a pitch for an innovative idea at an "Ideas Fair", *p. 63*
- Present a problem and list solutions, *p. 57*
- Choose an invention from a science fair to present to the class, *p. 58*

Keys to success

- **Strategy: convaincre à l'oral**, *p. 62*
- **Mind map:** problems, ideas, attitudes, *p. 60*
- **Grammar:** structures causatives, *p. 61*
- **Sounds:** accent contrastif, *p. 61*

Volunteers working in the Summer in the City program, which puts students to work on community improvement projects, Detroit, Michigan.

1 Basics

List all the words that come to mind when you think about your future (interests – work – hopes and fears).

WORKSHEET 5

2 Discover

Classe 1 Piste 24

Listen and **pick out** words associated with the future (lifestyle – employment – needs – solutions). **Compare** these visions of the future with your own.

▶ *In my opinion, the future will have…* • *Maybe there's going to be…* • *I guess we won't…*

Game 3 Play

Word game: Make up portmanteau words to refer to inventions that will definitely change our lives in the future. The others have to **guess** what they will be useful for. *Example: a sollphone → a solar cellphone.*

Écouter • Lire • Parler

Teens' ideas

1 vidéo Improving eating habits

1. Watch the video without the sound and take notes (speaker – people – places – activities – food).

2. Watch again with the sound. Pick out stressed words and classify them (food – health – activities – difficulties).

3. Médiation Use what you have understood to sum up the goals of the organisation.
▶ *It wants to make people... • It would like young people...*

4. Say whether you would like to work in this field and explain why / why not.

Haile Thomas is a certified nutrition health coach working with school children.

2 vidéo Seeing clearly

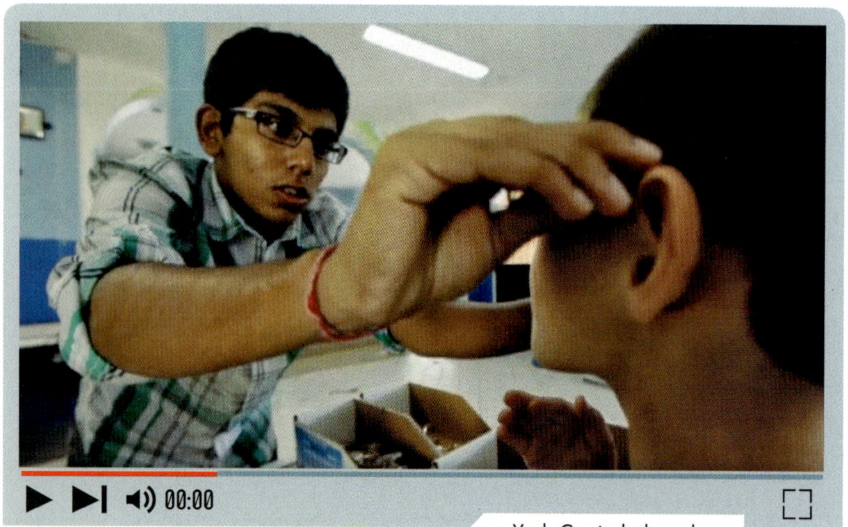

Yash Gupta helps a boy try on his new glasses.

1. Watch the video without the sound. Take notes about what you see (people – activities – environments). Use your notes to explain Yash's idea.

2. Watch the 1st part again with the sound and focus on numbers. Say what they refer to.

3. Watch the 2nd part and focus on Yash's experience and what it taught him.
▶ *Having no glasses let him discover... • The experience made him...*

4. Médiation Explain how Yash manages to convince us with his pitch that his idea is valid.

3 Protecting villages

1. **Look** at the picture, **read** the caption and **guess** the boy's job.
2. **Read** the text and **pick out** information about the boy (name – age – occupation – origins).
3. **Find** information about his invention (initial problem – idea – invention).
4. **Focus on** references to places. **Use** them to **describe** the impact of his invention.
5. Médiation — **Imagine** you are Richard. **Present** your idea to another village that is having the same problem.

CULTURE QUEST

Find out about what Richard is doing now.

Keywords: Richard Turere – Lion Lights – BBC.

Richard Turere with his father's cows, 2016

One of the talks from the TED[1] stage in Long Beach, Calif., this week came from Richard Turere, an inventor. He is a Maasai from Kenya. And he's 13.

"From ages 6 to 9, I started looking after my father's cows," Richard says. "I'd take them out in the morning and bring them back in the evening. We put them in a small cow shed[2] at night," and that's when the trouble would start. Lions would jump in the shed and kill the cows, which are enclosed and an easy target. (...)

One night he was walking around with a flashlight and discovered the lions were scared of a moving light. A light went on inside him and an idea was born. Three weeks and much tinkering[3] later, Richard had invented a system of lights that flash around the cow shed, mimicking a human walking around with a flashlight. His system is made from broken flashlight parts and an indicator box from a motorcycle.

"The only thing I bought was a solar panel," which charges a battery that supplies power to the lights at night, Richard says. He calls the system Lion Lights. (...)

His simple solution was so successful, his neighbors heard about it and wanted Lion Lights, too. He installed the lights for them and for six other homes in his community. From there, the lights spread and are now being used all around Kenya. Someone in India is trying them out for tigers. In Zambia and Tanzania they're being used, as well.

Nina Gregory, "All Tech Considered", NPR, March 1, 2013

1. Teens from all over the world participate every year in TED conferences.
2. shed (n.): *abri*
3. tinker (v.): *bricoler*

Need help?

- conservation = preservation
- deprived = poor with no resources
- endangered = threatened
- harmonious = balanced
- innovative = new
- renewable: *renouvelable*
- reusable = can be used again
- overseas: *à l'étranger*
- expand = develop
- lack = not have enough
- waste: *gaspiller*

Prepare your project

Pairwork — With a partner, present a problem (economic – social – environmental…) to your class and list three possible solutions.

▶ *This problem is ours to solve!*

Écouter • Lire • Parler

Young inventors

CULTURE QUEST

Discover more about the yearly Google Science Fair and the teen winners.

Keywords: Google Science Fair – teen winners.

1 vidéo Lighting the way

1. Guess the content of the video using the photo and the caption.

2. Watch the 1st part and pick out information about the inventor (name – age – home – family – interests). Describe her attitude.

▶ *She seems to be… • I'd say that she is… • She is undoubtedly…*

3. Watch the 2nd part. Focus on what you see to understand her invention. Note down information about its potential impact.

4. Give your opinion about Ann's pitch: convincing? unconvincing? Justify.

5. Write a 5-line paragraph in which you imagine going a week without electricity.

Young inventor Ann Makosinski, winner of the 2013 Google Science Fair, and her flashlight

Need help?

- display board: *tableau d'affichage*
- drought [draʊt]: *sécheresse*
- family origins
- dedicated = devoted to a task
- enthusiastic = very motivated
- scientific
- come up with = find
- change of pace = live at a different speed

Prepare your project

Choose an invention from a science fair and present it to the class (name – description – purpose – advantages). Try to persuade the class to vote for it.

▶ *This invention is the best because… • It makes us understand… • It lets you see…*

2 Changing lives in South Africa

DOSSIER documentaire

Classe 1 Piste 25

1. **Describe** the photo and **guess** what the girl is talking about.
2. **Read** the text and **pick out** information about the girl (name – education – place of living).
3. **Find** references to nature. Use your notes to **identify** the problem she noticed and what her invention does.
4. **Listen** to the audio and **pick out** information about the girl (age – likes – ambitions).
5. **Listen** again. **Focus on** references to the problem her country is experiencing, and **say** what she wants to do and have other young South Africans do.
   ▶ *Kiara wants to have other teens… • She wants to make them…*
6. **Make** a 1-minute presentation of a problem that you would like to find a solution to.

Kiara Nirghin was winner of the 2016 Google Science Fair thanks to an invention to combat drought.

Kiara Nirghin was leafing through a newspaper one day when she noticed several stories about farmers struggling with drought[1]. Nirghin, a high school junior in Johannesburg, had known South Africa was in the midst of an intense drought, but in that moment she realized the problem extended far beyond her country: "It's affecting the whole world. And to this point, there hasn't been something that has revolutionized drought."

Nirghin set about brainstorming on how to ensure that crops[2] have access to water – even during the most severe stretches of dry weather. Her simple solution earned her the grand prize at the Google Science Fair in September. (*Scientific American* co-sponsors the awards.)

For her project, Nirghin created a biodegradable and superabsorbent material that can be "planted" alongside crops to create "mini reservoirs of water in the soil," she explained in her presentation. First she boiled orange peels in water to produce a liquid rich in pectin, a highly absorbent carbohydrate. Then she combined the pectin with pieces of dried orange peels and avocado skins, baked the mixture to remove moisture and crushed it all into a powder. Finally, she mixed the powder with more peels and skins. The resulting polymer could hold 300 times its weight in water. In tests, the invention kept soil moist – and plants grown with it were taller and healthier and produced more flowers.

Catherine Caruso, *Scientific American*, Dec. 1, 2016

1. drought (n.): *sécheresse*
2. crop (n.): *récolte*

Grammar

Les structures causatives

Her research **made** Kiara **realise** that people needed help.

➥ *Grammar p. 61*

Mémoriser • Prononcer • Écrire

Words, words, words

➥ *Faire une carte mentale p. 234*
➥ *Mémoriser et enrichir son lexique p. 235*

Quizlet
quizlet.com/skysthelimit2e

Classe 1 Pistes 26-28 | 16 18

Créez votre propre carte mentale à partir de ce que vous avez vu en classe. Vous pourrez ensuite l'enrichir à l'aide de celle-ci. Écoutez les mots et répétez-les pour bien les prononcer. Écrivez-les aussi plusieurs fois pour mémoriser leur orthographe.

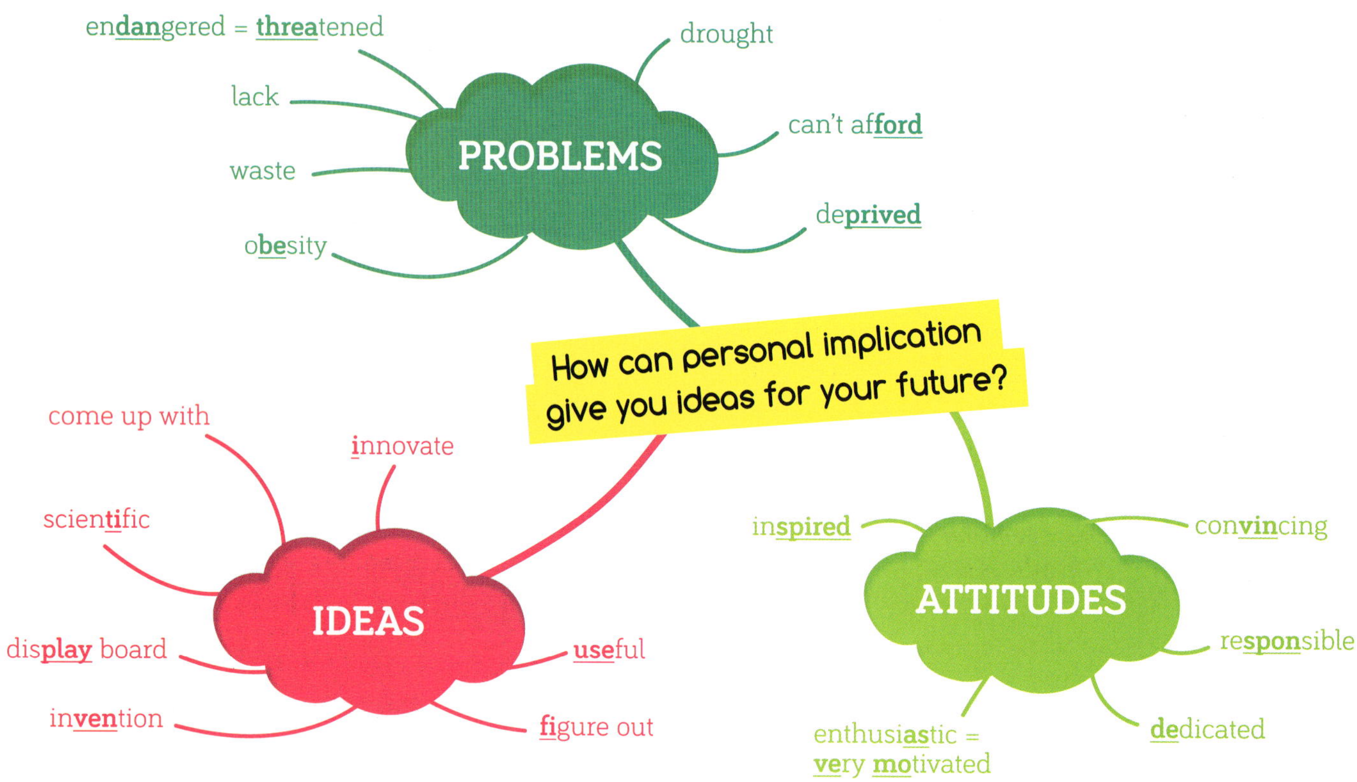

More words

Les pronoms possessifs

Repères, p. 256

– This idea is **ours** and we must develop it!
– The responsibility for preparing a pitch is **yours**.
– People used to think that a job was **theirs** for life.

L'essentiel

Les **pronoms possessifs** sont *mine*, *yours* (singulier et pluriel), *his*, *hers*, *ours* et *theirs*. Ils peuvent remplacer un adjectif possessif + nom, sauf pour *its* car il n'y a aucun pronom possessif correspondant.

1. Complétez les phrases avec le pronom possessif approprié : *mine – yours – his – hers – ours – theirs.*

He has made this decision. The decision is (?).
→ *The decision is his.*

a. That's my business. It's (?).
b. This office belongs to us all. It's (?).
c. Richard told the interviewer that the cattle were (?) to guard.
d. Ann's invention is (?) to develop into a sustainable business.
e. I'm not going to steal your idea! Obviously it's (?) to keep!
f. (?) was a really exceptional display board which they had spent weeks creating.
g. I had the best ideas. The best ideas were (?).
h. It's our project about innovation. The project is (?).

Grammar

Les structures causatives

Repères, p. 262

- Her research **made** Kiara **realise** that people needed help.
- The politician **let** the protester **give** his opinion.
- I will **have** him **postpone** the meeting to a later date.
- They **forced** us **to wait** for two hours.

L'essentiel

• Dans les **structures causatives** (faire faire qqc à qqn), le sujet est à l'origine de l'action mais ne l'accomplit pas lui-même.

• On utilise des verbes tels que *let*, *make* et *have*. Ils sont suivis soit de la **base verbale d'un 2e verbe**, soit d'un **verbe à l'infinitif avec *to***.

• Lorsque le sujet du 2e verbe est un pronom, c'est un **pronom complément** (*make him / her / them do sth*).

Attention : L'ordre des mots n'est pas le même qu'en français.

1. Faites des phrases avec les verbes *make* – *let* – *have*.

The police (*she – write a statement*).

→ *The police made her write a statement.*

a. We (*they – vote*) a new law to protect the coasts.

b. They (*we – speak*) before the whole assembly.

c. He (*she – start*) recycling.

d. They (*I – realise*) that I could do something about it.

2. Utilisez *have*, *make* ou *let* pour reformuler les réponses entre parenthèses.

Did you make the sign yourself? (*No, we asked a local artist…*)

→ *No, we had a local artist make it.*

a. Did you give a speech at the TED Conference? (*No, I forced my colleague…*)

b. Do they write all their campaign materials themselves? (*No, they allow volunteers…*)

c. Will he visit the new plantations soon? (*No, he'll encourage his associate to do it…*)

d. Are you going to write to Yash? (*No, you are welcome to…*)

3. Traduisez les phrases avec l'aide des amorces.

Je vais laisser parler mon ami. (*I will let…*)

→ *I will let my friend speak.*

a. Ils l'ont obligé à refaire sa présentation. (*They forced…*)

b. Leurs remarques me font penser à une autre solution. (*Their remarks make…*)

c. Dites-lui de m'appeler si elle trouve une nouvelle idée. (*Have her…*)

Sounds, sounds, sounds

L'accent contrastif

Repères, p. 247

L'essentiel

• En anglais, on utilise l'**accentuation** qui permet d'insister sur un mot : *She uses her website to give <u>her</u> opinion.* (Et pas l'opinion de quelqu'un d'autre.)

• L'accentuation peut porter sur n'importe quel mot de la phrase : *She uses her <u>website</u> to give her opinion.* (Son site web, et pas un autre média.)

Attention : Évitez de traduire littéralement du français (« c'est moi qui / c'est lui qui ») et pensez à l'accentuation : C'est lui qui a posté la photo. → *<u>He</u> posted the photo.*

Classe Piste 29 — 19

1. Écoutez la phrase, prononcée de trois manières différentes. Déterminez laquelle est neutre et lesquelles ont un élément accentué. Expliquez l'impact de ces accents contrastifs sur le sens.

I would define my generation as very creative.

Classe Piste 30 — 20

2. Lisez les phrases et les informations entre parenthèses. Identifiez les mots sur lesquels portera l'accent contrastif et lisez à voix haute. Écoutez et vérifiez.

a. The environment should be everybody's concern. (*It's not just a matter for activists.*)

b. She spent 7 hours on her project! (*Not 5 or 6 hours.*)

c. I think young people need to respect older generations. (*It may not be your opinion, but it is mine.*)

STRATEGY — CONVAINCRE À L'ORAL

Pour convaincre à l'oral, il faut :

1 ... être préparé(e) :

- Vérifiez que vous **maîtrisez votre sujet** (faits – chiffres – arguments).
- Veillez à avoir des **sources fiables**.
- **Organisez vos idées**, supprimez tout ce qui est hors sujet ou redondant.

Résumez en une phrase votre message pour vous assurer qu'il est clair.

2 ... choisir un vocabulaire adapté :

- **Utilisez :**
  - des **adverbes** pour insister sur une idée ;
    absolutely • really • undoubtedly...
  - des **expressions** pour attirer l'attention sur un point ;
    What you need to know is... • Without a doubt... • There is no denying...
  - des **questions** pour interpeller votre public en veillant à l'intonation.
    How can we accept that...? • How long will it take us to...? • Where are the...?

3 ... impliquer vos auditeurs :

- Maintenez un **contact visuel** avec vos auditeurs.
  Is that something you can accept?
- Adressez-vous directement à eux et commencez avec une **phrase** qui **attire tout de suite leur attention**.
  What I want to tell you about is...
- Posez-leur des **questions**.
- **Associez-les** à votre projet.
  We need to work together... • All of us...

4 ... être à l'écoute et argumenter :

- **Répondez** aux questions et **respectez** toutes les opinions.
  I can understand your point of view, however...

Your project

Present the pitch for an innovative idea

Your class is holding an "Ideas Fair": create a pitch for an innovative idea and present it. Try to win the first prize.

At a high school Science Fair, Massachusetts, USA, 2016

1 Find a solution to make tomorrow's world a better place.

- **Think of a situation that needs improving:** environment – society – everyday life, etc.
- **Find a solution:** a way to save energy – an idea for recycling – an invention that will make life easier. Be creative but keep it simple!

2 Decide what you will include.

- Write a **description** of the problem and what your idea or invention is (problem it will solve – where – when – impact).

3 Prepare your pitch.

- Decide which **visual aids** will make your points clearer.
- Think of a **striking opening**: a quote – a question – a surprising fact…
- **Organise** your ideas so as to be **concise and coherent**.
- **Practise** your pitch out loud (record yourself).
- **Stress keywords** and use a **dynamic tone**.
- **Imagine answers** to the audience's questions.

4 Deliver your pitch at the Ideas Fair.

- **Pitch your idea.** Take care to **stay within the timeframe** you have been given (max 1-2 minutes).
- **Make eye contact with your audience.** Make sure everyone speaks.
- **Answer** your classmates' questions.

5 Vote for the best idea.

- The class will **vote** for the best idea(s)! The five **most convincing ideas** can be posted on a class blog or on Padlet.

Keys to success

- **Utilisez le vocabulaire du chapitre :** problèmes, idées, attitudes.
  ➥ *Words, words, words, p. 60*
- **Utilisez les structures causatives.**
  ➥ *Grammar, p. 61*
- **Pensez à utiliser l'accent contrastif.**
  ➥ *Sounds, sounds, sounds, p. 61*
- **Servez-vous des conseils pour convaincre à l'oral.**
  ➥ *Strategy, p. 62*
- **Pensez à utiliser les conseils pour s'exprimer en public.**
  ➥ *Strategy, p. 233*

Entraînement aux épreuves communes

Au cours de l'année de 1re, deux épreuves porteront sur la compréhension de l'oral, la compréhension de l'écrit et l'expression écrite. Nous vous proposons un entraînement « en douceur » à ces épreuves.

- ***Épreuve 1 – 1re partie*** ➥ *p. 64-65*
- ***Épreuve 1 – 1re et 2e parties*** ➥ *p. 128-129*
- ***Épreuve 2 – 1re et 2e parties*** ➥ *p. 180-181*

▶ **1re partie de l'épreuve 1 :** compréhension de l'oral.
– Le document pourra être un audio ou une vidéo.
– Le titre du document vous sera communiqué en début d'épreuve.
– Il faudra rendre compte en français de ce que vous avez compris.
▶ **2e partie de l'épreuve 1 :** expression écrite : deux sujets au choix.

Compréhension de l'oral

Classe 3 · Piste 52 · 108

Sujet **Girls think of a new invention to help homeless people**

Vous allez **écouter trois fois** un document audio avec une pause entre chaque écoute.
À l'issue de la 3e écoute, vous devrez **rendre compte en français** de ce que vous avez compris.

▶ Les clés pour réussir

Attention à bien gérer votre temps entre la compréhension de l'oral et l'expression écrite.

Vous avez des connaissances, mobilisez-les !

- **Relisez la stratégie** de compréhension d'un document audio ou audiovisuel. ➥ *p. 30*

Concentrez-vous sur ce que vous comprenez, certains mots vous échapperont peut-être, c'est normal !

- Pour vous préparer à l'écoute, **appuyez-vous sur les connaissances de l'axe étudié**, Axe 2 : Les univers professionnels, le monde du travail, séquences *Transition Year Ireland* (➥ *p. 44*) **ou** *Finding your way* (➥ *p. 54*).

Avant l'écoute.

- **Anticipez :** lisez le titre et imaginez le contenu du document audio / vidéo.
- **Notez** au brouillon **toutes les idées** qui vous viennent à l'esprit.

Girls think of a new invention to help homeless people

teenagers? / students? → Girls
innovation / technology → new invention
housing / poverty → homeless

Pendant l'écoute.

1re écoute

– Identifiez **le type de document sonore :** *documentary – interview – dialogue...*
– **Concentrez-vous** sur les **indices sonores :** *sound effects – music – number and types of voices...* et / ou **visuels :** *places – people – attitudes – actions.*
– **Identifiez le sujet du document** à partir de ces premiers éléments.
– **Notez les mots** que vous avez compris.

Vous pouvez prendre des notes en anglais ou en français, selon ce qui est le plus simple pour vous.

2e écoute

– **Complétez vos notes :** mots accentués – mots répétés – nombres.
– Commencez à **organiser vos notes** selon **votre propre logique :** classement par thématiques – personnes qui parlent – parties 1, 2, 3... Une organisation sous forme de **tableau** peut être utile.
– Commencez à **faire des liens** entre **ce que vous savez** et **ce que vous avez compris**.

3e écoute

– **Complétez** une nouvelle fois vos notes selon l'**organisation** que vous aurez choisie et **ajoutez des mots** à vos différentes rubriques.

Ne cherchez pas à tout comprendre, vous pouvez compenser l'inconnu grâce à ce que vous savez déjà.

Entre les écoutes.

Vous avez **une pause** entre chaque écoute. Profitez-en pour :
– **mettre en relation** les éléments repérés ;
– **revoir vos notes**, les classer, ajouter de nouveaux mots ;
– vous **préparer à l'écoute suivante** en gardant à l'esprit les points à éclaircir.

Après la dernière écoute.

Avant la reformulation

– **Regroupez les éléments** selon votre logique.
– Vérifiez la **cohérence** de l'ensemble.

La reformulation

– Préparez votre **compte-rendu en français**.
– Évoquez la **nature du document**, son **thème**, le **nombre de personnes** qui parlent et les **idées** principales.
– Rédigez dans une **langue simple**.

Évitez de traduire mot à mot ce que vous avez entendu : concentrez-vous sur le sens global et reformulez avec vos propres termes.

– **Ne cherchez pas à donner votre avis :** il faut uniquement rendre compte de ce que vous avez entendu.
– **Relisez** votre résumé pour être sûr(e) qu'il est compréhensible et cohérent.

Pour la 2e partie de l'épreuve 1, rendez-vous → p. 128-129, avec un autre exemple de sujet.

Axe 3 : Le village,

le quartier, la ville

5 Life on the US Coasts, *p. 68* Séquence +

What are the cultural identities of the East and West Coasts?

6 Five senses in Mumbai, *p. 84*

How can the five senses contribute to discovering a city?

Axe 3 : Le village, le quartier, la ville

5 Life on the US Coasts

What are the cultural identities of the East and West Coasts?

Your project

Create and present a slideshow about a place on the East or West Coast, *p. 83*
- Compare places from each coast, *p. 71*
- Make an oral presentation about a film or a series, *p. 75*
- Record a presentation about a music style, *p. 77*

Keys to success

- **Strategy: parler à partir de notes**, *p. 82*
- **Mind map:** ethnic diversity, cultural diversity, living conditions, *p. 78*
- **Grammar:** comparatif et superlatif, verbes prépositionnels, phrases exclamatives, *p. 80*
- **Sounds:** syllabes accentuées, *p. 81*

Séquence +

1 Basics

List all the words that come to mind when you think of American coasts (people – places – history…). WORKSHEET 6

2 Discover

Classe / Piste 31

Match each picture with a coast (East or West) then **listen** to the speakers. **Pick out** keywords (places – people – activities…). Sum up what characterises each coast and compare.

▶ *It's more… than… • It's not as… as… • Compared to…*

Game 3 Play

Memory game: List as many States in the US as you can in three minutes. The team that names the most wins.

Parler • Échanger

Different diversities (1)

1 Coasts overview

1. **Share** what you know about the coasts (history and geography). **Compare** the figures. **Make** a list of what you find striking.
   ▶ *The population is much larger in… than… • It's the largest…*
2. **Describe** the dishes and **match** them with their origins when possible.

Many Chinese and Japanese immigrants arrived through Angel Island, San Francisco, 1910-1940.

The Bracero program brought over 4 million Mexican workers to the US, 1942-1964.

Asian food, LA

Fusion food: Asian style nachos, LA

Smoothies were invented in the 1930s in California.

Estimated population 2017

- West Coast: **51 million**
  about **15%** of the US population
- California State: **37.3 million**
  57% White
  37% Hispanic or Latino
  16% other
  13% Asian
  6% African American

Sources: census.gov – suburbanstats.org

Need help?

- co**he**sion = **u**nion
- dish
- **re**cipe ['resəpi]
- soul [səul] food = tra**di**tional **A**frican-A**me**rican food
- influ**en**tial = have an **im**pact
- mouth-**wa**tering = **tas**ty
- skilled ≠ un**skilled**
- **e**migrate ≠ **im**migrate
- fit in = con**form**
- o**ri**ginate = come from
- **se**ttle = come to live
- give something a go / a whirl / a shot = try something
- wave of immi**gra**tion: *vague d'immigration*

CULTURE QUEST

Watch a video about New Haven pizzas.
Keywords: Frank Pepe - New Haven - pizza - history - secrets - WTNH.

MAINE

NH* MA* Boston 673,000 NY* CT* RH*

New York City 8.5 million

PA* NJ* Philadelphia 1.5 million

MD* DE* Washington D.C. 680,000

Ellis Island = gateway for 12 million immigrants (Italian, German, Irish, Russian...), 1892-1954

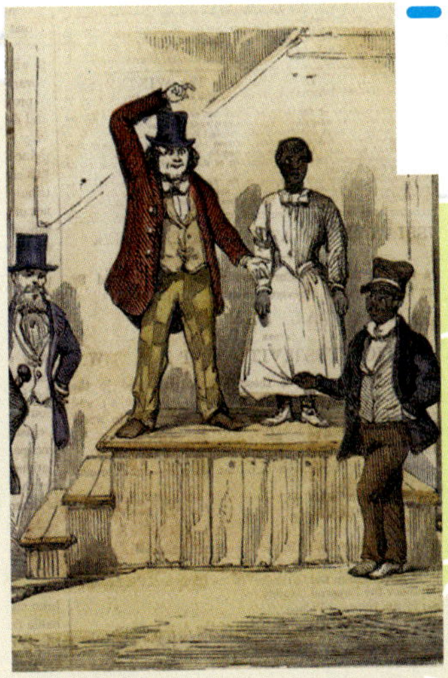

By the 1860s, there were almost 4 million slaves in the USA.

5 hours by plane (2019)

VA* NC*

Pastrami on rye, in Jewish delicatessens in NYC

The hamburger named after the "Hamburg steak", NYC, 19th century

African American soul food in Charleston, South Carolina

SC* GA* FLORIDA

ATLANTIC OCEAN

Estimated population 2017

- **East Coast: 117 million** about **36%** of the US population
- **New York State: 19.4 million**
  - 65% White
  - 17% Hispanic or Latino
  - 15% African American
  - 7% Asian
  - 7% other

Sources: census.gov – suburbanstats.org

* = original 13 colonies: New Hampshire – New York – Massachusetts – Connecticut – Rhode Island – Pennsylvania – New Jersey – Maryland – Delaware – Virginia – North Carolina – South Carolina – Georgia

Miami 500,000

Prepare your project

Find information (food – population – climate…) about a place on the map and present it without naming it. The class will guess the name. Then compare the places.

▶ *California is much bigger than… • New York is far more populated than…*

Different diversities (2)

2 Golden State HISPANICS

Classe 1 Piste 32

1. Comment on the picture and guess the content of the audio.
2. Listen and pick out information about Claudia Otero (job – origin).
3. Find references to language and say what has changed.

Hispanics waving Mexican and American flags in Los Angeles

Did you know?

Hispanics in **California** make up **37%** of the total population, which is the highest total number of Hispanics of any US State. Spanish is the State's second most spoken language. About 28% of Californians speak Spanish at home as a first language.

Sources: census.gov – suburbanstats.org

3 The wealth of a nation

Classe 1 Piste 33

1. Describe and comment on the photo.
2. Listen to the writer Thomas Steinbeck and pick out stressed words. Classify them (nationalities – culture – wine – fishing industry – orchard (*verger*) culture).
3. Sum up his opinion about the impacts of immigration on a country. (Médiation)

Dorothea Lange, *Japanese agricultural workers packing broccoli near Guadalupe*, California, 1937

Grammar

Les verbes prépositionnels

– She wasn't discriminated against.
(V. + prép.)

➥ *Grammar p. 81*

4 New York City vs Hartford

1. Describe the photo and imagine where the young women are going.

2. Read and find information about the narrator (probable age – family situation).

3. Make a list of all the places mentioned and situate them on a map. Say what they mean to the narrator.

4. Compare New York City and Hartford (activity – population – lifestyle).
▶ *Hartford is…* + adj. + *-er than…* • *New York must be a lot* + adj. + *-er than…*

5. Pick a dream place to live (town, city or country) and give five reasons why it's the best.

1945. Sara Smythe is in her early twenties. She has recently settled in New York…

The reason I didn't have a boyfriend was a simple one: at that juncture in my life, I was simply too busy. I had my job. I had my first apartment: a small studio, on a beautiful leafy[1] corner of Greenwich Village called Bedford Street. Most of all, I had New York – and that was the best romance imaginable. Though I'd visited it regularly over the years, living there was another matter altogether – and there were times when I literally thought I had landed in a playground for adults. To someone raised within the sedate[2], conservative, meddlesome[3] confines of Hartford, Connecticut, Manhattan was a heady[4] revelation. To begin with, it was so amazingly anonymous. You could become quite invisible, and never feel as if anyone was looking over your shoulder in disapproving judgement (a favorite Hartford pastime). You could stay out all night. Or spend half a Saturday losing yourself in the eight miles' worth of books at the Strand Bookshop. (…)
The sense of freedom was extraordinary. I was no longer under parental supervision. I was paying my own way in life. I answered to nobody. And thanks to my brother Eric I had a direct entrée into Manhattan's more esoteric underside. He seemed to know every arcane resident of the city. Czech translators of medieval poetry. All-night jazz disc jockeys. Emigré German sculptors. Would-be composers who were writing atonal operas about Gawain[5]… in short, the sort of people you would never meet in Hartford, Connecticut.

Douglas Kennedy, *The Pursuit of Happiness*, 2001

Stanley Kubrick, *Showtime in Manhattan*, NYC, 1946

1. leafy (adj.) = with many leaves
2. sedate (adj.) = calm
3. meddlesome (adj.) = intrusive
4. heady (adj.) = exciting
5. Gawain (n.): *Gauvin (chevalier de la Table ronde)*

Need help?

- **ashamed** ≠ proud
- **coastal** = be**side** the sea
- **diff**erent from ≠ **si**milar to
- **to**lerant = **o**pen-**min**ded
- une**vent**ful ≠ **bu**zzing
- ap**prove** of ≠ disap**prove** of
- dis**cri**minate against = treat (un)**fair**ly
- **in**tegrate = be**come** a part of
- share **bor**ders with = have the same **bor**der as
- **sparse**ly **po**pulated ≠ **dense**ly **po**pulated

Écouter • Écrire • Parler

LA and NYC on screen

Did you know?

The term "**La La Land**" refers to the city of Los Angeles partly because of the place name (LA) and partly because of the supposedly frivolous and eccentric behaviour of the city's movie community.
It now often means being "out of touch with reality".

1 vidéo A love letter to LA

1. **Comment** on the photo. Imagine what aspect of Los Angeles the film is about.
2. **Watch** the video without the sound and check. **Make** a list of the types of places shown.
3. **Watch** with the sound and **put** the places in the order in which they appear, then **pick out** information about them: Griffith Observatory / Planetarium – Lighthouse Jazz club – music venues – Hermosa Beach – Watts Towers – Angels Flight.
4. **Pick out** three elements in the video that would make you want to visit LA.

Opening scene from the film *La La Land* (2016), with the city of Los Angeles in the background

2 Celebrating the BIG apple

1. **Say** what you know about the TV series you see and react.
   ▶ *It's such an old… • I have never heard of… • I used to… • What an amazing…! • How funny…!*
2. **Use** the captions to **locate** the places on a map of New York City.
3. **Use** the Internet to **watch** extracts from other series set in NYC. **Keywords:** 15 – TV shows – visit – New York – nycgo. Say if they make you want to visit New York.
4. **Make** a list of your favourite TV series. Find out where they are set.

CULTURE QUEST

Find out where exactly the series *Friends* and *How I Met Your Mother* were shot.
Keywords: *Friends* or *How I Met Your Mother* – shooting – filming locations – studio – apartments – soundstage.

How I Met Your Mother (2005-2014), set in the Upper West Side

Need help?

- **back**drop: *décor*
- cast: *distribution*
- di**rec**tor: *réalisateur/-trice*
- **high**way = main road
- pro**du**cer: *producteur/-trice*
- a **se**ries: *une série*
- **cloud**less = without clouds
- **da**ted = old-**fa**shioned
- **i**conic = emble**ma**tic
- star in = play a **lea**ding role
- shoot = film
- on lo**ca**tion ≠ in the **stu**dio

The Get Down (2016-2017), set in the Bronx

Mr Robot (since 2015), set in Coney Island, Lower Manhattan, the Queens, etc.

Jessica Jones (since 2015) set in Hell's Kitchen, East Village, etc.

Friends (1994-2004), set in Greenwich Village

Brooklyn Nine-Nine (since 2013), set in... Brooklyn!

Prepare your project

Find at least five films or series set in NYC and LA on the Internet. Choose one and make a 3-minute oral presentation about it (filming locations – plot – places that can be seen…). The class will guess which one it is.

Grammar

Les phrases exclamatives

– What an amazing series! (an amazing series: GN)

➡ *Grammar p. 81*

Écouter • Lire • Partager • Parler

Legendary places and music

Différenciation

You are going to learn about East and West coast music styles.
Work on one of these topics to find the link between place and music.
Step 1: Pick out information and take notes (music style – origin – famous people – events – interesting information).
Médiation **Step 2:** GROUPWORK **Share your findings.** WORKSHEET 10

TOPIC 1 California cool

DOSSIER documentaire — Classe Piste 34 — WORKSHEET 7

1. Read the text.

2. Listen to Ray Manzarek and **sum up** the recording.
▶ *One of the biggest… • One of the most…*

Jim Morrison mural in Venice Beach (LA), by the artist Rip Cronk

Known around the world as one of L.A.'s quintessential bands, The Doors formed in 1965 after UCLA[1] alums[2], singer Jim Morrison and keyboardist Ray Manzarek, met in Venice Beach. As The Doors, the quartet of Morrison, Manzarek, guitarist Robby Krieger and drummer John Densmore became one of the best-selling bands in history. Regarded as one of the most influential rock acts of the 1960s, The Doors have been listed by many critics and magazines as one of the greatest music acts of all time. The band's eponymous debut album, **L.A. Woman**, and **Strange Days** were listed in *Rolling Stone's* 500 Greatest Albums of All Time. The Doors were inducted into the Rock and Roll Hall of Fame in 1993. (…) Fifty years to the day of the release of The Doors debut album, Jan. 4 was declared "Day of The Doors" in the City of Los Angeles.

discoverlosangeles.com, Jan. 2018

1. UCLA = University of California, Los Angeles
2. alum (n.) = a graduate of a university

TOPIC 2 West Coast RAP

WORKSHEET 8

1. Read about the man in the photo and **sum up**.
▶ *He's famous for… • He comes from… • His work was recognised…*

2. List all the American rappers you know.
Say what you know about them and guess where they are from.

Like many other rappers Kendrick Lamar comes from Compton, a hub-city near downtown LA, known for its violence in the 1980s.

In news that caught many off guard[1], celebrated Compton-born rapper Kendrick Lamar was awarded the Pulitzer[2] on Monday for his work on his 2017 album *Damn*. With the announcement, the committee praised Lamar's album as "a virtuosic song collection unified by its vernacular authenticity and rhythmic dynamism that offers affecting vignettes capturing the complexity of modern African-American life."
Translation: It's an amazing album that documents South L.A. black life with wildly accomplished beats and verses.

Randall Roberts, *Los Angeles Times*, April 16, 2018

1. catch off guard (exp.) = surprise 2. Pulitzer = a very famous American award

TOPIC 3

vidéo

Birth of Hip Hop

DOSSIER documentaire

WORKSHEET 9

1. **Describe** the invitation.
   ▶ *Back in the 70s… • People used to invite… • They had to communicate via…*

2. **Watch** the video about the history of hip hop.

3. **Read** the information box below and **sum up**.

CULTURE QUEST

Find out where other famous American music styles come from.

Keywords: music – United States – punk – rock – gospel – folk – blues – jazz.

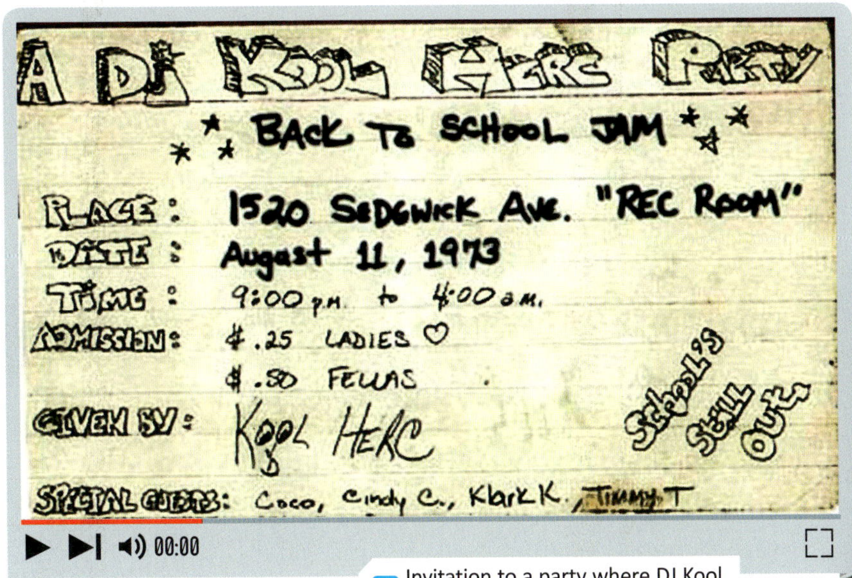

Invitation to a party where DJ Kool Herc performed for the first time in the Bronx, NYC

In the 1970s, gangs developed all over the Bronx because of urban deterioration. For hip-hop historian Marcus Reeves this context was at the origin of today's hip-hop culture. The new cultural movement came "out of the gangs to counteract the violence".

1520 Sedgwick Avenue: the apartment building that was once the home of DJ Kool Herc, in a social housing area of the Bronx, NYC.

Need help?

- band = group
- down**town** = **ci**ty **cen**tre
- **ly**rics = song words
- crime-**rid**den = full of crime
- hand**writ**ten ≠ typed
- run-down = neg**lec**ted
- hand out = dis**tri**bute
- in**spire** = **in**fluence
- re**late** to = link to
- **trig**ger = pro**voke**
- instru**men**tal break
- re**lease** an **al**bum: *sortir un album*

Prepare your project

Record a short presentation about a music style from the East or West Coast.

Mémoriser • Prononcer • Écrire

Words, words, words

➥ *Mémoriser et enrichir son lexique p. 235*

Quizlet
quizlet.com/skysthelimit2e

Classe 1 — Pistes 35-43 — 21 29

Créez votre propre carte mentale à partir de ce que vous avez vu en classe. Vous pourrez ensuite l'enrichir à l'aide de celle-ci.
Écoutez les mots et répétez-les pour bien les prononcer.
Écrivez-les aussi plusieurs fois pour mémoriser leur orthographe.

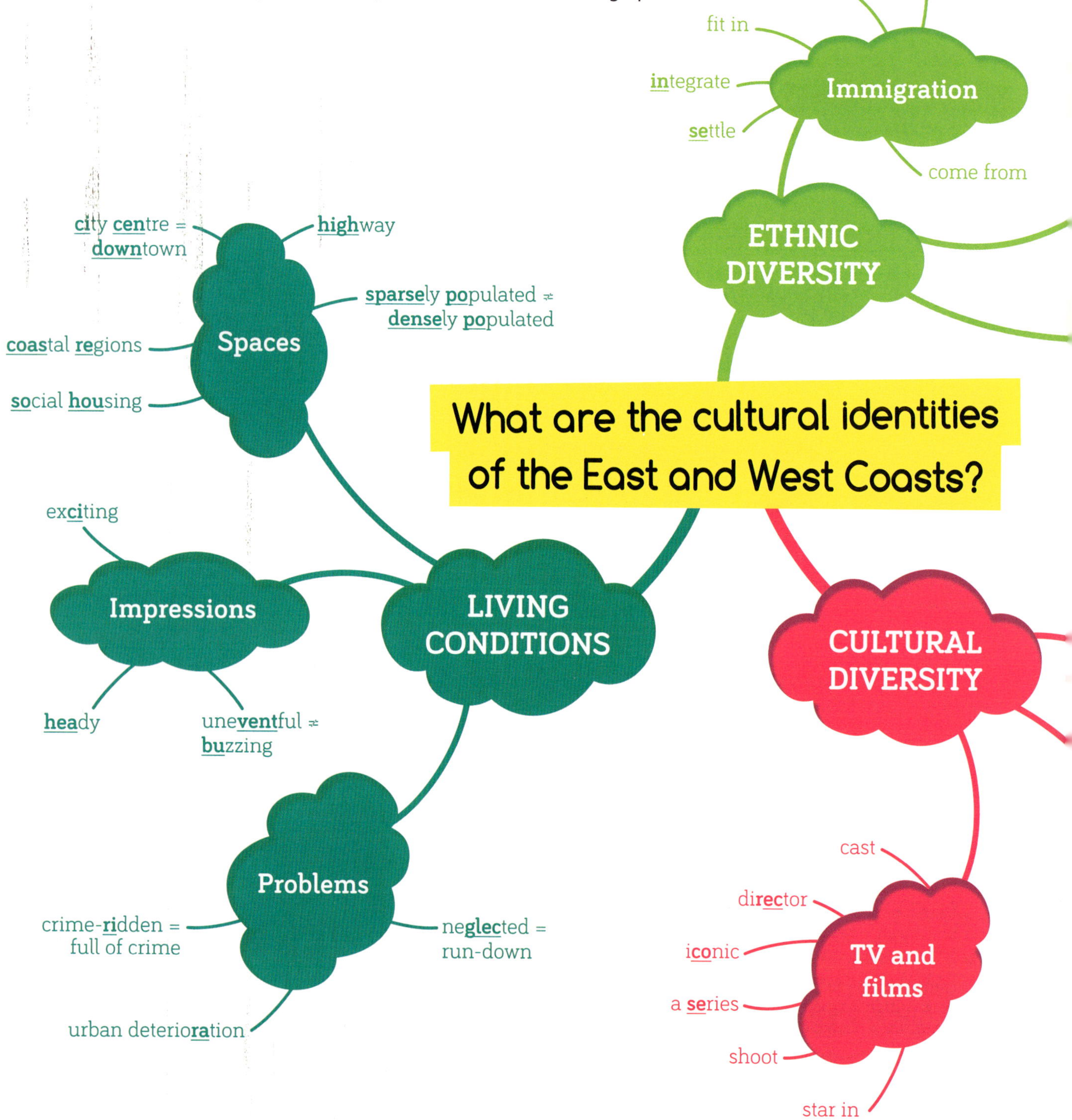

Reactions
- discriminate against
- approve of ≠ disapprove of
- open-minded
- treat (un)fairly

Impacts
- relate to
- provoke
- influential = have an impact
- inspire

Music
- instrumental break
- band
- lyrics
- release an album

Food
- dish
- recipe
- fusion food
- mouth-watering = tasty

More words

Les nombres Repères, p. 257

According to the 2010 Census, 37,253,956 people resided in California. Back in 1900 the population was under 1.5 million. Twenty years later, only 0.5% declared themselves to be Native American. At 38.9% the Hispanic population make up the largest ethnic group in the state. In 1990, the percentage was much lower.

L'essentiel

- La **ponctuation** pour les nombres est différente en anglais :
  - un espace dans un nombre en français devient une virgule (non dite à l'oral) ;
  - une virgule en français devient un point (*point* à l'oral).
- Un **zéro devant un point** se dit *nought* = 0.7% = *nought point seven percent.*
- Un **zéro après un point** se dit *oh* = 5.02 = *five point oh two.*

1. a. Écrivez les nombres en chiffres.
twenty point three oh four – one billion, twenty-three million, three hundred and twenty thousand, four hundred and two – nought point eight one two – three hundred thousand and twenty-three

b. Écrivez les nombres en lettres. Entraînez-vous à les dire à haute voix.
150,265 – 14.8 – 0.75 – 20.03 – 12,358,241 – 650.304 – 10,999 – 152,203,651,201 – 0.024

Les nationalités Repères, p. 257

Many **Chinese immigrants** and **Japanese immigrants** entered the US through Angel Island. Immigrants such as **the Irish**, **the Italians**, **the British and the Russians** had to pass through Ellis Island to enter the USA.

L'essentiel

- Les **adjectifs de nationalité** sont invariables et commencent par une majuscule (*American citizens*).
- Les **noms de nationalité** se terminant par *-ish* ou *-ese*, *-ch* ou *-sh* ne prennent pas de *-s* au pluriel.

2. Classez dans un tableau les noms et les adjectifs de nationalité des pays mentionnés ci-dessous.
The people that make up the East and the West Coasts of the USA today came from all over the world: England, The Netherlands, France, Ireland, Germany, Portugal, Italy, Russia, Vietnam, Sudan, Kenya, Mexico and China… The list is almost endless.

Country	Noun	Adjective
England	*The English*	*English*

Observer • Retenir • Appliquer

Grammar

Le comparatif et le superlatif Repères, p. 258

– The West Coast is **sunnier than** the East Coast.
– LA is **more populated than** San Francisco.
– Philadelphia is the **best** place to discover the Philly Cheese Sandwich.
– New York is **the most fascinating** city I have ever visited.
– I am **less attracted** to punk music **than** to hip-hop.
– *Friends* is **as good as** *How I Met Your Mother.*

L'essentiel

- **Le comparatif de supériorité**
  – Pour les **adjectifs courts** : on ajoute *-er* à l'adjectif + *than* ;
  – Pour les **adjectifs longs** : on utilise *more* + adj. + *than.*

  • Une et deux syllabes se terminant par *-y*, *-le*, *-ow* et *-er*.
  • Autres adjectifs à deux syllabes et adjectifs à trois syllabes et plus.

- **Le superlatif**
  – Pour les **adjectifs courts**, on ajoute *the* à l'adjectif + *-est* ;
  – Pour les **adjectifs longs**, on utilise *the most* + adj.

- **Le comparatif d'égalité** : quelle que soit la longueur de l'adjectif, on utilise *as* + adj. + *as.*

- **Le comparatif d'infériorité** : quelle que soit la longueur de l'adjectif, on utilise *less* + adj. + *than.*

Attention : Il y a des adjectifs irréguliers :
good → *better* → *the best*
bad → *worse* → *the worst.*

1. Remplacez les adjectifs entre parenthèses par des comparatifs (infériorité – / égalité = / supériorité +) ou des superlatifs (++).

California is almost (*big* =) France.
→ *California is almost as big as France.*

a. These quesadillas are (*tasty* +) the ones I had in New York.
b. The tacos at Las Cuatro Milpas in San Diego are (*good* ++) I have ever eaten.
c. Pizzas on the West Coast are not (*good* =) on the East Coast but they are much (*healthy* +).
d. Martin Scorsese's *Gangs of New York* is much (*exciting* +) Woody Allen's *Manhattan*.
e. The film *Baywatch* received four nominations, including (*bad* ++) picture and (*bad* ++) actor for Zac Efron.
f. Living in a coastal small town is (*stressful* –) living in New York.

2. Complétez en insérant les comparatifs et superlatifs appropriés.

a. The Notorious BIG, Nas, Jay-Z and Busta Rhymes are among the (*famous* ++) rappers of the East Coast.
b. They are widely recognised as the (*good* ++) East Coast rappers.
c. There is also 50 Cent, but he is a bit (*popular* –).
d. On the West Coast, Tupac Shakur, Ice Cube, Snoop Dog and Dr. Dre are certainly (*well-known* =) their East Coast equivalents but it seems West Coast rap was a (*big* +) commercial success.

3. Complétez les phrases avec le mot approprié en faisant les changements nécessaires.

high – populated – many – small – large

The coastal States are much (+) than the inland States of the US.
→ *The coastal States are much more populated than the inland States of the US.*

a. Together, they make up more than half of the US population although the territory is much (–).
b. Both the East and the West Coasts are multicultural coasts, but there is a (+) proportion of Hispanics in California than in South Carolina.
d. On the other hand, there is a (+) African American population in South Carolina than in California.
d. There are (=) Asians in the State of Washington as in the State of New York.

Les verbes prépositionnels

Repères, p. 253

– She wasn't **discriminated against**.
V. + prép.

– I **disagree with** her.
V. + prép.

L'essentiel

Certains verbes ont besoin d'une préposition pour introduire leur complément. La préposition est inséparable du verbe dont elle dépend et est placée à sa droite.

4. Complétez avec la préposition qui convient : *to – on – against – with – of – down*. Vérifiez dans un dictionnaire si nécessaire.

I'm not sure I approve (?) this new law.
→ *I'm not sure I approve of this new law.*

a. Hispanics are sometimes discriminated (?).

b. Many people disagree (?) the idea that one coast is better than the other.

c. Compared (?) the past, there is more diversity today.

d. He drove (?) from Seattle to spend a week in San Diego.

e. The music people like can depend (?) where they come from.

f. If you think (?) the history of music, you realise that new styles are always related (?) past styles.

Les phrases exclamatives

Repères, p. 260

– **What an amazing series!**
GN

– It has **such beautiful music!**
GN

– **How interesting** this film is!
adj.

– It is **so romantic!**
adj.

L'essentiel

- Avec ***what*** et ***such***, l'exclamation porte sur un groupe nominal.
- Avec ***how*** et ***so***, l'exclamation porte sur un adjectif.

Attention : Ne pas confondre les exclamatives en *How* (*How clever he is!*) et les questions (*How clever is he?*).

5. Proposez une ou plusieurs phrases exclamatives.

I love this man, he's a great actor.
→ *He is such a great actor!* (GN) / *What a great actor he is!* (GN) / *How great an actor he is!* (adj.)

a. I find this rock group absolutely amazing.

b. Californian smoothies are really delicious.

c. I think these song lyrics are shocking.

d. In my opinion, this is an excellent idea.

e. I love this book about New York! It's wonderfully written.

f. This is the best pizza I have ever eaten.

Sounds, sounds, sounds

Les syllabes accentuées

Repères, p. 246

L'essentiel

En anglais, lorsqu'un mot comporte plus d'une syllabe, l'une d'entre elles est toujours accentuée. Il faut insister sur cette syllabe accentuée. Si besoin, on peut écouter les mots à l'aide d'un dictionnaire en ligne (dictionary.cambridge.org).

California – Washington – Oregon

Classe 1 – Piste 44 – 30

1. Écoutez les mots suivants.

American – Chinese – ninety – eighteen – Hispanic – musical – essential – emigrate

2. Répétez les mots en insistant sur la syllabe soulignée. Enregistrez-vous et corrigez si nécessaire.

Classe 1 – Piste 45 – 31

3. Écoutez et notez les mots que vous entendez. Soulignez les syllabes accentuées. Entraînez-vous à les dire en insistant sur la syllabe accentuée.

STRATEGY
PARLER À PARTIR DE NOTES

Pour réussir à parler à partir de notes, il faut :

1 ... organiser vos idées :

- Faites **un plan** avec des **mots-clés.**
- Mettez en valeur les **mots importants** (couleur / encadré / souligné...).
- Prévoyez une **phrase d'accroche** et une **phrase de conclusion.**

Let's begin! • *Shall we start?*

I'd like to finish by saying... • *Thank you for your attention.*

Apprenez-les par cœur pour être à l'aise au début !

2 ... vous entraîner :

- Faites des **phrases** à partir des mots-clés.

Écrivez-les pour vous entraîner, puis servez-vous uniquement du plan.

- **Accentuez** les mots importants dans les phrases.
- Utilisez des **mots de liaison** pour rendre la présentation fluide.

Consequently... • *On the other hand...* • *Of course...*

Notez-les sur votre plan pour y penser !

- Pensez aux phrases de **transition.**

I will now talk about... • *My second topic is...* • *Finally...*

3 ... savoir faire passer votre message :

- Parlez **assez fort** et au **bon rythme** (ni trop lent, ni trop rapide).
- Marquez des **pauses.**
- Regardez l'auditoire pour **capter son attention.**
- Prenez le **temps de réfléchir** en utilisant des *gap fillers* pour enchaîner / préciser vos idées, ou revenir sur un point.

Well... • *I mean...* • *You know...* •

Where was I? • *Have I said that already?* • *Thanks for helping me out!*

ET SURTOUT, RESTEZ ZEN !

Your project | Create and present a slideshow

Prepare a slideshow about a place on the East or West Coast (neighbourhood, town, state...) and present it to your classmates.

Cable car with Alcatraz Island in the background, San Francisco, California, USA

1 Choose the information and documents you want to include in your presentation.

- **Use the following keywords to help you conduct your research:** food – music – films and series – famous people – population – history.
- **Vary your documents:** photos – interviews – maps – timelines – statistics – trailers…

2 Prepare your slideshow.

- **Keep the contents of your slides** simple, attractive and clear (maximum 10 slides). Include keywords and pictures that will help your audience understand the main points.
- **Compare your chosen place with what you have learnt** in this chapter to give a wider context.

3 Prepare your oral.

- **Prepare an outline and notes.** (No sentences!)
- **Check your pronunciation and your grammar** when you're not sure.
- **Practise speaking** without reading your notes. (You can record yourself.)
- **Use your slides** to illustrate what you're saying.

4 Present your slideshow to the class.

- **Speak clearly** and emphasise the important words. Be ready to **answer questions**.

Keys to success

- **Utilisez le vocabulaire du chapitre :** diversité ethnique, diversité culturelle, conditions de vie.
  ➥ *Words, words, words p. 78*
- **Écrivez correctement les nombres et les nationalités et veillez à bien les prononcer.**
  ➥ *More words p. 79*
- **Pensez à utiliser le comparatif et le superlatif.**
  ➥ *Grammar p. 80*
- **Faites des phrases exclamatives pour être plus convaincant(e).**
  ➥ *Grammar p. 81*
- **Accentuez correctement les mots de plus d'une syllabe.**
  ➥ *Sound, sounds, sounds p. 81*
- **Appliquez les conseils pour parler à partir de notes.**
  ➥ *Strategy p. 82*

Axe 3 : Le village, le quartier, la ville

6 Five senses in Mumbai

Your project

Prepare a short video presenting a place using your senses, *p. 93*
– Record a commentary about the sounds of a place, *p. 88*

Keys to success

- **Strategy: réaliser une courte vidéo**, *p. 92*
- **Mind map:** street life, urban art, five senses, *p. 90*
- **Grammar:** cause et conséquence, *p. 91*

How can the five senses contribute to discovering a city?

Martin Roemers, *Metropolis*, 2016

1 Basics

List all the words that come to mind when you think about Indian street life (people – places – activities – sounds). WORKSHEET 11

2 vidéo Discover

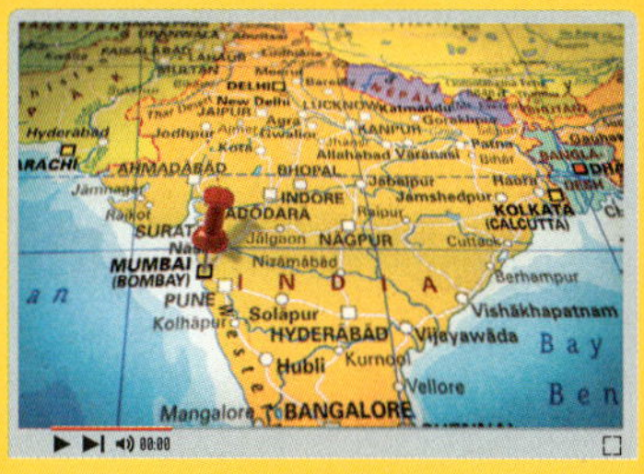

Watch and **pick out** references to Mumbai's characteristics.
Imagine what it feels like to live in a place like Mumbai.

▶ *As Mumbai is a huge city… • Since it is very crowded… • Because of the number of inhabitants…*

Game 3 Play

Long list game: List as many Indian references (cities – celebrities – dishes – movies…) as you can. The group with the most references wins.

Lire • Écouter • Écrire

A feast for the senses (1)

1 vidéo Moving art DOSSIER documentaire

1. Use the photos and the captions to **imagine** the purpose of this art project.

2. **Read** the text and **pick out** references to art. **Say** what is unusual about this form of art (place – senses…).

▶ *Usually you can't… • You don't expect… • The colours are so… that…*

3. **Watch** the video and find references to taxis in Mumbai. **Explain** their importance in the city.

4. Médiation **Pick out** examples of interior designs. **Use** your notes to sum up Sanket Avlani's purpose with his project.

An auto rickshaw (often used as taxis in Mumbai) with interior artwork

Imagine sliding[1] into a taxi and realizing, once you settle down, that you are sitting on top of a bright blue landscape with carefully painted horses leaping[2] across the seat. In front of you, the blue background continues behind a group of faceless figures. (...) The ceiling scene is depicted in the style of ancient frescoes. As you take in all the little details of the design, you almost forget that you are riding in a cab. You almost forget your original destination. This is the experience of riding in a cab transformed by Taxi Fabric.

Eva Recinaos, creators.vice.com, Jan. 31, 2016

1. slide (v.): *se glisser*
2. leap (v.) = jump

Mumbai's iconic taxis are becoming works of art.

2 Walls becoming art

1. **Describe** the picture, **read** the caption and **imagine** who the man painted on the wall could be.
2. **Read** the text and check. **Make** a list of the different topics that have inspired street artists in Mumbai.
3. **Write** a 5-line text considering the positive and negative impacts of street art in a city.
   ▶ *As it has become very popular… • However, some people might say…*

A mural depicting a scene from the 1975 film *Deewaar*

Mumbai is the undoubted artistic capital of India. In fact, it is one of the most important artistic hotspots in Asia. It isn't just the scores of galleries and museums where the city's pulsating art scene is at display but rather it is home to some of the city's finest artwork – raw, relevant and most accessible – present on its very own streets. There exist various degrees of work within the city's street art scene (…).

Much like the case in the rest of the country, a good section of Mumbai's street art depicts Bollywood, which isn't surprising considering the cultural influence and power held by the film industry. While some works pay tribute to[1] movies, others idolize stars with larger-than-life[2] depictions. Amitabh Bachchan[3], or Big B as he is fondly known among fans, is a common sight. The city itself is one of the most common subjects depicted in various forms. Some look back at the Bombay[4] of the past with the iconic ode to the city's maritime history adorning the walls of Lion Gate in Fort. It is also common to find commentaries on contemporary life – sometimes ridiculing it, sometimes just mirroring its absurdity.

Sridevi Nambiar, theculturetrip.com, Sept. 26, 2016

1. pay tribute to (exp.): *rendre hommage à*
2. larger-than-life (adj.): *plus vrai(e) que nature*
3. Amitabh Bachchan = famous Indian actor (born 1942)
4. Bombay = former name of Mumbai (the name changed in 1996)

Need help?

- canvas: *toile pour peinture*
- design / designer
- fabric: *tissu*
- rickshaw
- sight
- taxi driver
- touch

- amazed = surprised
- lively = colourful
- unusual = out of the ordinary

- decorate = embellish
- promote

- convey a message: *véhiculer un message*
- create social bonds: *créer des liens*
- intend to do sth = plan to do sth
- it is meant to = its purpose is to
- strike up a conversation = start a conversation

Grammar

La cause et la conséquence

As Mumbai is a very colourful city, it is a pleasure for the senses.

➥ *Grammar p. 91*

A feast for the senses (2)

CULTURE QUEST

Discover the sounds of Mumbai.

Keywords: sounds - Mumbai - interactive - Tapan Babbar.

3 Turning sound into music

DOSSIER documentaire

Classe 1 Piste 46

Artist Sandunes working in the streets of Mumbai

1. **Describe** the picture. **Use** what you see and the introduction to **deduce** what the woman is doing.
2. **Read** the introduction and the text to check. **Find** information about the woman and link her to places and sounds.
3. **Listen** to Sandunes talking about her work. **Pick out** stressed words and **classify** them into references to Mumbai and to sounds.
4. Pairwork — **Agree** on a list of five other places in a city and say what sounds you could collect there.

As the commercial and entertainment capital of India, Bombay[1] is one of the densest amalgamations of sights, smells, sensations and sounds on the planet. Who better then, than Bombay-based producer Sanaya Ardeshir, aka Sandunes, to take us around the city and explore its rich sonics (…).

Ableton: Were you yourself surprised by the variety of timbres, rhythms and melodies that your city offered up?

Sandunes: (...) I expected to gather a lot of different textural and rhythmic information but I didn't quite expect it to all be so usable or musical! The process of actually looking for sound in a relatively "normal" environment has definitely changed the way I hear things in my city. (...)

Ableton: Which of the sounds did you end up using in the track you made (...)?

Sandunes: (...) My most favourite finds were the hits from the potato chopping[2] at the Byculla veggie market, the crates[3] being unloaded from trucks and tossed on the ground from the Dadar flower market, a lot of the bell/clings from the metal mill[4] too, and most of the "groove" is from the hammering[5] and breaking up of all the (stolen?) car parts at Chor Bazaar.

ableton.com, Dec. 20, 2016

1. Bombay = former name of Mumbai (the name changed in 1996)
2. chop (v.) = cut into pieces
3. crate (n.): *cageot*
4. metal mill (n.): *usine métallurgique*
5. hammering (n.): *martèlement*

Prepare your project

Choose a place and record the sounds you hear. Make a 1-minute recording about what you found.

Need help?

- aroma = fragrance
- flavour = taste
- street vendor
- mouth-watering: *appétissant*
- smelly = stinky
- spicy
- sweet ≠ sour
- tasty = delicious
- unpleasant = disagreeable

4 Breathing Bombay

1. **Describe** the picture. **Read** the first sentence of the text and **imagine** the different smells the narrator is going to talk about.
2. **Read** the text and **focus on** references to smell. **Classify** them (concrete / abstract – positive / negative). **Sum up** the overall impression of the city.
3. **Write** a text that describes the different smells in a place of your choice.

Vendors at a flower market, Mumbai

The first thing I noticed about Bombay[1], on that first day, was the smell of the different air. (...) I know now that it's the sweet, sweating smell of hope, which is the opposite of hate; and it's the sour[2], stifled[3] smell of greed[4], which is the opposite of love. It's the smell of gods, demons, empires, and civilisations in resurrection and decay. It's the blue skin-smell of the sea, no matter where you are in the Island City, and the blood-metal smell of machines. It smells of the stir[5] and sleep and waste of sixty million animals, more than half of them humans and rats. It smells of heartbreak, and the struggle to live, and of the crucial failures and loves that produce our courage. It smells of ten thousand restaurants, five thousand temples, shrines[6], churches, and mosques, and of a hundred bazaars devoted exclusively to perfumes, spices, incense, and freshly cut flowers. (...) Whenever I return to Bombay, now, it's my first sense of the city – that smell, above all things – that welcomes me and tells me I've come home.

Gregory David Roberts, *Shantaram*, 2003

1. Bombay = former name of Mumbai (the name changed in 1996)
2. sour (adj.): *aigre*
3. stifled (adj.): *qui étouffe*
4. greed (n.): *avidité*
5. stir (n.) = movement
6. shrine (n.): *lieu saint*

5 vidéo Street food

1. **Watch** the video and **take** notes on what you hear and see. **Pick out** information about Vada Pav (ingredients – flavours).
2. **Use** your notes to **compare** what you see in the video with street food in your country. **Pick** your favourite street food and check with your classmates to find the most popular one.

Street food, Mumbai

Mémoriser • Prononcer • Écrire

Words, words, words

➥ *Faire une carte mentale p. 234*
➥ *Mémoriser et enrichir son lexique p. 235*

Quizlet
quizlet.com/skysthelimit2e

Classe 1 — Pistes 47-49 — 32 34

Créez votre propre carte mentale à partir de ce que vous avez vu en classe. Vous pourrez ensuite l'enrichir à l'aide de celle-ci. Écoutez les mots et répétez-les pour bien les prononcer. Écrivez-les aussi plusieurs fois pour mémoriser leur orthographe.

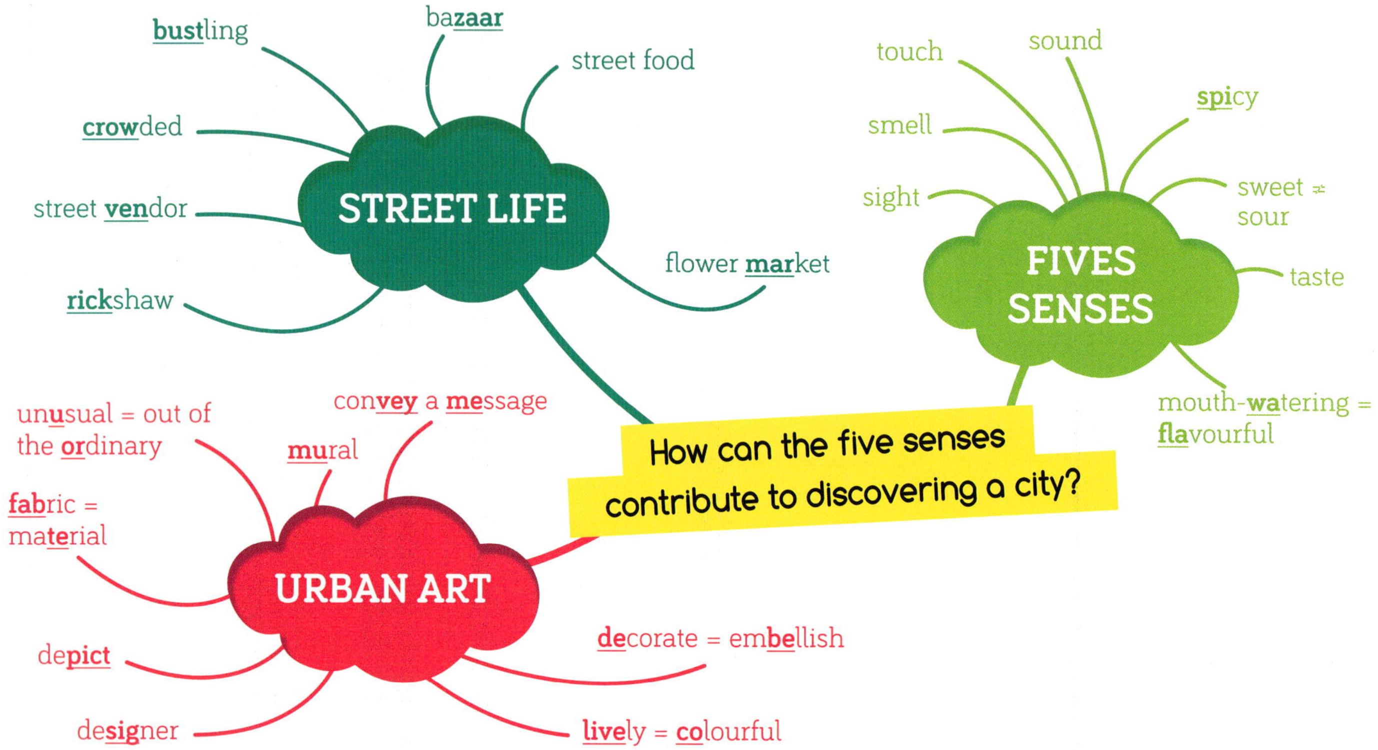

More words

Les suffixes *-ful* et *-less*

Repères, p. 260

– It is amazing how **colourful** Mumbai is!

– You should be very **careful** to avoid carts when you cross the streets.

– I thought the food would be **tasteless** but it is quite the opposite!

L'essentiel

Les **suffixes**, qui s'ajoutent à la droite du mot-racine, permettent la création de nouveaux mots.

- Le suffixe *-less* indique l'idée d'être « dépourvu de », alors que *-ful* indique celle d'être « pourvu de ».
- La catégorie grammaticale du mot est en fonction du suffixe. Avec les suffixes *-ful* et *-less*, on forme des adjectifs : *doubt* = nom → *doubtful* = adj.

1. Complétez ces phrases à l'aide d'un des mots de la liste auquel vous aurez ajouté le suffixe *-ful* ou *-less*.
sleep – end – use – joy – wonder

They had a (?) time discovering this city. It was fantastic.
→ *They had a wonderful time discovering this city. It was fantastic.*

a. He spent a (?) night strolling in the streets of Mumbai.
b. It was very (?) to follow this guide as we discovered incredible places in the city.
c. The people who welcomed us and showed us around were so welcoming and (?).
d. The trip to Mumbai was really long: it was so long it seemed (?) so I was glad when we finally arrived there.

Observer • Retenir • Appliquer

Grammar

La cause et la conséquence

Repères, p. 262

- **As** Mumbai is a very colourful city, it is a pleasure for the senses.
- The dish was **so** spicy **that** I had to stop eating.
- I thanked the guide **for showing** us amazing places in the city.
- The city is very noisy **because of** the huge number of inhabitants.

L'essentiel

Pour relier deux propositions, on peut utiliser **des mots de liaison**.

- **Pour exprimer la cause**, on peut employer : *because, since, as, because of, due to, for* + V-ing.
- **Pour exprimer la conséquence**, on peut employer : *consequently, as a consequence, so, that's why, therefore, so* + adj. + *that*.

Attention : Certaines expressions sont suivies d'un groupe nominal (*I couldn't cross the street because of / due to the traffic*) alors que d'autres sont suivies de propositions (*As / Since it is a big city, you need several days to visit Mumbai*).

1. Remplacez les mots de liaison soulignés par une expression sans changer l'ordre des propositions.

Since Bollywood movies are very popular, you should try one.
→ *As Bollywood movies are very popular, you should try one.*

a. Because the city is very noisy, I couldn't sleep with the windows open.
b. Sandunes was fascinated by the sounds of Mumbai, therefore she collected them to produce a song.
c. Due to its number of inhabitants, Mumbai looks crazy and chaotic.
d. The fabrics are colourful and original, that's why they are unforgettable.

2. Reliez les phrases à l'aide d'un mot de liaison exprimant la cause ou la conséquence. Faites les ajustements nécessaires.

Street artists created murals in Mumbai. The walls were too dull.
→ *As the walls were too dull, street artists created murals in Mumbai.*

a. Taxis are a good place to deliver a message. They are used by a lot of people.
b. It is difficult to choose. There is such a variety of street food!
c. The flower market was really big. It took us the whole morning to go around.
d. There are so many different sounds in the city. It can be confusing.

Sounds, sounds, sounds

Les mots accentués

Repères, p. 247

L'essentiel

- L'anglais est une langue accentuelle : dans une phrase, les **mots accentués** sont les mots lexicaux (noms, verbes, adjectifs). Les mots grammaticaux (articles, pronoms, etc.) sont, quant à eux, en général inaccentués : *Mumbai is a lively city that never sleeps.*

Classe 35 – Piste 50

1. Écoutez et lisez les phrases. Décrivez les mots soulignés et les autres mots à l'aide des vignettes.

accentué | non accentué | mot lexical | mot grammatical

If you go to Mumbai, there are so many things to discover. It is a place that invites you to a real feast for the senses. You can be amazed by the colours of the murals as well as surprised by the number of street vendors or the variety of sounds that the city has to offer.

Classe 36 – Piste 51

2. Servez-vous de la règle pour identifier les mots accentués dans les phrases. Lisez-les à haute voix puis écoutez pour vérifier.

These amazing taxis that display so many different fabrics and atmospheres were not only designed for artistic reasons. When people use them, they can also discover the different messages that the artists want to convey.

STRATEGY RÉALISER UNE COURTE VIDÉO

Pour réaliser une courte vidéo, il faut :

1 ... anticiper son contenu :

- Assurez-vous d'avoir compris en quoi consiste **la vidéo** à produire (jeu de rôle – interview – reportage...).
- **Réfléchissez au sujet** (personnages – lieux : extérieur / intérieur).
- **Faites des repérages** pour sélectionner le ou les lieu(x) de tournage.
- Décidez **qui sera dans la vidéo** (vous, d'autres personnes connues ou inconnues) ou s'il y aura simplement une **voix-off**.

2 ... préparer votre script :

- Partez de vos **notes**. Veillez à **limiter** la longueur des phrases.
- Indiquez les **noms des personnes qui parlent** avant chaque intervention.
- **Annotez le texte** avec des indications pour les participants : ton – attitude – position – expression...
- Vérifiez dans un dictionnaire la **prononciation des mots**.

3 ... préparer votre matériel vidéo :

- Choisissez le **matériel** pour filmer (caméra – téléphone).
- Vérifiez que la **lumière est bonne**.
- Vérifiez votre **prise de son** : votre voix ne doit pas être parasitée par des bruits de fond.

N'oubliez pas de vérifier que votre batterie est suffisamment chargée.

4 ... faire votre vidéo :

- Veillez à ne pas apparaître à **contrejour** ou **surexposé(e)**.
- Vous pouvez **varier les plans** (gros plan, plan panoramique, zoom...).
- **Filmez sans trembler :** faites appel à un ami si besoin, vous pouvez aussi utiliser une perche à selfie ou un pied pour votre caméra.
- Veillez à être **audible**, on doit pouvoir vous comprendre dans l'intégralité de la vidéo.
- Si vous réalisez votre vidéo sur plusieurs jours, pensez à faire les **raccords** (vêtements, plans).

5 ... visionner votre travail final :

- Assurez-vous de l'**adéquation** entre l'image et le son.
- Demandez-vous si votre **vidéo répond bien aux critères imposés**.
- Faites des **coupes** si besoin.

Your project — Present a place in a video

Choose a place that you can describe through one or more of the five senses and present it in a video.

1 Choose a place not far from you.

- **Pick a place** that you could link with one or more of the **five senses** (market – train station – road – beach, etc.).

2 Prepare your notes.

- **Think** of the way the place you have chosen can **stimulate** the senses (sound – sight – smell – taste – touch).
- **Write down ideas** and **keywords**.

3 Prepare your video.

- **Decide** on the structure of your video (voice over – with or without journalist – different scenes – places – sounds).

4 Prepare your script.

- Check the **pronunciation** when you're not sure.
- **Practise speaking** without reading your notes.

5 Make your film.

- Don't speak too fast, use your hands and your facial expressions to help **communicate your ideas**.
- **Check** the lighting and the sound quality.
- When you have finished, **watch your film** and **make cuts** if necessary.

6 Present your video to the class.

- **Share your contribution** with the class (blog – Padlet…).

Keys to success

- **Utilisez le vocabulaire du chapitre :** art de la rue, art urbain, cinq sens.
  ➡ *Words, words, words, p. 90*
- **Pensez à exprimer la cause et la conséquence.**
  ➡ *Grammar, p. 91*
- **Pensez à l'accentuation des mots.**
  ➡ *Sounds, sounds, sounds, p. 91*
- **Utilisez les conseils pour réaliser une vidéo.**
  ➡ *Strategy, p. 92*

Axe 4 : Représentation

de soi et rapport à autrui

7 Our fashion matters, p. 96
Séquence +
What do our clothes say about us and our society?

8 Self(ie)-portraits, p. 112
Séquence +
How are portraits, self-portraits and selfies related?

Vers le BAC Entraînement à l'épreuve 1 p. 128

Axe 4 : Représentation de soi et rapport à autrui

7 Our fashion matters

What do our clothes say about us and our society?

Your project

Groupwork **Prepare and conduct a survey about clothing and the fashion industry**, *p. 111*
- Interview your classmate, *p. 99*
- Prepare a multiple choice questionnaire, *p. 101*
- Analyse and share the results of a survey, *p. 105*

Keys to success

- **Strategy: interagir à l'oral**, *p. 110*
- **Mind map:** clothes, fashion and styles, fashion industry, *p. 106*
- **Grammar:** forme interrogative, similarités et différences, conseil, *p. 108*
- **Sounds:** intonation des questions, *p. 109*

Martin Parr, Fashion shoot in London, 2013

Séquence +

1 Basics

Write a list of all the items of clothing that you can think of.

WORKSHEET 12

2 Discover

vidéo

Do you know JNCOs?
Watch the video.
Pick out keywords and use them to **describe** this item of clothing and the teenagers' reaction.

3 Play

Game

Guess who game: Prepare a written description of what you and the people sitting near you are wearing. Hand it in to the teacher, then listen to another description and guess who it is.

▶ *It's a girl. She's wearing…* •
The boy behind her is wearing… •
Is he / she wearing…?

Parler • Écouter • Échanger

What fashion means to me

1 What's my style?

1. Look at the pictures and **pick out** the style you relate to the most and the least. **Describe** them and say why.

► *You'd never catch me wearing a… • I really identify with…*
It would / wouldn't suit me because…

2. **Sum up** what fashion means to you.

► *For me, fashion is… • In my opinion, fashion isn't… • Fashion should / shouldn't…*

Need help?

- **bla**zer ['bleɪzə] = a light **ja**cket
- **fa**shion-**vi**ctim: *victime de la mode*
- **hoo**die: *sweat à capuche*
- **track**suit ['træk,suːt]: *survêtement*
- **trai**ners (GB) = **snea**kers (US)
- trend = **fa**shion
- **bo**ring = un**in**teresting
- **com**fy = **com**fortable
- smart = in**for**mal
- **time**less ≠ not af**fec**ted by **chan**ges in **fa**shion
- **tren**dy ≠ old-**fa**shioned
- all-time **fa**vourite ≠ **ab**solute **fa**vourite

CULTURE QUEST

Listen to two songs about fashion.
Keywords: The Kinks – David Bowie – fashion.

2 My favourite item of clothing

Classe 2 Piste 1

1. **Read** the quotes and guess the item of clothing.
2. **Listen** and check. **Pick out** stressed words then classify them (item of clothing – feelings).
3. **Say** who you identify with the most.

Grammar

La forme interrogative

– **What do you like wearing** the most?
Wh- + aux. + sujet + BV

➡ *Grammar p. 108*

Prepare your project

Pairwork

Bring in a photo of your all-time favourite item of clothing.
Get ready to answer questions about it. (What? Where? How long? Why?)
Now interview your classmate.

Parler • Écrire • Échanger

Fashion (r)evolution

1 A fashion controversy

1. Describe the three women.

2. Use the photos and the texts to say what type of women they represent.

3. Pick out words and expressions revealing their opinions. Compare them.
▶ *Constance is classier than… • Katharine isn't as… • Lilian is the most…*

4. Write a short presentation about someone who doesn't follow fashion.

Katharine Hepburn (...) refuses to be quoted on trousers as on all other subjects, but one thing is certain – Katharine Hepburn would not choose to wear them because they were the style, or refrain from wearing them because they were unconventional. She does as she chooses without reference to the rest of the world.

Movie Classic, Mar.-Jul. 1933

"Trousers for women are incredible, ridiculous and absurd!"

says Constance Bennett, whose clothes have been the envy of half the girls of America. "I can't imagine wearing such atrocities. Such a style will never please American men."

Movie Classic, Mar.-Jul. 1933

Constance Bennett: one of the most popular and best-paid actresses of the 1920s and 1930s

Katharine Hepburn: one of the most famous and popular Hollywood actresses of all time, *Philadelphia Story*, 1940

Lilian Harvey: Anglo-German actress famous in Hollywood in the 1930s

Lilian Harvey is horrified to find Hollywood going into pants just as she has arrived with forty-five separate dresses and suits complete with hats, shoes, bags and gloves to match every one. (…) "Trousers for women? But no!" she shivers. "Men were intended to wear the pants in the family. Mannish trousers, coats and vests have not the least feminine appeal."

Movie Classic, Mar.-Jul. 1933

Need help?

- <u>eve</u>ning gown: *robe de soirée*
- suit [suːt] / <u>trou</u>ser-suit: *tailleur-pantalon*
- <u>tom</u>boy = a girl who acts / <u>dre</u>sses like a boy
- <u>trend</u>setter ≠ <u>fa</u>shion-<u>fo</u>llower
- chic = <u>e</u>legant
- <u>cla</u>ssy = chic
- <u>da</u>ring: *osé*
- dressed up: *sur son trente et un*
- <u>man</u>ly = like a man
- dress down = dress <u>ca</u>sually
- <u>fo</u>llow a trend = <u>co</u>py a new <u>fa</u>shion

2 Fashion cycles

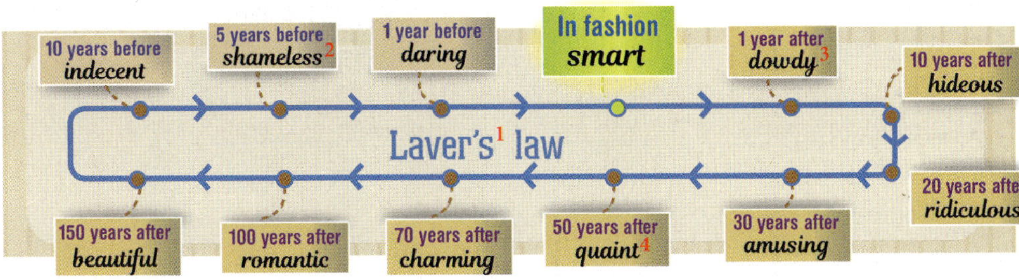

1. James Laver, inventor of the concept (1937)
2. shameless (adj.) = without shame
3. dowdy (adj.) = unattractive
4. quaint (adj.) = old-fashioned but nice

1. Pick an adjective from the scale to qualify the clothes of the two actresses at the time. Imagine a woman dressed like them today: choose an adjective to qualify her style.

Groupwork

2. Think about an item of clothing present or past (19th century top hat, 1920s flapper-dress, 1950s bomber-jacket, 1960s mini-skirt…) and match it to the scale. Agree on an adjective for each.

▶ *Back in the 20s… • This used to be… • Nowadays, it is considered…*

Prepare your project

Groupwork

Prepare a multiple choice questionnaire about how people relate to fashion and interview your classmates.

Grammar

Similarités et différences

– <u>Contrary to C. Bennett</u>

contrary to + nom

K. Hepburn is wearing trousers.

➥ *Grammar p. 109*

Lire • Partager • Écrire

Fast fashion

Différenciation

You are going to learn about fast fashion and its impact on society. Work on one of these topics to find out about the human cost of our clothing choices.

Step 1: Find information and take notes (working conditions – child labour – prices – disparities).

Step 2: GROUPWORK Share your findings. WORKSHEET 16

Médiation

Did you know?

Fast fashion (like fast food) is a tendency to design, manufacture and market clothes very quickly and sell them at very cheap prices.

Need help?

- brand: *marque*
- fabric = material
- garment = item of clothing
- manufacturer: *fabricant*
- retailer: *détaillant*
- striking: *frappant*
- surprising = unexpected
- just over ≠ just under
- on average: *en moyenne*
- roughly [ˈrʌflɪ] = approximately = about

TOPIC 1 Who made my clothes?

Classe 2 Piste 2

WORKSHEET 13

1. Read the poem and find answers to the questions asked.

2. Use the answers to write your own verse of a poem.

► *A young girl sewed the seams. Her friend…*

Who sewed the seams[1]
Who stitched[2] the tag[3]
Whose fingers bled
Whose fault is this
(…)

Who's overdressed
Who's oppressed
Who's high on fashion
Who's high on fumes[4]

Whose dress is to die for
Who shops to live
Who gets the bargain[5]
Whose life's on sale

Who's always searching
Who's never satisfied
Who's got nothing to wear
Who cares

Who sets the price
Who pays the cost
Who's asking
Who needs to know
(…)

Who are you
Who are you wearing?

Sasha Haines-Stiles, *Money Fashion Power*, fashionrevolution.org, 2017

1. seam (n.): *ourlet*
2. stitch (v.) = sew (*coudre*)
3. tag (n.): *étiquette*
4. fumes (n.) = pollution in factory towns
5. bargain (n.): *une bonne affaire*

TOPIC 2 Inside the factory

WORKSHEET 14

1. Compare the photos of the two girls and note down your thoughts.
► *Both girls are… • Unlike the girl on the left…*

2. Read the text to discover more about the life of factory workers in manufacturing countries.

3. Imagine a secret message Nasima sews into a pair of trousers destined for America.

Nasima and Sonia were the fastest finishing team[1] at Millennium[2] (…). Nasima had followed her mother into the factory as soon as Sonia was old enough to attend school. Sonia had joined them when she was thirteen, though her employment documents recorded her age as fifteen, the legal minimum in Bangladesh. The hours were brutal, the influx[3] of overseas[4] orders relentless[5], and the wages subsistence level and often paid late. But it was honest work, steady work, and with three of them collecting paychecks, the money had multiplied, allowing the boys to stay at school. (…)

Nasima (…) slid another waistband[6] and label into the machine. The pants were bright red and sized to fit a girl about six years old. How much would the child's parents pay in America? Five dollars? Ten? Fifteen? It was a guessing game she sometimes played to break the monotony. The fabric[7] was nice. Twelve, she guessed. At her current wage of forty-two cents an hour, Nasima had to work four days to earn such a sum, but she felt no bitterness[8]. Nor did she wonder – as she had when she was younger – how Americans could afford such luxuries. The West had grown rich, while much of the world remained poor.

Corban Addison, *A Harvest of Thorns*, 2017

1. finishing team (n.): *équipe chargée des finitions*
2. Millennium (n.) = name of a factory
3. influx (n.) = arrival in large numbers
4. overseas (adv.) = from abroad
5. relentless (adj.) = non-stop
6. waistband (n.): *ceinture d'un vêtement*
7. fabric (n.) = material
8. bitterness (n.): *amertume*

TOPIC 3 Fast fashion facts

WORKSHEET 15

1. Read the quotation and examine the illustration. Write down your first reaction.

2. Sum up what you have understood about the fast fashion industry.

3. Design a fairer T-shirt.

"170 million children work, many in the clothing industry."
Source: International Labour Organisation, 2017

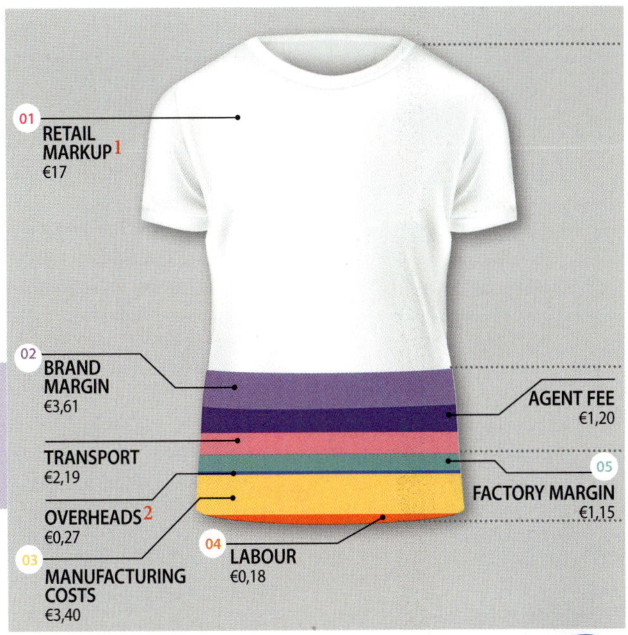

Source: Fashion Revolution

1. markup (n.): *majoration*
2. overheads (n.): *frais généraux*

Écouter • Écrire • Échanger

Ethical fashion

Did you know?

Ethical fashion (or slow fashion) covers a range of issues such as quality over quantity, working conditions, exploitation, fair trade, sustainable production, the environment, and animal welfare.

1 Get involved

1. **Describe** the pictures and **comment on** the caption.
2. Focus on the labels and **list** the information you can find.
3. *Pairwork* **Imagine** a company's reply to #whomademyclothes?
   ► *Dear X,… • Thank you for the interest… • Contrary to what you think, …*

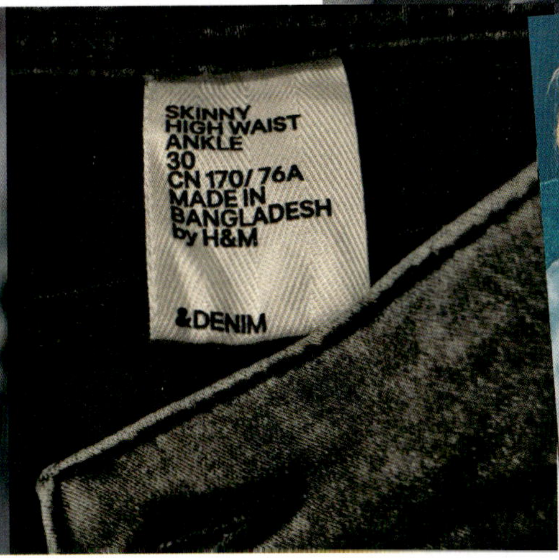

People took photos of themselves showing the label of an item of clothing and sent it to the company with #whomademyclothes?

2 vidéo Advice from a YouTuber

1. **Watch** a YouTuber's video about ethical fashion. **Identify** the date and the event mentioned.
2. **List** the solutions she suggests.
3. **Use** the advice to **prepare** a short message to the company of your choice.
   ▶ *Why don't you…? • You should… • Why not…?*

Grammar

Le conseil

– You **should choose** a company that has more ethical principles.

➥ *Grammar p. 109*

Verena Erin, ethical and sustainable fashion YouTuber at *My Green Closet*

Prepare your project

Take photos of various clothing labels.
Analyse the information you have found (manufacturing / distributing countries – material – languages – other information) and share them with the class.

Need help?

- child labour: *travail des enfants*
- company = firm
- fair trade: *commerce équitable*
- label: *étiquette*
- welfare: *bien-être*
- ethical = fair
- sustainable: *durable*
- convey a message
- get involved = participate

Mémoriser • Prononcer • Écrire

Words, words, words

➥ *Mémoriser et enrichir son lexique p. 235*

Quizlet
quizlet.com/skysthelimit2e

Classe 2 — Pistes 3-10 — 37 44

Créez votre propre carte mentale à partir de ce que vous avez vu en classe. Vous pourrez ensuite l'enrichir à l'aide de celle-ci. Écoutez les mots et répétez-les pour bien les prononcer.
Écrivez-les aussi plusieurs fois pour mémoriser leur orthographe.

What do our clothes say about us and society?

CLOTHES

- Items of clothing
  - **bla**zer
  - **track**suit
  - suit
  - **hoo**die
  - **trou**sers (GB) = pants (US)
  - jeans
  - **trai**ners (GB) = **snea**kers (US)

FASHION AND STYLES

- Styles
  - smart ≠ in**for**mal
  - **time**less
  - dressed up ≠ **ca**sual
  - **cla**ssy
  - **tren**dy ≠ old-**fa**shioned
  - chic = **e**legant
  - **man**nish = **tom**boy
- Behaviour
  - **fa**shion-**vi**ctim
  - **fa**shion-**fol**lower
  - i**den**tify with
  - **fol**low a trend
  - set a trend = **trend**setter
- Opinions
  - a**mu**sing
  - **da**ring
  - **hor**rified
  - **hi**deous
  - ri**di**culous
  - **bo**ring = un**in**teresting

THE FASHION INDUSTRY

- People and places
  - con**su**mer
  - **re**tailer
  - the **clo**thing **in**dustry
  - **fac**tory
  - over**seas** = from a**broad**
  - manu**fac**turer

Description
- wide-legged
- baggy
- manly ≠ feminine
- comfy = comfortable

Actions and goals
- sustainable production
- fair wages
- get involved
- convey a message
- ethical fashion = slow fashion

The issues
- subsistence level
- child labour
- working conditions
- exploitation
- the environment
- quality over quantity

More words

L'ordre des adjectifs Repères, p. 258

Funny black and white striped cotton trousers

> **L'essentiel** Pour faire une description, l'**ordre des adjectifs** est le suivant : *avis • taille • couleur • motif • tissu.*

1. Mettez les adjectifs dans le bon ordre pour compléter les phrases.

silk – green – beautiful – long
I found a (?) scarf at the market. → *I found a beautiful long green silk scarf at the market.*

a. *bright-green – cotton – flowery – amazing*
Look at this (?) shirt!

b. *canvas – old-fashioned – pin-striped – baggy*
I found these (?) trousers at the vintage store.

2. Classez les mots ci-dessous en fonction de leur catégorie (opinion, taille, etc.). Vous pouvez vous servir d'un dictionnaire si besoin. Puis, choisissez un vêtement et décrivez-le en détail. Ajoutez d'autres mots que vous avez appris dans ce chapitre.

slate-grey – royal-blue – striped – short – over-sized – gorgeous – loose – cotton – tartan – leather – beautiful – denim – stunning – ugly – dress – flowery – shirt – baggy – boring – stylish – scruffy – suit – massive – coat – tight

Les adjectifs composés en *-ed* et *-ing*

Repères, p. 257-258

> a **short-sleeved** top a **ong-lasting** style
> adj. + nom + *-ed* adj. + V-*ing*

> **L'essentiel** Si l'**adjectif composé** commence avec un adjectif et se termine par un nom ou un verbe, il faut ajouter *-ed* au nom et *-ing* au verbe.

3. Reformulez les phrases.

It's a shirt with long sleeves. → *It's a long-sleeved shirt.*

a. These are trousers with wide bottoms. They are…
b. My top looks original. It's an…
c. My shirt has a small collar. It's a…
d. The skirt is smart but the fashion is old. It's a smart but…
e. The T-shirt fits loosely. It's a…

Grammar

La forme interrogative Repères, p. 258

» Les questions en *Wh-*

– **What do you like** wearing the most?
Wh- + aux. + sujet + BV

– **Where did you buy** this hat?
Wh- + aux. + sujet + BV

– **How often you do buy** new trainers?
Wh- + aux. + sujet + BV

– **Why aren't these clothes** more comfortable? → Because they're too tight.
Wh- + *be* + sujet

– **What are you going** to do about the problem?
Wh- + *be* + sujet + V-*ing*

– **Who wore** my jacket?
Wh- + V

» Les *yes / no questions*

– **Does she like** wearing skinny jeans?
aux. + sujet + BV

– **Won't they go** to the fashion show? → No, they won't.
aux. + sujet + BV

– **Have you ever wondered** where your clothes come from?
aux. + sujet + adv. + V (p. passé)

L'essentiel

- Il y a deux types de questions en anglais :
  - Les questions en ***Wh-*** (questions ouvertes), qui commencent par un mot interrogatif.
  - Les ***yes / no questions*** (questions fermées), auxquelles on répond par oui ou non.

  L'ordre des mots est le même dans les deux types de questions : auxiliaire + sujet + verbe.

Attention : Si la question porte sur le sujet, il n'y a pas d'inversion auxiliaire-sujet.

1. Mettez les mots dans l'ordre pour former une question.

is – jacket – where – my – ? → *Where is my jacket?*

a. is – coat – whose – this – ?
b. you – come – meeting – don't – ? – why – the – to
c. ? – often – do – how – buy – clothes – new – you
d. the company – ethical fashion – ? – become – ever – interested in – will
e. possible – ? – ethical – it – be – is – both – to – fashionable – and

2. Posez une question pour avoir l'information qui manque.

They decided to (?). → *What did they decide to do?*

a. He bought (?) at the shops yesterday.
b. He saw (?), who was shopping too.
c. I'm thinking of going to (?) tomorrow, if I have the time.
d. Mary says she will write (?) to the company to ask them to stop manufacturing abroad.
e. (?) says she will sign an online petition.

3. Voici des réponses. Quelles étaient les questions ?

My jacket? I got it in a little shop in London.
→ *Where did you get your jacket?*

a. Tonight? I think I'm going to watch that new documentary about fast fashion.
b. Bangladesh? It's close to India.
c. I can't remember exactly, but I'd say I've been a member of this association for about three years.
d. It's just my opinion, but yes I do. The reason I think people should get involved is because it's an important issue.

Similarités et différences Repères, p. 263

– **Contrary to C. Bennett** K. Hepburn is wearing trousers.
Contrary to + nom
– John is wearing trousers **whereas Joe is wearing jeans**.
whereas + phrase
– **Both Kim and Katie are** trendy. **Both of them like** clothes.
Both + nom + V (pl.) — *Both of* + pronom + V (pl.)
– **Neither Kim nor Katie buys** fast fashion. **Neither of them agrees** with it.
Neither + nom + V (sing.) — *Neither of* + pronom + V (sing.)

L'essentiel
- Pour exprimer la **similarité**, on utilise : *both / neither (of them), all of them / none of them.*
- Pour exprimer la **différence**, on emploie les mots de liaison *whereas, contrary to, unlike* ainsi que *compared to.*

Attention : Après *whereas*, on trouve une phrase. Après *contrary to, unlike* et *compared to*, on trouve un nom.

4. Reformulez à l'aide des structures suivantes.
both of them – neither of them – all of them – none of them – neither… nor
Jim, Mo and Jack are wearing hats. → *All of them are wearing hats.*

Jim and Jack don't like caps. Jim and Jack don't have boots. Jim and Jack are wearing shoes. Jim and Jack aren't wearing jeans.

5. Trouvez une fin logique aux phrases ci-dessous.
Joe hates ties. Mike loves ties. *Contrary to…*
→ *Contrary to Joe, Mike loves ties.*

a. Joe is a smart dresser but Mike is a much smarter dresser.
Compared to…

b. Mary likes fashion from the 70s. Joan prefers the 90s.
… whereas…

c. Mary likes wearing black. Joan likes wearing red.
Unlike…

Le conseil Repères, p. 253

– You **should choose** a company that has more ethical principles.
– **Why don't you check** the labels of your clothes?
– **Why not send** a message to one of the companies?
– **How about suggesting** that they pay fair wages?

L'essentiel
- Pour **donner un conseil**, on peut utiliser *should* ou *could* + BV.
- On peut aussi utiliser : *Why don't you…* + BV? *Why not* + BV? ou *How about* + V-ing?

6. Réécrivez les phrases en remplaçant *could* ou *should* par une autre structure exprimant le conseil.
It's cold outside. You should wear a warmer coat.
→ *It's cold outside. Why not wear a warmer coat?*

a. Couldn't we do some shopping this afternoon?

b. Shouldn't you ask him first?

c. You really don't have anything to wear for this job interview. You should buy a suit.

Sounds, sounds, sounds

L'intonation des questions Repères, p. 247

L'essentiel
- Les ***yes / no questions*** ont en général une intonation montante en fin de phrase ↗.
- Les **questions en *Wh-*** se terminent par une intonation descendante ↘.

Classe 2 Piste 11 — 45

1. Écoutez et repérez l'intonation des questions suivantes. Répétez.

a. Do you like my new jacket?

b. Where did you buy this hat?

c. Can I borrow your coat?

d. How long have you had it?

Classe 2 Piste 12 — 46

2. Dites à haute voix toutes les questions des exercices 1 à 3 en respectant l'intonation. Écoutez pour vérifier.

STRATEGY INTERAGIR À L'ORAL

Pour réussir une interaction orale, il faut :

1 ... bien comprendre : → Faites **reformuler** ou **reformulez** vous-même.

Oh! You mean…?

Could you rephrase your question, please?

Can you repeat, please?

If I understand you well, what you mean is…

2 ... réagir : → **Utilisez** des **réponses courtes**, des **phrases simples**, des ***question-tags***.

Yes, I am. • Of course I do. • No, I don't.

Why not? • That's crazy! • Unbelievable!

Once a week. • Never. • It is, isn't it?

3 ... hésiter : → Laissez-vous le temps de répondre en utilisant des **marqueurs d'hésitation**.

I'd say that… • I suppose… • The thing is…

I'm not sure. Well… • Er… you know… • Let me think…

4 ... relancer : → Vous pouvez **relancer la conversation / poursuivre le questionnement**.

What about you? • May I ask you one more question?

When…? • How long…? • Have you ever…?

5 ... et être convaincant(e) : → **Insistez** sur les **mots importants** ou les **auxiliaires**.

Les gestes peuvent parfois aider à faire passer le message !

I <u>do</u> think that… • I <u>can't help</u> thinking that… • Are you <u>sure</u>?

Your project — Prepare and conduct a survey

Groupwork

Interview your classmates about their clothing habits and the problems of the fashion industry.

Negotiation over a pair of Air Jordans, New York

1 Design the survey.

- **Get into groups.**
  Choose the themes of your survey (3-4): personal style – favourite clothes – shopping habits – origins – working conditions – responsibilities (companies, governments, consumers…) – suggestions.
- **Agree on** a list of 10 questions (2 or 3 for each theme) and **prepare** a survey grid.
- Ask your teacher for help.

2 Test the survey.

- **Test** the **questions** on your own group.
- **Correct** your **grid**.

3 Conduct the survey.

- **Interview** other groups in the class.
- **Fill** in the **grid**.

4 Analyse the results.

- **Read** the results.
- **List** the general **trends** and **pick out** the **exceptions**.
- **Prepare** to present your **results** and **compare** them with those of the other groups.

Keys to success

- **Utilisez le vocabulaire du chapitre lié à la mode :** les vêtements, la mode et les styles, l'industrie de la mode.
  ➥ *Words, words, words, p. 106*
- **Posez des questions en utilisant l'intonation appropriée.**
  ➥ *Grammar, p. 108*
  ➥ *Sounds, sounds, sounds, p. 109*
- **Employez plusieurs adjectifs et des adjectifs composés.**
  ➥ *More words, p. 107*
- **Pensez à exprimer des similarités et des différences.**
  ➥ *Grammar, p. 109*
- **Appliquez les conseils pour interagir à l'oral.**
  ➥ *Strategy, p. 110*

Axe 4 : Représentation de soi et rapport à autrui

8 Self(ie)-portraits

1 Basics

List all the words you know about art (people – techniques – colours – works of art).

WORKSHEET 17

2 vidéo Discover

Watch the video.
Pick out names, marking events, dates and numbers. Use them to **make a timeline** of the history of photographic self-portraits.

Game 3 Play

Guessing game: Describe a famous person without giving their name.
Include something in your description that represents the person (symbol – object). The class will **guess** who it is.

▶ *He's got… • She's holding a X… • The basketball symbolises…*

Your project

Record a short commentary about your self-portrait for an audioguide, *p. 127*

– Write about a photo of yourself, *p. 117*
– Record a short presentation about an artist, *p. 119*

Keys to success

- **Strategy: améliorer sa prononciation**, *p. 126*
- **Mind map:** art, photography and technology, description, *p. 122*
- **Grammar:** présent simple et en *be* + V-*ing*, souhait, but, *p. 124*
  Sounds: -*s* à la 3e personne, *p. 125*

Séquence +

Andy Warhol,
Self-Portrait, 1966

How are portraits, self-portraits and selfies related?

Parler • Lire • Écrire

Looking at myself

1 Seeing my reflection

1. Describe the painting.
► *In the background / foreground / middle... • The landscape is... • The characters look...*

Pairwork

2. Read the *Did you know?* Then agree on a possible interpretation of the painting.
► *The artist represents... • The man's attitude is symbolic of... • The woman looks... • Her expression suggests...*

John William Waterhouse, *Echo and Narcissus*, 1903

Did you know?

In Greek mythology, **Narcissus** was famous for his beauty. When he first saw his reflection in a pool of water, he realised how handsome he was. He was so absorbed with his reflection that he stopped eating and died. Today the word "narcissistic" means being absorbed with yourself.

Need help?

- bare-**foo**ted = not **wea**ring shoes
- **fa**scinated = ab**sorbed**
- **hand**some = good-**loo**king (for a man)
- **hope**less ≠ **hope**ful
- **na**ked ['neɪkɪd]: *nu(e)*
- ob**sessed**
- stretched [stretʃt] out: *allongé(e)*
- **thought**ful = **pen**sive
- up**set** = dis**tressed**
- lean **for**ward: *se pencher en avant*
- lie down: *se coucher*
- reach out: *tendre la main*
- see one**self**: *se voir*

2 Stopping time

1. **Suggest** three things the character in the picture might be thinking.

2. **Read** the 1st paragraph. **Focus on** movements and feelings.
Pick out the reason(s) that provoked Dorian's emotions.

3. **Read** the 2nd paragraph. **Say** how he feels now. Guess what has happened.

4. **Read** the 3rd paragraph. **Search** for reasons that explain his feelings.

5. **Make** a list of three magic wishes that you have and share them with your classmates.
▶ *I wish… • If only…*

Ben Barnes in the film *Dorian Gray* by Oliver Parker, 2009

Dorian Gray is a handsome young man whose portrait was drawn by artist Basil Hallward. He has just discovered the painting at the artist's London studio.

Dorian made no answer, but passed listlessly[1] in front of his picture, and turned towards it. When he saw it he drew back, and his cheeks flushed[2] for a moment with pleasure. A look of joy came into his eyes, as if he had recognised himself for the first time. He stood there motionless[3] and in wonder, dimly conscious that Hallward was speaking to him, but not catching the meaning of his words. The sense of his own beauty came on him like a revelation. He had never felt it before. (…)

As he thought of it, a sharp pang of pain struck through him like a knife, and made each delicate fibre of his nature quiver[4]. His eyes deepened into amethyst, and across them came a mist of tears. He felt as if a hand of ice had been laid upon his heart. (…)

"How sad it is!" murmured Dorian Gray, with his eyes still fixed upon his own portrait. "How sad it is! I shall grow old, and horrible, and dreadful. But this picture will remain always young. It will never be older than this particular day of June… If it were only the other way! If it were I who was to be always young, and the picture that was to grow old! For that – for that – I would give everything! Yes, there is nothing in the whole world I would not give! I would give my soul for that!"

Oscar Wilde, *The Picture of Dorian Gray*, 1890

1. listlessly (adv.) = without energy
2. flush (v.) = turn red
3. motionless (adj.) = without movement
4. quiver (v.): *trembler*

Grammar

Le souhait

– If only he would look at me!

➥ *Grammar p. 125*

Representing yourself

CULTURE QUEST

Find information about the artists you don't know (place of birth – death – other types of works of art).

1. **Name** the different types of art you can see (drawing – engraving – sculpture – painting – photography).

2. **Match** the artists with their self-portraits. **Use** the captions and quotations to help you.

Pairwork

3. **Prepare** a detailed description of one of the self-portraits. **Describe** it to your classmate and have him / her **guess** which picture you described.

4. **Compare** the two self-portraits you chose with the corresponding photos. **Note down** the differences and **imagine** why the artists portrayed themselves this way.
▶ *He / She may want to symbolise / represent…*

A

Louise Bourgeois (1911-2010)
French-American artist
“The strong figure on the right is the father, and the softer figure on the left is the mother. And there, in between, this creature appears. It is simply a self-portrait.”

Self-portrait as a Heel, 1982

2

1

Untitled, #213, 1989

B

Francis Bacon (1909-1992)
British artist
“I loathe[1] my own face, and I've done self-portraits because I've had nobody else to do.”

1. loathe (v.) = hate

3

Self-portrait, 1966

4 Self-portrait, 1990

C
Erik Olson (1982-)
Canadian artist

D
Cindy Sherman (1954-)
American artist

“I feel I'm anonymous in my work. When I look at the pictures, I never see myself; they aren't self-portraits. Sometimes I disappear.”

E
Alexander Calder (1898-1976)
American sculptor

5 Self-portrait, 2013

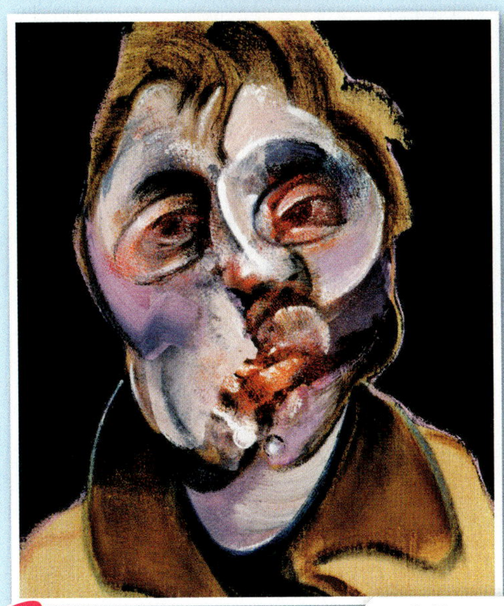

6 Self-portrait, 1969

F
Jean-Michel Basquiat (1960-1988)
American artist and graffiti artist

“I like kids' work more than work by real artists any day.”

Need help?

- graf**fi**ti
- oil **pain**ting
- sketch: *croquis*
- **wa**tercolour
- wire: *fil de fer*
- **ab**stract ≠ **fi**gurative
- **ima**ginative = in**ven**tive
- made out of
- **ob**vious = **e**vident
- sur**pri**sing = unex**pec**ted
- in stark **con**trast with = ex**treme**ly **dif**ferent from
- **si**milar to = like
- the **o**pposite of = the **con**trary of

Prepare your project

Bring in an old photo of yourself and write a short commentary about it.

▶ *You can see me here… • I look happy…*

Display your photo and description in the class. See if you recognise your classmates.

Écouter • Écrire • Partager • Parler

Visions of the world

Différenciation

You are going to learn about two photographers.
Work on **one of these topics** to find out more about how their self-portraits express a vision of the world.

Step 1: Pick out information and take notes (artist's life – country – style – techniques used – possible message).

Step 2: GROUPWORK Share your findings. WORKSHEET 20

Médiation

Did you know?

South Africa was colonised by the Dutch (17th century) and the British (19th century). The Afrikaaners (whites of Dutch descent) implemented a system of racial segregation (called apartheid) from 1948 to 1991.

TOPIC 1 Symbolic self-portraits

Classe 2 Pistes 13-14 WORKSHEET 18

1. Compare and contrast the two (self-)portraits.

2. Listen to the recording and read the *Did you know?* to find out more about the artist.

Mohau Modisakeng wearing a trilby hat (left) and blinkers (right), 2016

Mohau Modisakeng was born in the township[1] of Soweto, on the outskirts[2] of Johannesburg, South Africa, in 1986. His work is included in public collections such as the Johannesburg Art Gallery or the Saatchi Gallery in London.

1. township (n.) = poor black urban ghetto in South Africa
2. outskirts (n.): *périphérie*

Need help?

- **gar**ment = item of **clo**thing
- **do**minated
- op**pressed**
- sym**bo**lic = repre**sen**tative
- as**pire** to = aim to
- **co**py = **i**mitate
- **e**cho = re**call**
- **fo**cus on = **con**centrate on
- **high**light = under**line**
- look like = re**sem**ble
- re**flect** on = think a**bout**
- re**late** to = i**den**tify with
- **sym**bolise = stand for

Grammar

Le but

He represents himself **in order to express** what he feels.
in order to + BV

➥ *Grammar p. 125*

TOPIC 2 An urban self-portrait

WORKSHEET 19

1. **Describe** the photo and **guess** where and when the scene takes place.

2. Use the short biography to **imagine** why Vivian Maier represented herself in this environment.

3. **Check out** the artist's self-portraits on Vivian Maier's official website. **Find** information (people – places – things – techniques used – how she represented herself).

Vivian Maier, *Self-Portrait*, 1950s

Vivian Dorothy Maier (1926, Bronx, New York – 2009) worked as a nanny for 40 years. In her free time she would take lots of pictures.

It was only after her death in 2009, when her photographs were purchased at auction (= *aux enchères*), shown on Flickr and quickly went viral, that her work became known and admired.

Need help?

- camera: *appareil photo*
- photograph
- photographer
- photography
- reflection: *reflet*
- shop window: *vitrine*
- window-shopping: *lèche-vitrines*
- cut off from = isolated from
- drawn towards = attracted to
- photographic
- out of focus = blurred
- illustrate = explain
- stroll: *flâner*
- at first glance: *au premier coup d'œil*
- keep one's distance = avoid

Prepare your project

An art-gallery has asked you to make a short presentation about an artist. Prepare a 1-minute recording about one of the artists you discovered.

Parler • Écouter • Échanger

The age of the selfie

CULTURE QUEST

Search the web for information about the monkey's selfie.

Keywords: monkey – steal – camera – snap – 2011 – David Slater – Sulawesi – NPR – copyright – selfie – viral.

1 Selfies are everywhere

1. Describe the photos on both pages.

2. Make a list of their common points and differences.

3. Agree on the answers to the quiz questions. (Groupwork)

▶ *Out of… • More than / Less than… • The percentage of people… • On average…*

4. Compare the results with your own habits.

Social media QUIZ

Choose the correct answer.

1 Average number of Snaps per day:
- 3 million
- 30 million
- 300 million
- 3 billion or more

2 In 2015
- more
- less

people died from taking selfies than from shark attacks.

3 Percentage of Snapshat photos that are selfies:
- ≤ 25%
- between 25 and 50%
- between 50 and 75%
- ≥ 75%

4
- 24 million
- 240 million
- 2.4 billion
- 24 billion

selfies were posted on Google servers in 2015.

5 Percentage of US teens that use Snapchat daily:
- 0-25%
- 25-50%
- 50-75%
- 75-100%

6 Proportion of teens who have already taken selfies in the UK:
- 5/20
- 10/20
- 15/20
- 19/20

7 As of December 2016, there were over
- 106 million
- 282 million
- 541 million selfies on Instagram

Barack Obama pretending to take a selfie in front of Kehinde Wiley's official portrait of him, 2018

2 vidéo Can a selfie be a work of art?

1. **Guess** the content of the video.

2. **Watch** it without the sound and check.

3. **Watch** with the sound and **pick out** information about the event mentioned (people – places – theme – number of entries). **Sum up** what you've understood.

4. **Compare** Nigel Hurst's and Andrew Garritty's opinions about the roles smartphone photography can play.
▶ *According to… • Unlike…, X says that… • Both X and Y say that…*

Groupwork
5. **Debate** about whether or not a selfie can be a work of art then **vote** with the rest of the class.

From Selfie to Self-Expression, exhibition at the Saatchi Gallery, London, 2017

Grammar

Le présent simple et le présent en *be* + V-*ing*

In this photo, the monkey **is smiling**.

➥ *Grammar p. 124*

Need help?

- de**vice**: *appareil*
- **fea**ture = charac**teris**tic
- **sel**fie stick: *perche à selfie*
- dis**po**sable = **throw**away
- short-**las**ting = e**phe**meral
- swipe: *faire glisser (sur un écran)*
- at arm's length: *à bout de bras*
- make **fa**ces: *faire des grimaces*
- take a **pho**to of one**self**: *se prendre en photo*

Mémoriser • Prononcer • Écrire

Words, words, words

➥ *Mémoriser et enrichir son lexique p. 235*

Quizlet
quizlet.com/skysthelimit2e

Classe 2 Pistes 15-22 — 47 54

Créez votre propre carte mentale à partir de ce que vous avez vu en classe.
Vous pourrez ensuite l'enrichir à l'aide de celle-ci.
Écoutez les mots et répétez-les pour bien les prononcer.
Écrivez-les aussi plusieurs fois pour mémoriser leur orthographe.

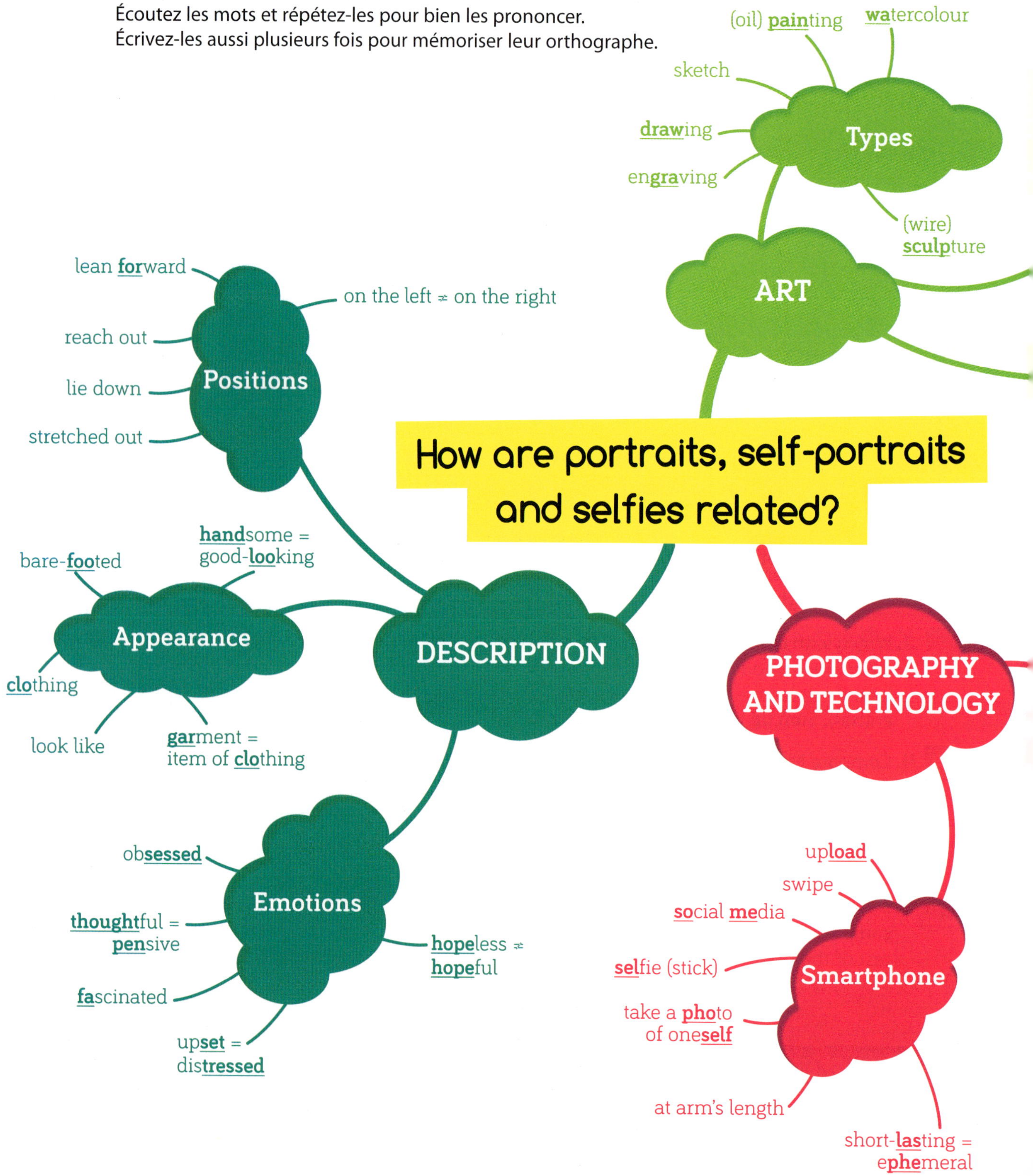

Qualifying

- in stark contrast with ≠ similar to
- obvious = evident
- surprising = unexpected
- abstract ≠ figurative
- imaginative = inventive

Interpreting

- represent
- highlight = underline
- symbolise = stand for
- illustrate = explain
- relate to = identify with

Photography

- photo(graph)
- snap(shot)
- camera
- device
- out of focus = blurred
- disposable = throwaway

More words

Analyser une image

American Gothic selfie (adapted from Grant Wood, *American Gothic*)

The phone on the right of the picture **stands for** / **represents** / **symbolises** / **is symbolic of** new technology. The style of the painting **makes us think of** / **reminds us of** the famous painting by Grant Wood. The contrast between the style of the painting and the smartphone **highlights** / **emphasises** / **underlines** the way society has changed. The artist **depicts** / **shows** / **represents** two characters taking a selfie in order to make **us reflect on** / **think about** the impact selfies have on the way we see ourselves.

1. Reliez chaque expression à un synonyme et sa traduction.

stand for •	• draw attention to •	• *réfléchir à*
evoke •	• signify •	• *suggérer*
highlight •	• consider •	• *attirer l'attention sur*
reflect on •	• suggest •	• *signifier*

2. Commentez le tableau en complétant le texte : remplacez les numéros par une expression que vous avez apprise.

In the (1) there is a blue sky and what seems to be a church. This church may (2) the fact that American society is very religious. In the (3) there is a couple who look very serious and thoughtful. This (4) the severe, puritan impression that the painting gives. The mobile phone (5) modern-day life, which contrasts starkly with the couple and their environment. The artist probably wants to (6) how omnipresent technology has become in our lives today.

3. Écrivez une courte description et analyse de l'image page 113 ou d'un autre tableau de ce chapitre.

Observer • Retenir • Appliquer

Grammar

Le présent simple et le présent en *be* + V-*ing*

Repères, p. 249

- Many people **visit** art museums when they **travel**.
- He **knows** what he **likes**.
- He **doesn't like** modern art.
- I'**m visiting** a museum at the moment, can I call you later?
- In this photo, the monkey **is smiling**.

L'essentiel

Contrairement au français, il existe plusieurs temps du présent en anglais.

• Le **présent simple** sert à exprimer les **goûts**, les **opinions**, les **vérités générales** et les **habitudes**.

- À la forme affirmative, il n'y a pas d'auxiliaire.
- À la forme interrogative et négative, on utilise l'auxiliaire *do* / *does*.

• Le **présent en *be* + V-*ing*** sert à exprimer une **action en cours**, à **décrire quelque chose** et à **exprimer une intention**. On utilise l'auxiliaire *be* à toutes les formes (***am*** / ***is*** / ***are***).

Attention : Les verbes d'état (*be, belong, seem*...) et de goût / d'envie (*love, want*...) ne s'emploient pas à la forme *be* + V-*ing*.

1. Mettez les verbes entre parenthèses à la forme du présent simple qui convient.

I usually (*visit*) museums in the morning, when there (*be*) not too many people.

→ *I usually visit museums in the morning, when there are not too many people.*

a. She (*take*) a lot of selfies whenever she is on a trip.

b. Modisakeng (*be*) an artist who (*use*) self-portraits as a message.

c. It (*not always be*) easy to recognise Cindy Sherman on her self-portraits.

d. On this self-portrait, Francis Bacon (*no look*) very happy, does he?

2. Mettez les verbes entre parenthèses à la forme du présent en *be* + V-*ing* qui convient.

The man in the picture (*look at*) a sculpture.

→ *The man in the picture is looking at a sculpture.*

a. (*you / go*) to your art class next Saturday?

b. I (*just / watch*) a documentary about Vivian Maier.

c. What (*Vivian Maier / do*) in this photo?

d. She (*stand*) near a shop-window.

e. He (*not / pay*) any attention to what the guide is saying.

3. Voici des réponses. Utilisez les mots entre parenthèses pour retrouver les questions.

I think it is a good idea. (*What – you – think – about going to the exhibition tonight?*)

→ *What do you think about going to the exhibition tonight?*

a. Because he loves art. (*Why – John – want – to paint his own portrait?*)

b. Not often, only when I'm on a night out. (*You – often – take – selfies?*)

c. *The Picture of Dorian Gray*. (*What – book – you – read?*)

d. I think he's trying to take a selfie while cycling! (*What – that man – do?*)

4. Complétez les phrases en mettant le verbe à la forme qui convient : présent simple ou présent en *be* + V-*ing*.

She (*stand*) in front of a shop-window.
She (*probably / want*) to buy what she sees in it.

→ *She is standing in front of a shop-window.*
She probably wants to buy what she sees in it.

a. In this photo, I (*sit*) on a bench (*read*) a book. But I (*not / do*) that very often. It (*not / represent*) who I am.

b. People sometimes (*think*) museums can be boring, but I (*love*) going to modern art museums, they (*often / exhibit*) works of art I (*find*) funny and original.

c. Look at him! He (*ride*) his bike and (*take*) a selfie! It's dangerous!

d. (*you / go*) to the exhibition with me tomorrow? You can come with your friend if she (*like*) the artist.

5. Écrivez trois phrases sur ce que vous faites habituellement à cette heure-ci et trois phrases sur ce que vous êtes en train de faire.

→ *Usually, at this time of the day I… • At the moment, I…*

Le souhait Repères, p. 252

– **If only he would** look at me!
– I **wish I could** paint.
– I **wish he listened** to me!
– **If only I were** an artist!

L'essentiel : Pour **exprimer le souhait**, on utilise *wish* ou *if only* + V au prétérit modal ou *would* / *could* + BV.
Attention : Pour le verbe *be* au prétérit modal, on utilise *were* à toutes les personnes.

6. Complétez les phrases avec le verbe à la forme qui convient.
They wish they (*have*) a portrait of their daughter.
→ *They wish they had a portrait of their daughter.*

a. I wish you (*know*) how long the exhibition lasts.
b. If only my parents (*take*) me to the museum more often!
c. She wishes she (*not have to*) leave so early, the private viewing (= *vernissage*) has only just begun.

Le but Repères, p. 262

– He represents himself **in order to express** what he feels.
in order to + BV
– He practised a lot **to become** an artist.
to + BV
– He worked hard **so that people would know him**.
so that + phrase

L'essentiel : Pour **exprimer le but**, on utilise : *in order* / *to* + BV ou *so that* + phrase.
Attention : On ne peut pas utiliser *for*, sauf lorsqu'il y a deux sujets (*for sb to do sth*).

7. Complétez avec *to, in order to* ou *so that*.
I need to know a lot about this painter (?) do my oral presentation.
→ *I need to know a lot about this painter in order to do my oral presentation.*

a. How about going to the museum (?) I can finally see this exhibition!
b. He decided to give up his job (?) concentrate on his work as an artist.
c. He needs a lot of time alone (?) be creative.

8. Reliez les phrases avec *to, in order to* ou *so that*. Faites les changements nécessaires.
I chose warm colours for my painting. I wanted to represent Africa.
→ *I chose warm colours in order to represent Africa.*

a. He wants to come with us. He says he can tell us all about the artist.
b. The artist used red and yellow. He wanted to symbolise warmth and light.
c. You should read a book about this painter. You would learn a lot about him.

Sounds, sounds, sounds

Le -*s* à la 3e personne Repères, p. 246

L'essentiel :
- Le -*s* final s'entend toujours en anglais.
- Il y a trois prononciations possibles pour le **-*s* à la 3e personne du singulier** : [s], [z] ou [ɪz].
- La prononciation est différente en fonction du son de la dernière syllabe de la base verbale.

Classe 2 – 55 – Piste 23

1. Écoutez les mots suivants et classez-les en fonction de la prononciation du -*s* final : [s], [z] ou [ɪz].
seems – symbolises – hates – loves – wishes – paints – draws – describes

Classe 2 – 56 – Piste 24

2. Lisez les phrases en veillant à bien prononcer le -*s* final pour les verbes soulignés. Puis écoutez et vérifiez.
This photo <u>shows</u> my mum leaving the house early on a Sunday morning. The sun <u>illuminates</u> the street. I chose it because she <u>likes</u> to go for a walk on her own now and then. It <u>represents</u> her need to be alone. She never <u>manages</u> to go for a walk during the week because she <u>uses</u> her car a lot and <u>comes</u> home quite late.

3. Faites des phrases sur les goûts et les habitudes d'un(e) ami(e) avec les verbes suivants. Veillez à bien prononcer le -*s*.
like – love – wish – want – play – practise

STRATEGY AMÉLIORER SA PRONONCIATION

Pour bien prononcer, il faut...

1 ... respecter les particularités de l'anglais oral :

→ **Accentuez :**
- le **mot le plus important** dans la phrase ;
- les **mots lexicaux** dans la phrase (noms – verbes – adjectifs) ;
- une **syllabe** dans tous les mots qui ont plus d'une syllabe.

I **love** this **pho**tograph. It **shows** my **fa**ther when he was a **teen**ager. The **photographer** is his **bro**ther.

→ **Faites les liaisons** entre les mots.

→ **Pensez à l'intonation** pour les questions.
Do you like going to the museum? ↗
➥ *Strategy, p. 45*

N'hésitez pas à exagérer l'accentuation des mots pour que ça « sonne anglais ».

2 ... savoir comment les mots se prononcent :

→ **Vérifiez la prononciation des mots.** Certains mots ne se prononcent pas comme ils s'écrivent.

pear ≠ hear

Quand vous n'êtes pas sûr(e), servez-vous d'un dictionnaire en ligne (par exemple dictionary.cambridge.org). Vous pourrez écouter le mot et voir sa transcription phonétique.

3 ... s'entraîner :

→ **Enregistrez-vous :** écoutez et vérifiez que le **débit** et le **rythme** sont adaptés, que les mots importants sont audibles.

→ **Demandez à d'autres de vous écouter :** vérifiez qu'ils ont compris ce que vous vouliez dire.

→ **Recommencez l'enregistrement** jusqu'à ce que vous soyez content(e) de ce que vous entendez !

Your project | Talk about your self-portrait

Your class has decided to make an audioguide for an exhibition of the self-portraits you made. Record a commentary about your own self-portrait.

Student making a self-portrait out of clay (*argile*)

1 Choose your medium.

- You can use a mixture of **different mediums** (photo – painting – drawing – sculpture – collage – video – app – software – cartoon). **Be imaginative!**
- **Remember:** you don't need to be technically skilled to create a work of art!

2 Create your self-portrait.

- **Think about what you want your self-portrait to look like.**
  – Figurative or abstract?
  – Which colours / forms / objects / words represent you best and why?
  – **Include** at least one symbol in your self-portrait.

3 Decide on the contents of your audioguide.

- **Describe** your self-portrait in detail. Write about the techniques, the colours and the symbols you used and **explain why**.

4 Record your audio guide.

- **Rehearse** (= *Répétez*) numerous times before recording your final version. The **key criteria** to a good audioguide: clarity – pronunciation – intonation – rhythm – fluidity – tone.

Keys to success

- **Utilisez le vocabulaire du chapitre :** art, photographie et technologie, description.
  ➡ *Words, words, words, p. 122*
- **Utilisez le vocabulaire pour décrire une image.**
  ➡ *More words, p. 123*
- **Pensez à utiliser les temps du présent.**
  ➡ *Grammar, p. 124*
- **Prononcez correctement le -*s* à la 3e personne du singulier.**
  ➡ *Sounds, sounds, sounds, p. 125*
- **Servez-vous des conseils pour améliorer votre prononciation.**
  ➡ *Strategy, p. 126*

Entraînement aux épreuves communes

▶ **1re partie de l'épreuve 1 :** compréhension de l'oral.
– Le document pourra être un audio ou une vidéo.
– Le titre du document vous sera communiqué en début d'épreuve.
– Il faudra rendre compte en français de ce que vous avez compris.

▶ **2e partie de l'épreuve 1 :** expression écrite : deux sujets au choix.

Compréhension de l'oral

Classe 3 Piste 53 9

Sujet

Narcissistic, maybe. But is there more to the art of the selfie?

Vous allez **écouter trois fois** un document audio avec une pause entre chaque écoute.
À l'issue de la 3e écoute, vous devrez **rendre compte en français** de ce que vous avez compris.

▶ **Les clés pour réussir** ➡ *Comprendre un document audio ou audiovisuel p. 30*

Attention à bien gérer votre temps entre la compréhension de l'oral et l'expression écrite.

Expression écrite

Sujet 1

Can selfies be a form of art? Give your opinion.

▶ **Les clés pour réussir**

Analysez le sujet.

– Relevez les **mots-clés** du sujet.
– Identifiez bien la **nature** du sujet et la **tâche** à accomplir.

Can selfies be a form of art? Give your opinion.

Réfléchissez.

– **Notez tous les mots** qui vous viennent à l'esprit pour chaque mot-clé : pensez à ce que vous avez vu en cours (idées, exemples, lexique…).

N'hésitez pas à faire une carte mentale pour classer vos idées ! ➡ *Faire une carte mentale p. 234*

– Listez les **expressions utiles** pour exprimer une opinion nuancée : *In my opinion…* • *As far as I'm concerned…* • *I can understand that…*

Organisez vos idées.

– Faites un **plan structuré**.

Rédigez.

– Rédigez votre **introduction** (le thème – les grandes lignes de votre plan). Trouvez une **phrase d'accroche** qui retiendra l'attention du lecteur : citation – question – idée généralement acceptée…
– **Développez** chaque partie en veillant à garder une idée principale par paragraphe.
– Soignez vos **transitions** : *Let's move on to…* • *Moreover…* • *Furthermore…* • *Last but not least…*

– Illustrez votre propos avec des **exemples**.
– Rédigez une **conclusion** (répondre à la question que vous vous êtes posée – ouvrir sur un sujet plus large).

Finalisez votre copie.

– **Relisez-vous**. Vérifiez que vous avez bien respecté le nombre de mots autorisé (± 10 %).

ou

Sujet 2

Read the opinions of three high-school students and say which one you agree with the most. Support your answer with arguments.

In my opinion, everything can be art, including selfies.
Amy, 16, Minnesota

I don't think selfies are art, I think they are narcissistic.
Riley, 18, Maine

It depends on the selfie. Some are art, some are not.
Ethan, 15, New Mexico

▶ Les clés pour réussir

Analysez le sujet.

– **Identifiez** le **point commun** entre les citations.
– Relevez les **mots-clés** de chaque citation et comparez-les.
– Prenez en compte le **contexte proposé**.

– *In my opinion, everything can be art, including selfies.*
– *I don't think selfies are art, I think they are narcissistic.*
– *It depends on the selfie. Some are art, some are not.*

Réfléchissez.

– **Positionnez-vous** : quelle citation semble correspondre le plus à ce que vous pensez ?
– Trouvez des **arguments** pour défendre la citation choisie.
– Cherchez des **contre-arguments** pour justifier pourquoi vous n'êtes pas d'accord avec les autres citations.

Pensez à vous appuyer sur ce que vous avez étudié (idées, documents, exemples…).

Organisez vos idées.

– Faites un **plan structuré**.

Rédigez.

– Rédigez votre **introduction** (thème des citations – votre position – les grandes lignes de votre plan).
– **Développez** chaque partie en veillant à avoir une idée principale par paragraphe.
– Illustrez votre propos avec des **exemples**.

Pensez aux ***expressions utiles*** *pour exprimer votre opinion :* accord : *I completely agree with… • I believe…* – désaccord : *How could X possibly think that…?*

– Soignez vos **transitions** : *Let's move on to… • Moreover… • Furthermore… • Last but not least…*
– Rédigez une **conclusion** (les points principaux du développement – ouverture sur un sujet plus large).

Finalisez votre copie.

– **Relisez-vous**. Vérifiez que vous avez bien respecté le nombre de mots autorisé (± 10 %).

Pour la 1re partie de l'épreuve 1, rendez-vous ➥ p. 64-65.

Axe 5 : Sports

et société

9 Extreme challenges, p. 132

What can we learn from people who push themselves beyond their limits?

10 The Great Game, p. 142

Séquence +

Why has football always been so important in British society?

Axe 5 : Sports et société

9 Extreme challenges

What can we learn from people who push themselves beyond their limits?

Your project

Groupwork

Narrate an extreme adventure in a journal and read those of your classmates, *p. 141*

– Imagine an entry in Usain Bolt's diary, *p. 135*

– Write the last two or three entries in Titus Oates' journal, *p. 137*

Keys to success

- **Strategy: comprendre un texte,** *p. 140*
- **Mind map:** nature, challenges, qualities, *p. 138*
- **Grammar:** prétérit simple et *present perfect, p. 139*

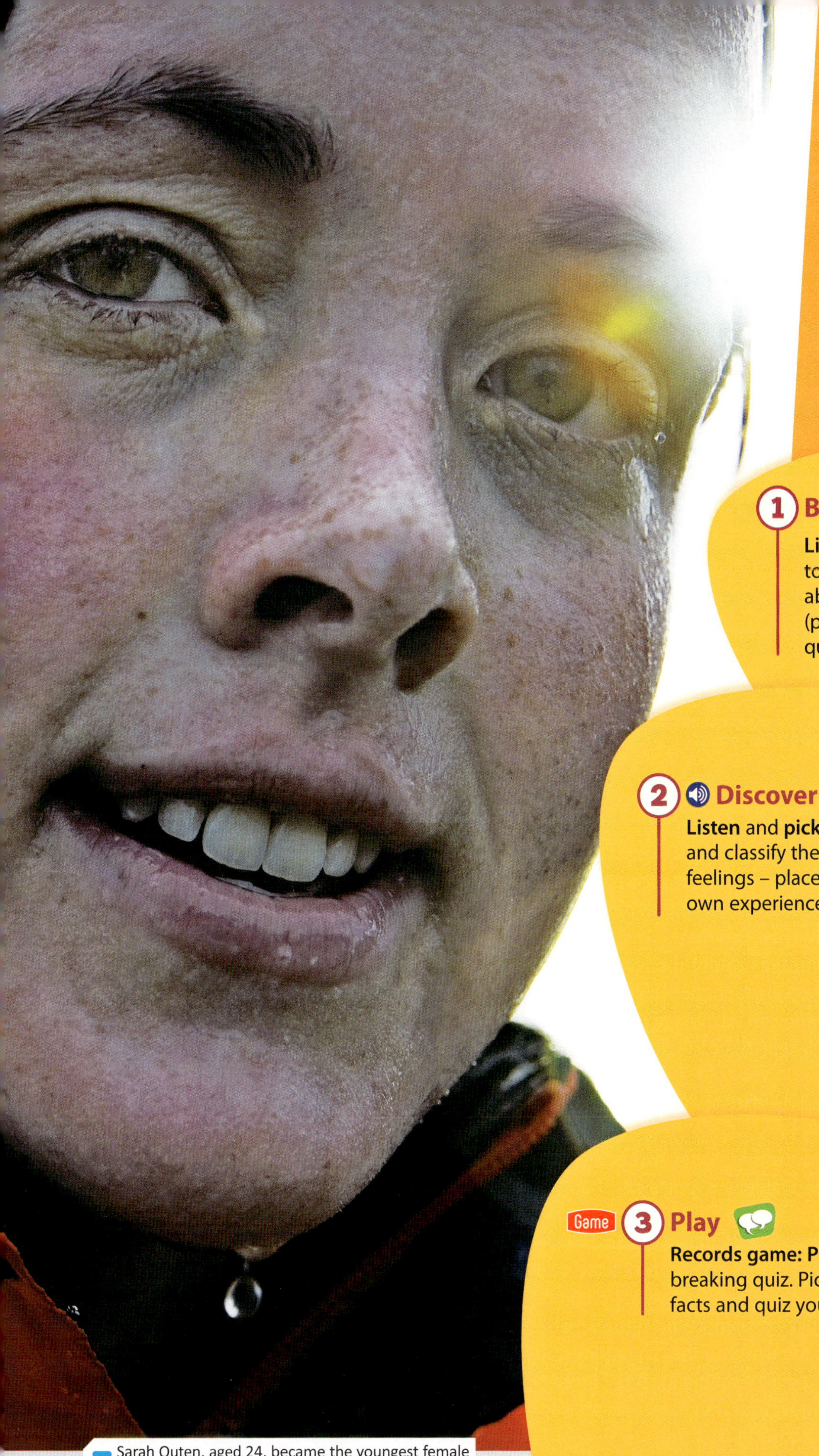

Sarah Outen, aged 24, became the youngest female to row alone across the Indian Ocean.

1 Basics

List all the words that come to mind when you think about extreme challenges (places – examples – feelings – qualities). WORKSHEET 21

2 Discover

Classe 2 Piste 25

Listen and **pick out** the stressed words and classify them (sports – activities – feelings – places). **Compare** with your own experience and feelings.

Game 3 Play

Records game: Prepare a record-breaking quiz. Pick record-breaking facts and quiz your classmates.

Lire • Écouter • Écrire

Competing to win

1 Faster than lightning

Jamaican Usain Bolt is an 11-time world champion, having broken 100m and 200m world records.

1. Say everything you know about the man in the picture. Read the caption and the source then guess what the text will be about.

2. Read the text and check. Pick out details about the narrator (likes – dislikes – talents).

3. Focus on references to places, sports accomplishments and time. Use what you have found to trace the evolution of the narrator over the years.
▶ *At first he was… • After a while he… • Just a few years later he…*

Pairwork
4. Discuss the reasons behind Usain Bolt's success.
▶ *What is special about Usain Bolt is that… • He wouldn't have succeeded if he hadn't…*

At school I was pretty good in class, especially math, and when lessons began I made an important discovery: man, I loved to compete! As soon as a problem went up on the chalkboard[1], I'd race to finish. Often NJ would battle me to see who could complete the sums first, and that's when a killer instinct showed up. Everything I got involved in, I did it to win. I had to win. First was everything, second only meant losing. And I really hated losing.
I cruised through my first few years at school, and sports quickly became my thing. Thanks to all that running around the wild bush in Coxeath I was fast. In cricket when I bowled[2] I could come down on the wicket hard, with speed, and I was quick in the field. My physical size gave me an advantage over the other pupils because I was growing into a tall kid, and at the age of eight I was taking wickets[3] off cricketers a lot older than me, guys that were 10 or 11 years old. I was already the same height as them and it wasn't long before I'd opened the batting[4] for Waldensia a couple of years earlier than most kids even made the team.
I was pretty good at sprinting, too. I had potential. I was quick on my feet and after I'd beaten Ricardo in the Waldensia sports day, I entered my first serious inter-schools race (where the prize was made out of tin and plastic rather than rice and peas), winning all my events. After a few more competitions in 1997, it was obvious to everyone that I was the fastest kid in Sherwood Content, and I later won the Trelawny parish champs[5] when I was 10. People were taking notice of what I could do and I was winning school race after school race. Our house creaked at the fittings[6] with all the plastic trophies and medals I was bringing back for winning this championship and that, but none of it was really serious to me. I just enjoyed running for fun. I loved the sensation of coming first in school races, of beating the other kids, but there was no way I could have seen that track and field was a serious future for me at that time. How could I? I was just a kid.

Usain Bolt, *Faster than Lightning,* 2013

1. chalkboard (n.): *tableau noir*
2. bowl (v.): *lancer*
3. take a wicket (exp.): *sortir un adversaire (cricket)*
4. bat (v.): *jouer le batteur*
5. champs (n.) = championships
6. creak at the fittings (exp.) = be completely full

2 A triumph of determination

DOSSIER documentaire — Classe 2 Piste 26

1. Describe the photo and imagine how the person in the picture feels. Explain why you think the person feels this way.

2. Read the text. Pick out references to places, time and weather. Find what Libby Riddles is famous for.
▶ *Despite the weather… • She went from being… • She is the first woman to have…*

3. Listen and use what you notice (number / tone of voices – background noises) to deduce what the recording is about.

4. Listen again and note down stressed words, focusing on references to Libby's exploit (weather conditions – distances – motivation...).

5. Group together your notes and use them to write a paragraph about Libby Riddles and her great accomplishment.

Médiation

Libby Riddles out racing with her dogs and sled, 1986

When the 1985 Iditarod Trail[1] Sled Dog Race began, Libby Riddles was a virtually unknown musher[2] living in Teller[3]. When the race ended, she was an international celebrity. By braving a storm that no other musher challenged, Riddles became the first woman to win the world's most significant dog sled race. During a year of terrible storms that periodically interrupted the event, the leading mushers halted in a village checkpoint. Only Riddles seized the moment and set out on the iffy[4] trail beyond Shaktoolik…

Alaska Sports Hall of Fame, 2019

1. trail (n.): *parcours*
2. musher (n.): *conducteur de traîneau tiré par des chiens*
3. Teller (n.) = small Eskimo village in Alaska
4. iffy (adj.) = uncertain

Prepare your project

Imagine an entry in Usain Bolt's diary on the day he decided that he wanted to be the fastest man in the world.
▶ *Dear diary… • I have come to a life-changing decision… • I will always remember today…*

Need help?

- athlete / athletics
- blizzard = snowstorm
- determination = perseverance
- sled: *traîneau*
- wilderness: *étendue sauvage*
- brave = courageous
- gifted = talented
- tough = difficult
- unprecedented = never done before
- achieve = accomplish
- blow: *souffler*
- howl: *hurler*
- overcome: *surmonter*
- win ≠ lose
- rough climate: *climat rude*

Extreme limits

CULTURE QUEST

Discover more about what happened to the members of the *Terra Nova* expedition.
Keywords: terrible race - the *Terra Nova* expedition - photos - 1910-1913.

1 Brave to the end

1. **Describe** the photo and **imagine** what the people you see are doing.
2. **Read** the introduction and **react**.
3. **Read** the text and **identify** the genre. **Find** information about the characters.
4. **Pick out** words and expressions that describe the place and the narrator's state of mind.
5. **Focus on** references to Oates (first name – events – problems – character). **Choose** two words to describe him: courageous – selfish – thoughtful (= *attentionné*) – pessimistic – heroic – persevering – cowardly (= *lâche*). **Explain** your choices.
6. (Pairwork) Use what you have understood in the last entry to **discuss** what may have happened afterwards.
   ▶ *Considering the ending they must have… • Perhaps they managed to….*

Geologist Thomas Griffith Taylor and meteorologist Charles Wright look out towards the *Terra Nova* ship, Jan. 5, 1911.

Scott and his team were hoping to be the first ever to reach the South Pole but on January 16th, 1912, just before reaching their destination, they made a terrible discovery: a team of Norwegians had got there four weeks earlier. Nonetheless, they decided to continue…

Wednesday, January 17 – (…) Well, it is something to have got here, and the wind may be our friend tomorrow. Now for the run home and a desperate struggle. I wonder if we can do it.

Friday, March 16 or Saturday 17 – Tragedy all along the line. At lunch, the day before yesterday, poor Titus Oates said he couldn't go on; he proposed we should leave him in his sleeping-bag. That we could not do, and we induced him to come on, on the afternoon march. In spite of its awful nature for him he struggled on and we made a few miles. At night he was worse and we knew the end had come.

Should this be found I want these facts recorded. Oates (…) has borne intense suffering for weeks without complaint, and to the very last was able and willing to discuss outside subjects. He did not – would not – give up hope till the very end. He was a brave soul[1]. This was the end. He slept through the night before last, hoping not to wake; but he woke in the morning – yesterday. It was blowing a blizzard. He said, "I am just going outside and may be some time." He went out into the blizzard and we have not seen him since.

Thursday, March 29 – (…) Every day we have been ready to start for our depot 11 miles away, but outside the door of the tent it remains a scene of whirling drift[2]. I do not think we can hope for any better things now. We shall stick it out to the end, but we are getting weaker, of course, and the end cannot be far. It seems a pity, but I do not think I can write more.

R. Scott

For God's sake look after our people.

Last entry

R. F. Scott, *The Diaries of Captain Robert Scott, 1910–1912*

1. soul (n.): *âme*
2. whirling drift (n.): *rafale de neige*

2 vidéo The silent hero

1. **Read** the cartoon and **pick out** information about Matthew Henson (job – skills – exploit).

2. **Watch** the video without the sound and **take** notes about what you see (people – places – events). Say what you can **deduce** about Matthew Henson's life.

3. **Watch** again with the sound. **Note down** stressed words and **divide** them into categories (numbers – places – people).

Médiation

4. **Use** what you have understood to **compare** Peary and Henson (occupation – ethnicity – character – recognition).

▶ *They have both managed to… • Contrary to Peary, Henson… • They had similar…*

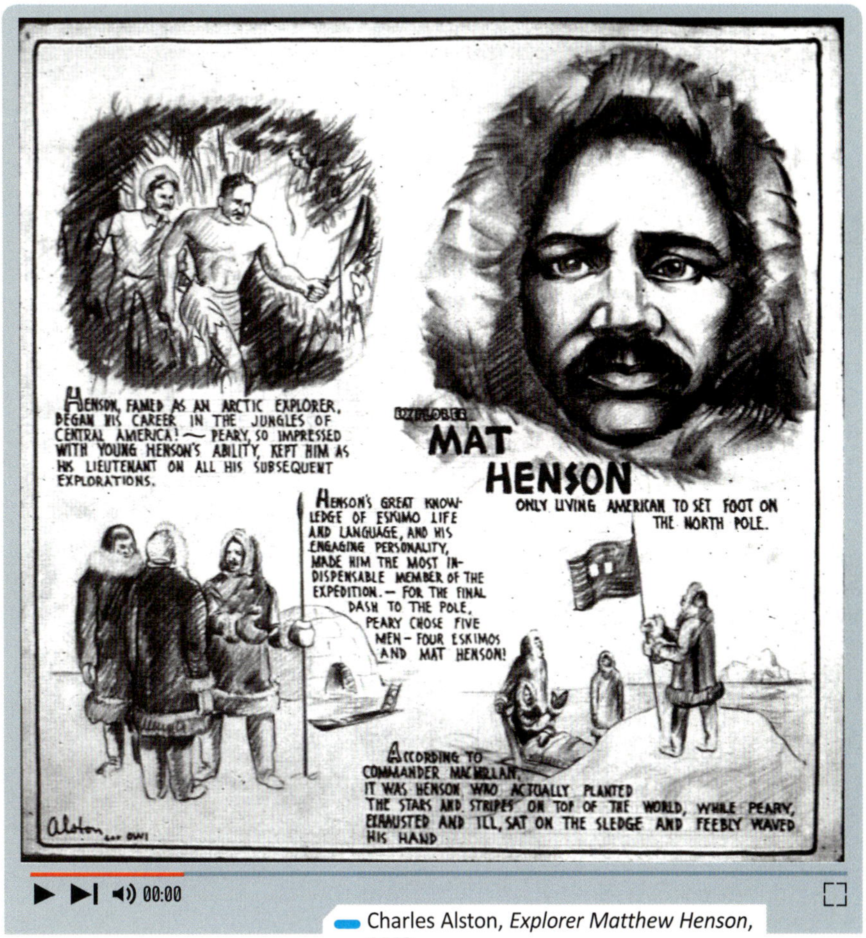

Charles Alston, *Explorer Matthew Henson*, 1943

Need help?

- award
- physical exhaustion: *épuisement physique*
- recognition: *reconnaissance*
- adventurous
- caring = thoughtful: *attentionné*
- posthumous: *posthume*
- selfless ≠ selfish
- dash = rush
- suffer ['sʌfə] from
- face the elements: *affronter les éléments*
- freeze to death = die of cold
- go unnoticed: *passer inaperçu(e)*
- pitch a tent: *monter une tente*
- stars and stripes = the American flag
- through thick and thin: *contre vents et marées*

Prepare your project

Write the last two or three entries in Titus Oates' journal before he went out into the blizzard.

Grammar

Le prétérit simple et le *present perfect*

– Ever since the blizzard **destroyed** our tent (V-ed) two days ago, this expedition **has been** awful. (*have* + part. passé)

➡ *Grammar p. 139*

Words, words, words

➡ *Faire une carte mentale p. 234*
➡ *Mémoriser et enrichir son lexique p. 235*

Quizlet
quizlet.com/skysthelimit2e

Classe 2 – Pistes 27-29 – 57 59

Créez votre propre carte mentale à partir de ce que vous avez vu en classe. Vous pourrez ensuite l'enrichir à l'aide de celle-ci. Écoutez les mots et répétez-les pour bien les prononcer. Écrivez-les aussi plusieurs fois pour mémoriser leur orthographe.

More words

Les adjectifs et les adverbes pour décrire

– The athlete was **incredibly inspiring** when he spoke about his life.
– You need to be **somewhat courageous** to climb a high mountain.
– There is an **absolutely amazing** view from here.

L'essentiel

• On peut utiliser un **adjectif** pour décrire une personne, une chose ou un événement.
• Un **adverbe** peut donner des précisions sur ce même adjectif : *She was **extremely** tired.*

Attention : Contrairement au français, les adjectifs sont toujours invariables en anglais.

1. Piochez dans les deux colonnes pour compléter les phrases. Aidez-vous d'un dictionnaire si besoin.

Adverbs	Adjectives
somewhat – quite – really – extremely – absolutely – incredibly – exceptionally	amazing – persevering – great – talented – courageous – awesome – inspiring

a. She walked for three days non-stop, which was (?).
b. Matthew Henson was (?) to continue exploring despite the lack of recognition.
c. The fact that they managed to cross the ocean in a small boat shows that they were (?).
d. I think you need to be (?) to travel to the North Pole.

Grammar

Le prétérit simple et le *present perfect*

Repères, p. 249

– Ever since the blizzard **destroyed** (V-ed) our tent two days ago, this expedition **has been** (have + part. passé) awful.

– She **started** (V-ed) running when she was 13 and she **has won** (have + part. passé) three gold medals so far.

– I **have trained** (have + part. passé) for three months so I hope to do well in the race.

– He **loved** (V-ed) climbing mountains as a young man but now he is too old.

L'essentiel

• Le **prétérit simple** (BV + *-ed*) sert à évoquer des moments passés, coupés du présent. Il est souvent utilisé avec des dates et des expressions qui situent l'événement dans le passé : *yesterday, last month, two hours ago, in 1989...*

• Avec le ***present perfect*** (*have / has* + part. passé), on fait le lien entre le passé et le présent. *Since* indique le point de départ d'un événement qui continue aujourd'hui.

Attention : Seul le contexte vous permet de choisir entre le prétérit et le *present perfect* pour traduire le passé composé en français :

Hier, **je suis allé(e)** faire du ski. → *Yesterday I **went** skiing.*

Jusqu'à présent, il n'**a** jamais **perdu**. → *Up to now, he **has** never **lost**.*

1. Complétez avec le prétérit ou le *present perfect*.

Merlene Ottey (*be*) born in 1960. → *Merlene Ottey was born in 1960.*

a. The 100m at the World Championship (*be contested*) by men and women since 1983.

b. Usain Bolt (*win*) the gold-medal for the 100m in 2008. In 2009 he (*break*) his own record.

c. The world record of 9.58 sec for the 100m (*not equal*) since 2009.

d. The American sprinter Carmelita Jeter is the only woman to (*win*) four medals in the history of the World Championship.

2. Mettez les verbes au prétérit ou au *present perfect*.

Dear diary,

I (*wake up*) this morning at 6 o'clock. After having my breakfast I (*decide*) to go for a run as usual, to train for the race. My father (*tell*) me I shouldn't go out in the rain! The truth is he (*never – understand*) how much I love athletics! I (*not – win*) any major competitions yet, but I know that I will one day. So, I (*ignore*) my father and I (*go*) for a run in the rain. And I (*not – fall*) ill! Actually, my mother (*be*) a sprinter when she (*be*) young and she (*tell*) me two years ago, when I (*start*) to get interested in athletics, that you (*have*) to suffer to succeed.

Sounds, sounds, sounds

La règle de *-ion*

Repères, p. 246

L'essentiel

L'accentuation des mots se terminant par ***-ion*** porte sur la syllabe qui précède cette terminaison : *competition, dedication.*

Cette règle s'applique par extension à d'autres terminaisons commençant par un *i* suivi d'une ou deux voyelles et éventuellement d'une ou deux consonnes (*-ious, -ian, -ial...*) : *conscientious.*

Classe 2 – Piste 30 – 60

1. Écoutez les mots et indiquez la syllabe accentuée. Puis écoutez à nouveau et répétez.

suspicion – ambition – champion – cautious – determination – anxious – special – preferential – historian – potential

Classe 2 – Piste 31 – 61

2. Servez-vous de la règle de *-ion* pour identifier les syllabes accentuées dans les mots suivants. Dites-les à haute voix puis écoutez pour vérifier.

competition – special – historian – dedication – contribution – unconscious – exploration – preferential – primordial – specialisation – technician – potential

STRATEGY COMPRENDRE UN TEXTE

Pour comprendre un texte, il faut :

1 ... anticiper :

- **Observez les informations** autour du texte : le titre – l'auteur – la date et éventuellement l'image qui accompagne le texte.
- **Imaginez le contenu** du texte et anticipez le lexique que vous pourriez rencontrer.

2 ... repérer quelques éléments-clés :

- À la 1re **lecture**, **vérifiez** si vos **hypothèses** étaient correctes.

Acceptez de ne pas tout comprendre. Cela ne vous empêchera pas de comprendre le sens général du texte.

- Concentrez-vous sur :
  - les **personnages** (noms – pronoms – relations entre les personnages) ;
  - les **lieux** (villes – pays – pièces d'une maison – mobilier ou toute autre information utile) ;
  - les **références temporelles** (dates – moments de la journée – époques).

Les majuscules, les chiffres et la ponctuation peuvent vous aider à comprendre les éléments essentiels.

3 ... chercher et relier d'autres éléments :

- À la 2e **lecture**, **classez** les **informations** : type de narration (1re / 3e personne) – personnages présents et mentionnés – lieux où se déroule l'histoire.
- Trouvez plus d'**informations** sur les **lieux** et les **personnages** et sur la **situation**.
- Cherchez d'**autres informations** sur les éléments repérés : personnages – lieux – actions – sentiments...

4 ... s'appuyer sur ce qu'on comprend :

- Utilisez les mots que vous comprenez pour **deviner le sens** des mots que vous ne connaissez pas (contexte – composition des mots – ressemblance avec le français...).
- Reliez les **adjectifs** et les **adverbes** aux personnages – lieux – événements qu'ils qualifient.
- Servez-vous des **champs lexicaux** pour vous aider à comprendre le sens implicite du texte.

Your project

Narrate and read an extreme adventure in a journal

Groupwork

Write the journal of people out on an extreme adventure and read those of your classmates.

Walking on an Alaskan glacier, USA

1 Choose the adventure.

- Decide **when and where the adventure takes place**: past – present; mountains – sea – desert – river…
- Choose **what exactly it consists in**: climbing to the top of a mountain – sailing across a sea – trekking across a continent…
- **Look for factual information to make your adventure realistic**: how far exactly – weather conditions – equipment necessary…

2 Develop your characters.

- Decide on **a name** – **age** – **personality** – **skills**… for the narrator.
- Create a **family** and a **short biography** for the narrator. Include the **motivations** for completing this adventure.
- If the narrator is travelling with a team, **draw character portraits** of each member.

3 Prepare to write.

- **List** some **ideas** for events along the journey: ordinary routines, spectacular successes, dramatic events, tragic moments…
- Choose a **starting point and dates** for each entry and decide on which days the events take place.

4 Write your entries.

- **Share out** the writing: one or two entries for each member of your group.
- Begin with the date and the place. Write in the **first person**, as in a letter.
- Describe the **day's events. Express thoughts and feelings** as well as **facts**.
- **Unite** the different entries and make sure that the **entries are coherent**. Correct any mistakes.

5 Share your journal with the class.

- **Share your journal** on the class blog or create a little paper booklet for your classmates to read.
- The class can **vote** for the most exciting / saddest / most frightening / original journal.

Keys to success

- **Utilisez le vocabulaire du chapitre :** nature, défis, qualités.
  ➥ *Words, words, words, p. 138*
- **Utilisez les adjectifs et adverbes pour vos descriptions.**
  ➥ *More words, p. 138*
- **Utilisez le prétérit simple et le *present perfect*.**
  ➥ *Grammar, p. 139*
- **Servez-vous des conseils pour comprendre un texte.**
  ➥ *Strategy, p. 140*
- **Servez-vous des conseils pour le travail en groupe.**
  ➥ *Strategy, p. 237*

Axe 5 : Sports et société

10 The Great Game

Your project

Prepare a display board about a team sport in an English-speaking country, *p. 157*
- Find information about a team sport, *p. 145*
- Find a significant event involving your team sport, *p. 146*
- Find out about the link between your sport and money, *p. 151*

Keys to success

- **Strategy: écrire un court texte factuel**, *p. 156*
- **Mind map:** national identity, role in society, sports and money, *p. 152*
- **Grammar:** articles, paradoxe, pronoms relatifs, *p. 154*

Why has football always been so important in British society?

Séquence +

Stuart Roy Clarke, *Looking Up; Sunderland v Coventry City*, Roker Park, 1996

1 Basics

Write a list of all the words you can think of linked to team sports.

WORKSHEET 22

2 Discover Classe 2 Piste 32

Listen and **pick out** keywords. **Classify** them using the following titles: football clubs / towns – positive / negative opinions and use them to **sum up** the recording.

Game **3 Play**

Guessing game: Create a list of all the British football teams you have ever heard of. Guess where these teams are located and **situate** them on a map. The group with the most correct answers wins.

Écouter • Lire • Partager • Écrire

A British institution

Différenciation

You are going to learn about the popularity of football in Britain.
Work on **one of these topics** to understand what has made football so popular over the years.

Step 1: Pick out information and take notes (players – fans – past / present – devotion – identity).

Médiation **Step 2:** GROUPWORK Share your findings. WORKSHEET 26

TOPIC 1 vidéo An old tradition

WORKSHEET 23

1. Watch the video about football in the past.

2. Use the following keywords to compare football in the past with football today: fans – football players.

▶ *Children used to… • Even though nowadays… • Just as in the past…*

Boys playing street football, London, 1961

TOPIC 2 Forever fans

Classe 2 Piste 33 WORKSHEET 24

1. Describe the painting (place – people – event) and comment on the quotation.

▶ *Although the weather is… • Some people are so crazy about football that…*

2. Listen to the recording to find out more about British fans.

Graham Twyford, *Carlisle: Saturday on Warwick Road*, 2017

“Some people believe football is a matter of life and death. I'm very disappointed with that attitude. I can assure you it is much, much more important than that.”

Ex-footballer and manager Bill Shankly

Did you know?

Although the term "**soccer**" was invented by the British, today it is used by Americans so as to distinguish football from American football.

TOPIC 3 A sense of belonging

WORKSHEET 25

1. Read the text to find out about how football can impact school life.

2. Sum up what you have understood.

Boys playing football: a common outdoor activity for school children

I was the only Arsenal supporter in the first year. (…) Arsenal's best-known player was probably Ian Ure, famous only for being hilariously useless and for his contributions to the television series *Quiz Ball.* But in that glorious first football-saturated term[1], it didn't matter that I was on my own. In our dormitory town no club had a monopoly on support and, in any case, my new best friend, a Derby County fan like his father and uncle, was similarly isolated. The main thing was that you were a believer. Before school, at breaktime and at lunchtime, we played football on the tennis courts with a tennis ball, and in between lessons we swapped Soccer Star stickers (…)

And so transferring to secondary school was rendered unimaginably easy. I was probably the smallest boy in the first year but size didn't matter, although my friendship with the Derby fan, the tallest boy by several feet, was pretty handy; and though my performance as a student was undistinguished (…) the lessons were a breeze[2]. Even the fact that I was one of only three boys wearing shorts wasn't as traumatic as it should have been.

This pattern has repeated itself several times since then. The first and easiest friends I made at college were football fans.

Nick Hornby, *Fever Pitch*, 1992

1. term (n.): *trimestre*
2. a breeze (exp.) = easy

Need help?

- coal mine: *mine de charbon*
- crowd: *foule*
- ice-breaker: *brise-glace*
- industrial environment
- terraced houses = houses that are joined together
- working class: *classe ouvrière*
- dedicated = loyal
- disillusioned [ˌdɪsɪ'luːʒənd] = disenchanted
- family-orientated = good for families
- lonely = isolated
- exclude = leave out
- fit in: *s'intégrer*
- get along with: *s'entendre avec*
- support: *soutenir*
- treasure ['treʒə]: *adorer*
- odd one out = different from everyone else

Prepare your project

Groupwork

Choose a team sport played in an English-speaking country (basketball – baseball – football – rugby – cricket…) and find information about it (history – rules – equipment – places – famous players). Illustrate your findings with photos, maps, quotations, timeline…

Grammar

Le paradoxe

– They decided to play outside in spite of the bad weather.
mot de liaison + GN

➡ *Grammar p. 154*

Lire • Écrire • Échanger

Bringing people together

Did you know?

When **World War I** broke out in 1914, many people thought it would be "over by Christmas". Instead, it lasted for four years, causing the death of tens of millions of soldiers and civilians.

1 A letter home

DOSSIER documentaire

1. Read the letter and create a timeline of the events. Imagine the hopes of the soldiers then guess what happened in the following days.
   ▶ *They must have wanted… • They probably hoped… • Instead of…*

2. Read the text and the *Did you know?* to check. Find information about the role football played at that moment.

3. Imagine the letter (5 lines) Clement Barker wrote home a month after this event.
   ▶ *Dear… • It's hard to believe… • In spite of… • What an amazing… • I wish… • Take care… • All my love…*

The 1914 Christmas truce, Sainsbury's ad, 2014

(...) on the 24th had a messenger come from the German lines, it said that if they did not fire Xmas Day, they (the Germans) wouldn't. So in the morning (Xmas day) a German looked over the trench – no shots – our men did the same and then a few of our men went out and brought the dead in (69) and buried them, and the next thing, happened a football kicked out of our trenches and Germans and English played football. Night came and still no shots. Boxing Day[1] the same.

1. Boxing Day (exp.) = 26th December

Staff Sergeant Clement Barker sent the letter home four days after Christmas 1914. It was only rediscovered in 2012.

This letter is of great historical value and the truce[1] was the last bit of chivalry[2] of the First World War. The war had already been costly but it was about to get far worse.
One of the reasons they were playing football was because they weren't able to communicate very well due to the language barrier. This was a way for them to share something. It wouldn't have been an organised match or anything, more of a free-for-all kick around. There is something appealing about the idea that nations could settle their differences in sport rather than war.

1. truce (n.): *trêve*
2. chivalry (n.): *comportement digne*

James Taylor, historian at the Imperial War Museum, *Daily Mail*, Dec. 23, 2012

Prepare your project

Groupwork

Search interesting facts, past or present, involving your chosen team sport. Share the information you have found with your team. Together, choose which facts to keep for your final project.

2 Uniting communities

1. **Read** the interview and **pick out** information about the street football tournament (name – places – aims).
2. **Focus on** references to people. **Take** notes on their differences and their difficulties.
3. **List** examples of the positive role football plays according to the interviewees.
   ▶ *Football is a sport that everyone… • People who play together share…*

Pairwork

4. **Interview** a classmate about her / his experience of team sports (yes / no – why / why not – names of team sports – how long – benefits – difficulties…).

Grammar

Les articles

– **Ø Street football** can be **a platform** to unite **Ø communities**.

➥ *Grammar p. 154*

SPORTbible: What is the Last Stand?

Gundeep Anand: The Last Stand is pretty much London's street football tournament right now. It started from Shepherd's Bush[1] just as a platform to unite communities through sport and break the social barriers. As you know we have teams from different parts of London, different cultures, different religions, different ethnicities, it's mad. We're just uniting people through sport.

Gundeep Anand, founder of The Last Stand, with Jay, Daniel and Ayman, three tournament players, West London

SPORTbible: Why is the tournament so important for young people?

Gundeep: The tournament's important because it brings a lot of people together. Whereas people from one sector or one aspect would never come together, or they would never meet or talk. The postcode thing[2], it's not hot right now in the news, but it still exists. There are people from certain areas that can't go to another area.

SPORTbible: What's the difference between street football and what we watch on TV?

Jay: For me, the massive difference between street football and the glamorous big stage of football is just opportunity. Opportunity is very very limited in the larger game, but street football? Anyone can turn up. Anyone can come here and play.

Daniel: I feel like street football is a chance for you to prove yourself to yourself and people around you in the streets. Where we come from, you know, football is in our blood. Literally, that's all we knew.

sportbible.com, Nov. 18, 2017

1. Shepherd's Bush (n.) = district in London
2. the postcode thing (exp.) = prejudice based on where you live

Need help?

- community spirit
- neighbourhood: *quartier*
- no man's land = unoccupied space between two armies
- peace [piːs] ≠ war
- truce = temporary end of fighting
- divided = separated
- bring together = unite
- in the same boat = have the same problems

CULTURE QUEST

Find out more about this street football tournament.

Keywords: Gundeep Anand – sportbible – The Last Stand.

Girls in the game

Did you know?

Women's football used to be extremely popular but then in 1921 it was banned by the Football Association (FA) because they considered it "unsuitable[1] for females". The ban lasted for 50 years. Today about 3 million women are active football players (biggest team sport in England).

1. unsuitable = inappropriate

1 Girls not allowed

1. Describe the photo and say what was surprising for the time. Read the *Did you know?* to find out more.

2. It's 1921 and you are in favour of women's football. Write a short message of complaint to the FA about their decision.
   ▶ *Let me say that…* • *I find such a decision…* • *Yours sincerely…*

"Dick, Kerr Ladies" drew a crowd of 53,000 on Boxing Day 1920.

2 Pushing for progress

Classe 2 Piste 34

1. Guess the content of the recording from the picture and the caption.
2. Listen and pick out the journalist's questions.
3. Listen to Niamh's answers to each of the questions separately and list the changes she mentions (for teenagers – grown-ups).
   ▶ *Contrary to the past…* • *Girls who play today…* • *The team that they play for…*
4. Groupwork — Search for information (dates – numbers – differences from country to country – famous examples…). Use your findings to prepare a quiz about the place of women in team sports. Test it on your classmates.

Niamh McKevitt was the first girl to officially play in a boys' football team between the age of 12 and 18.

3 vidéo FOOTBALL heroines DOSSIER documentaire

1. **Read** the text and **make** a list of all the words linked to football (people – stadium).

2. **Watch** the 1st part of the video and **pick out** the stressed words. **Use** the text and the tone to **deduce** the different feelings of the characters. **Choose** 3-4 adjectives that describe them.

3. **Watch** the 2nd part. **Pick out** information about Emma Clarke and Lily Parr.

4. **Choose** the words which best describe Emma Clarke and Lily Parr in your opinion and **explain** your choices: daring – crazy – courageous – eccentric – pioneers – shy – exceptional.

Keeley: Heart thumping with oxygenised blood,
adrenalin flooding[1] every little bit of me
and every little bit of me
is every little bit of the field in front of me.
I'm the white lines marking out the rules of my life
for the next 90 minutes.
The thick white net…
I'm the wind in my hair I can't clip back[2]…
I'm the text message beeping…
The spikes on the referee's[3] boots…
The adverts on the banner boards[4]…

Mickey: Picture it.
The pitch, huge…

Keeley: I'm my mum, up there, watching, alone…

Mickey: Huge and green…

Keeley: I'm every time someone's said "Take it on the chin"[5]…

Mickey: Green like polished emeralds…

Keeley: I'm me, Keeley, and I'm playing to win.

Mickey: Me,
and Keeley.
Thousands of faces
staring down at us,
dressed to represent the team
we've dreamed of representing
for what seems like centuries.
Me and Keeley,
eyes locked with the knot
of knowledge that you're about to make a future
full of hope for all those who come next,
with all the tools[6] at our toes…
Or so I thought.

Sabrina Mahfouz and Hollie McNish, *Offside*, scene 6, 2017

Tanya Loretta Dee and Jessica Butcher in Sabrina Mahfouz and Hollie McNish's play, *Offside*, 2017

1. flood (v.) = invade
2. clip back (v.): *attacher*
3. referee (n.): *arbitre*
4. banner board (n.): *panneau d'affichage*
5. take it on the chin (exp.): *encaisser sans broncher*
6. tool (n.): *outil*

Need help?

- equal opportunity: *égalité des chances*
- gender equality = the same rights for men and women
- Jersey [dʒɜːzi] = sports top
- locker room = changing room
- national anthem: *hymne national*
- role model = example
- proud [praʊd]: *fier / fière*
- uplifting = inspirational
- ban: *interdire*

Grammar

Les pronoms relatifs

– Girls who / that played football were criticised by society.
(Girls = antécédent humain)

➡ *Grammar p. 151*

A money-generating passion

1 Football Pools nostalgia

1. **Read** the text and **pick out** facts about the pools.
2. **Compare** the pools with football gambling today.
3. **List** the things that the writer likes about the pools.
   Use your list to **describe** the effect the pools had on society.
   ► *It made people… • Playing the pools helped to… • People who played were…*
4. **Read** the second text to **find out** the meaning of "Viv Nicholson-ness".

There's something quintessentially[1] British, roast-beefy and beige-tinted retro about "the pools[2]". A quick crammer[3] for the uninitiated (or annoyingly young): launched in 1923, (…) betting pools were a way of predicting football results in the hope of winning whopping[4] cash prizes. It spread nationwide like wildfire and became huge business by the 60s, 70s and 80s, with a peak of 10 million playing weekly. (…) It was then a Saturday afternoon ritual to huddle around[5] for the classified football results at 5 pm. (…) It seemed far more innocent than today's stats-fixated, faux-scientific football gambling.
Where's the romance in tapping away at a smartphone to predict the number of corners in the second half of Hull vs Stoke? Where's the fairytale, the family bonding, community spirit and sheer Viv Nicholson-ness of it?
(…) I miss those days.

Michael Hogan, *The Telegraph*, Sept. 5, 2014

1. quintessentially (adv.) = typically
2. pools (n.): *loto sportif*
3. crammer (n.) = lesson
4. whopping (adj.) = enormous
5. huddle around (exp.) = come together

2 A dream come true

1. **Read** the text and **note down** information about the people in the picture. **Use** the numbers to **sum up** what happened.
2. *Groupwork* **Create** your own football pools. **Guess** the results of some upcoming matches (win – draw – lose). **Find out** next week who wins the jackpot!
3. *Pairwork* You and your classmate have won £3.1 million. **Agree on** what to do with the money.

Viv Nicholson was a housewife and a factory-worker who became famous when she won the pools in 1961. When asked what she was going to do, she said: "Spend, spend, spend".

The week before we won, we desperately needed some money. My husband Keith was working on a night shift, for £7 a week, and I was earning £7 a week in a cake factory. After paying the bills, it was hard to make ends meet[1]. We weren't even eating very well. At least, I wasn't eating very well, because I had to keep my husband and my three children going, so one of us had to suffer.
We found out on Saturday evening that we'd won the pools, but we couldn't find the coupon. We weren't sure if we'd sent it off or not, but then the winning ticket turned up in Keith's trousers. It's unbelievable that I remember the exact amount we won so clearly – it was £152,300, 18 shillings and 8 pence[2]. Back then, even the 8 pence meant something.

Bulent Yusuf, *The Guardian*, July 6, 2017

1. make ends meet (exp.): *joindre les deux bouts*
2. the equivalent of £3.1 million today

3 A BIG business

1. **Agree on** the correct answers to the quiz questions.
2. **Read** the text. **Pick out** all the numbers and **say** what they refer to.
3. **Give** your opinion on the salary gap between men and women in football (5 lines).

Groupwork

The Man U Fact quiz

1 Manchester United was named the richest football club in:
- 2017
- 2018
- 2019

2 Its annual revenues are:
- under £300m
- between £300m and £600m
- over £600m

3 The club makes around:
- £50m
- £100m
- £200m in gate and matchday income[1]

4 Its revenue from TV and broadcasting amounts to:
- under £100m
- between £100m and £200m
- over £200m

5 Commercial, merchandising and sponsorship rights rake in:
- under £100m
- between £100m and £200m
- over £200m

6 The highest paid player in the team earns over:
- £100,000
- £200,000
- £300,000 a week

1. gate and matchday income (exp.): *argent généré par la vente des billets et les recettes le jour du match (nourriture, boissons…)*

Women's football salaries – the ultimate gender pay gap

Overall, a top bracket earner in women's football such as Manchester City and England's Steph Houghton, has the potential to earn around £70,000 per year including sponsors. In comparison, recent Everton signing, Wayne Rooney's current yearly salary tops an astonishing £13 million. While it's safe to say the popularity of women's football is increasing with better sponsorship deals, larger crowds and higher TV viewing figures, the dizzying[1] heights of the men's multi millionaire players do seem a long way off. But the question is, is Wayne Rooney really more than 186 times better than England women's best?

Daniel Draper, farleys.com, August 2, 2017

1. dizzying (adj.): *vertigineux*

Need help?

- betting = gambling
- income = revenue
- merchandise [ˈmɜːtʃəndaɪs]
- season ticket
- transfer fees: *indemnités de transfert*
- turnover: *chiffre d'affaires*
- exorbitant = excessive
- poverty-stricken
- generate = create
- rake in = earn (a lot of money)
- struggle = fight
- make a fortune [fɔːtʃuːn]
- make ends meet: *joindre les deux bouts*

Prepare your project

Use the keywords below to conduct some research about money in the sport you have chosen for your final project. Compare the past and the present.
Keywords: season ticket prices – players' salaries – amateur – professional – betting – merchandise – sponsoring – TV.

Words, words, words

➥ *Faire une carte mentale p. 234*
➥ *Mémoriser et enrichir son lexique p. 235*

Quizlet
quizlet.com/skysthelimit2e

Classe 2 Pistes 35-42 | 62 69

Créez votre propre carte mentale à partir de ce que vous avez vu en classe. Vous pourrez ensuite l'enrichir à l'aide de celle-ci. Écoutez les mots et répétez-les pour bien les prononcer. Écrivez-les aussi plusieurs fois pour mémoriser leur orthographe.

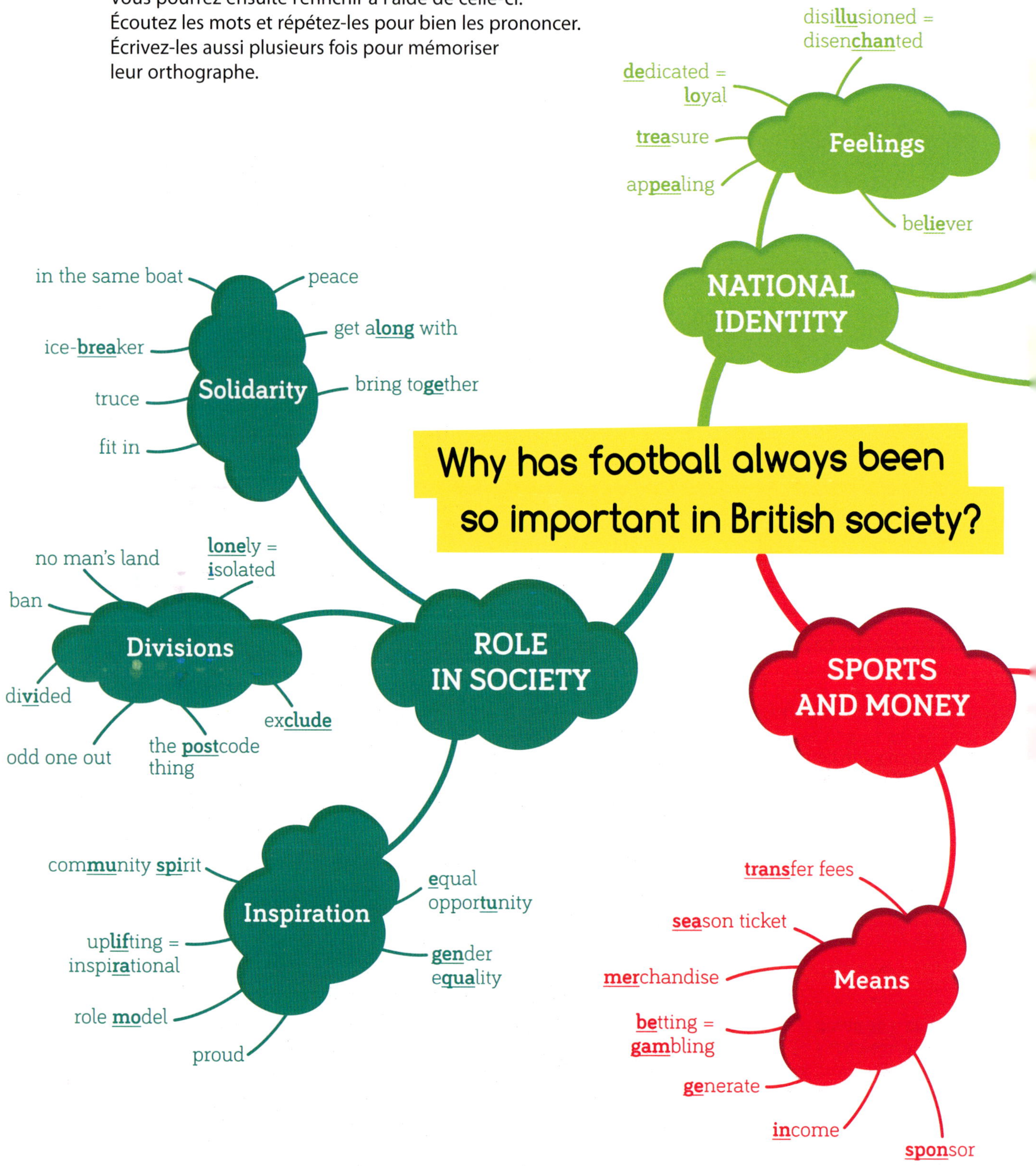

Urban life
- neighbourhood
- terraced houses
- poverty-stricken
- make ends meet
- industrial environment

People
- working class
- crowd
- fans = supporters
- family-orientated
- player

Money
- make a fortune
- struggle
- pay gap
- turnover
- exorbitant = excessive
- rake in

More words

Les indénombrables Repères, p. 257

– Playing **football** in a team requires **courage** and **tenacity**.
– **Money** is present in many sports today.
– Players should drink **water** before a match.

L'essentiel
- Contrairement aux noms dénombrables (= qu'on peut compter), les **noms indénombrables** sont toujours au singulier (ils ne prennent pas de *s*) et ne peuvent pas être précédés de l'article *a* ou d'un nombre. Ils désignent souvent une idée ou une notion abstraite, des matériaux, des aliments ou un ensemble.

1. Dénombrable ou indénombrable ? Vérifiez dans un dictionnaire si vous n'êtes pas sûr(e).
milk – table – furniture – tennis – knowledge – idea – bread – biscuit – talent – skill

2. Faites une liste de tous les noms dans le texte ci-dessous en séparant les dénombrables des indénombrables.
I've been playing basketball for five years. I believe it is a sport that needs not only skills but also intelligence if you want to become a good player.

Les quantifieurs Repères, p. 257

– He has many friends who watch **a lot of football** so they have **little time** to study.
– I invited **a few girls** to the sports field to play **some cricket** with us.
– I have **a little money** so I can buy the tickets, though there's not **much hope** that our team will win.

L'essentiel
- Les **quantifieurs** peuvent varier en fonction du type de nom :
- *too much* (trop) – *a lot of* – *some* – *a little* (un peu de / quelques) – *little* (peu de) + indénombrable (sans s) ;
- *too many* (trop) – *a lot of* – *some* – *a few* (un peu de / quelques) – *few* (peu de) + dénombrable (avec s).

3. Choisissez le quantifieur approprié.
a. I drank (?) orange juice. (*a lot of / many / few*)
b. It gave me (?) energy for the match. (*some / many / few*)
c. There were too (?) people in the crowd. (*some / many / few*)
d. I have (?) ideas that could improve your techniques. (*much / a few / a little*)

4. Complétez avec un quantifieur.
a. They have (?) hope of winning the championship. *(peu de)*
b. I ate (?) food and now I can't stand up. *(trop de)*
c. (?) football players make a fortune. *(peu de)*
d. (?) courage can go a long way. *(un peu de)*

Grammar

Les articles Repères, p. 256

– Ø **Street football** can be **a platform** to unite **Ø communities**.
– **The** team is called **Ø** Manchester United. **Ø** Teenagers all over **Ø** England dream of playing for this team.
– It was founded in 1878 in **Ø** Newton Heath, in **the** suburbs of **Ø** Manchester.
– **The** nickname "**the** Red Devils" comes from **the** devil on **Ø** Manchester United's club crest.

L'essentiel

Il y a trois articles en anglais : *a / an*, *the* et Ø (article zéro = pas d'article).

• ***A / An* est un article indéfini :** il mentionne un élément sans le distinguer des autres (comme « un(e) » en français).

• ***The* est un article défini** utilisé devant un élément spécifique déjà connu ou mentionné précédemment.

• **L'article Ø (= pas d'article)** est utilisé quand on parle d'une notion en général ou d'un groupe tout entier.

• **Attention :** L'article zéro ne peut pas être suivi d'un nom dénombrable au singulier, le nom est au pluriel : *Ø Tournaments are organised in many towns.*

1. *The* ou rien ? Complétez les phrases avec l'article *the* ou l'article zéro.

I walked onto (?) pitch and looked at (?) crowd.
→ *I walked onto the pitch and looked at the crowd.*

a. I've played (?) football for (?) years.
b. We read about (?) winner of the pools in (?) newspaper.
c. I didn't have time for (?) lunch as I was late for (?) match.
d. (?) situation has improved but we still need more (?) equality in sports.

2. Choisissez l'article approprié en fonction du contexte.

She plays (*a / the / Ø*) football in (*a / the / Ø*) club.
→ *She plays Ø football in a club.*

a. (*a / the / Ø*) team she plays for is mixed.
b. (*a / the / Ø*) boys and (*a / the / Ø*) girls play in her team.
c. In general, (*a / the / Ø*) sports are mixed these days.
d. (*a / the / Ø*) sport that is the most popular in Britain is (*a / the / Ø*) football.

3. Complétez les textes avec les articles (*a / an – the – Ø*).

a. Among (1) most valuable team sports teams ranked by (2) American magazine Forbes every year you can find (3) American football teams, (4) baseball and (5) soccer / football teams. It is not (6) surprise that (7) basketball teams like (8) New York Knicks are also very high in (9) 2017 ranking.

b. (1) Football is (2) sport which generates (3) money thanks to (4) sponsors and (5) selling of (6) merchandise. It takes (7) courage for (8) girls to play (9) football as sometimes (10) people think it's (11) boy's sport.

4. Traduisez les phrases suivantes.

J'adore le basket → *I love basketball.*

a. Je joue dans un club.
b. Les gens avec qui je joue sont tous plus âgés que moi.
c. C'est le club de ma ville.
d. Je ne joue pas au base-ball mais j'aimerais bien essayer.
e. En France, les gens ne connaissent pas le base-ball.

Le paradoxe Repères, p. 262

– **Though I'm not very good at football**, I like to play on Sundays.
(mot de liaison + phrase)
– They decided to play outside **in spite of the bad weather**.
(mot de liaison + GN)
– **In spite of being** fond of football, I never watch it on TV.
(mot de liaison + V-*ing*)

L'essentiel

• Pour **relier deux idées en apparence contradictoires**, on peut utiliser les mots de liaison :
- *in spite of / despite* (équivalents de « malgré ») + GN / V-*ing* ;
- *though / even though / although* (équivalents de « bien que ») + phrase.

5. Complétez à l'aide d'un mot de liaison.

(?) his bad luck, he won the pools.

→ *Despite of his bad luck, he won the pools.*

→ *In spite of his bad luck, he won the pools.*

a. He's quite good at team sports, (?) he never played when he was young.

b. She wasn't allowed to play football as a child, (?) that, she became a football star.

c. (?) she never talks about it, she dreams of becoming a famous football player.

6. Reliez les phrases à l'aide d'un mot de liaison exprimant le paradoxe. Faites les modifications nécessaires.

It's raining. Many people are going to the stadium.

→ *Although / Though / Even though it's raining, many people are going to the stadium.*

→ *In spite of the rain, many people are going to the stadium.*

a. My brother hates football. He watches all the important games with his friends on TV.

b. I have played cricket all my life. I'm not very good at it.

c. I love sport. I hate the way it has become a business.

Les pronoms relatifs Repères, p. 261

– **Girls who / that** played football
antécédent humain
were criticised by society.

– Today there are **many clubs which / that**
antécédent non humain
allow boys and girls to play together.

L'essentiel

• Les **pronoms relatifs** reprennent l'antécédent dans une phrase complexe :

– antécédent **humain** : on le remplace par *who(m)* ou *that* ;

– antécédent **non humain** : on le remplace par *which* ou *that*.

Attention : Si l'antécédent est suivi d'une virgule, on ne peut pas utiliser *that* : *The FA, which had forbidden women's football in 1921, only lifted the ban after 50 years.*

7. Complétez les phrases à l'aide du pronom relatif approprié. Parfois plusieurs choix sont possibles.

The players (?) are professional sometimes earn a lot of money. → *The players who / that are professional sometimes earn a lot of money.*

a. I went to the stadium (?) is in my town.

b. I talked to the goalkeeper, (?) told me he had been playing for five years.

c. Team sports, (?) are very popular in Britain, are often played in school.

d. He couldn't play the sport (?) he preferred.

8. Reliez les phrases à l'aide d'un pronom relatif. Faites les modifications nécessaires.

He played with a team. It was very famous.

→ *The team that he played with was very famous.*

→ *He played with a team that / which was very famous.*

a. John was English. He was the manager of the team.

b. She spoke to her friend. Her friend wanted to join the team.

c. He went to a school. The school offered many different team sports.

Sounds, sounds, sounds

Les lettres *h* et *k* Repères, p. 245

L'essentiel

• Certaines lettres ne se prononcent pas.

– Le plus souvent ***h*** est prononcé (*history, hotel, inhale...*) mais il y a des exceptions (*exhibit, honesty...*). Vérifiez dans un dictionnaire.

– Quand un mot commence par *kn-*, la **lettre *k*** est muette.

Classe 2 – Piste 43 – 70

1. Écoutez et notez si les lettres *h* ou *k* sont muettes.

knock – knowledge – kick – knees – kit – knife – known – knot – tightknit – goalkeeper – knuckles – honest – ghetto – heart – hopeful – honourable – rhythm – high – hour – exhausted – help – happy – half

Classe 2 – Piste 44 – 71

2. Lisez ces phrases à voix haute en faisant attention aux lettres *h* et *k*. Écoutez pour vérifier.

a. The goalkeeper broke his knuckles and his knees before the end of the first half.

b. It is not known when he will be back as he is exhausted but he hopes it will be soon.

STRATEGY ÉCRIRE UN COURT TEXTE FACTUEL

Pour réussir à écrire un court texte factuel, il faut...

1 ... bien délimiter le sujet :

→ **Choisir une thématique, un angle d'approche** précis.
American football – The place of women in basketball

2 ... faire les recherches nécessaires :

→ **Trouvez des informations** pertinentes et marquantes et éventuellement des citations.

→ **Variez** le type de **supports** (articles – infographies – interviews...).

→ **Vérifiez la fiabilité** des sources et croisez-les.

→ **Gardez la trace** de ces sources : noms des sites internet, auteurs, dates, etc.

3 ... organiser le contenu :

→ **Établissez un plan court et cohérent** : du plus simple (faits connus – vérités générales – informations simples comme les dates marquantes...) au plus complexe (faits qui nuancent le propos – cas particuliers...).

4 ... attirer l'attention du lecteur :

→ **Proposez une phrase d'accroche**, par exemple :
- → une question : *Did you know that...?*
- → une citation : *As Beckham once said...*
- → une anecdote : *I remember one Christmas years ago...*
- → une généralité : *Everybody thinks that...*
- → une phrase choc / exclamative : *How amazing!*

5 ... varier le lexique et prévoir des articulations logiques :

since – yet – for – first and foremost – secondly – however – until – last but not least

6 ... bien relire :

→ **Vérifiez l'orthographe et la correction grammaticale** ainsi que **la cohérence des propos.**

Your project — Prepare a display board

Groupwork

Participate in an exhibition. Prepare a display board about a team sport in an English-speaking country of your choice.

Display board, New York Yankees' baseball team, 1940s

1 Choose your team sport.

- **It must be a team sport** played in an English-speaking country. Examples: baseball – American football – basketball – rugby – hockey – hurling – netball – rounders – cricket…
  Choose a country, town or team that you would like to focus on.

2 Choose areas to research.

- **Use the chapter to choose aspects to explore** (history – impact on society – the place of women – the financial side…).
- **Group together** all the information found and **decide collectively** what to keep. You can add aspects of your own that particularly interest you.

3 Prepare your display documents.

- **Choose a main title** for your subject. Each member of the group **writes a short text** (4-5 lines) to present your team and explain your visuals. **Read the texts** written by other members of the group to check for mistakes. **Find titles** for each part.

4 Design your display board.

- **Include** a variety of documents (timelines – graphs – texts – quotes – interviews – photos – paintings…). **Make it colourful**, attractive and easy to read.
  Don't overload the display board and make sure that the title is **immediately visible**. **Practise** presenting it orally.

Keys to success

- **Utilisez le vocabulaire du chapitre :** identité nationale, rôle dans la société, argent et sport.
  ➥ *Words, words, words, p. 152*
- **Pensez à utiliser les indénombrables et les quantifieurs.**
  ➥ *More words, p. 153*
- **Utilisez les articles *a / an*, *the* et Ø.**
  ➥ *Grammar, p. 154*
- **Utilisez des pronoms relatifs.**
  ➥ *Grammar, p. 155*
- **Servez-vous des conseils pour écrire un court texte factuel.**
  ➥ *Strategy, p. 156*
- **Utilisez les conseils pour travailler en groupe.**
  ➥ *Strategy, p. 237*

Axe 6 : La création

et le rapport aux arts

Axe 6 : La création et le rapport aux arts

11 Glasgow: more than just bricks

What makes people become attached to buildings?

Your project

Write a text for a "Special Places" Memory Book, *p. 169*

– Write a tweet about your favourite building, *p. 163*

Keys to success

- **Strategy: écrire un texte personnel,** *p. 168*
- **Mind map:** urban architecture, living conditions, feelings, *p. 166*
- **Grammar:** prétérit simple, *p. 167*

Kibble Palace, designed by John Kibble, oasis in the West End of Glasgow

1 Basics

List all the words that come to mind when you think about buildings (famous ones – styles – insides – materials…). WORKSHEET 27

2 Discover

Classe 2 Piste 45

Listen and **pick out** references to places and buildings. **Pick out** words used to describe the buildings and their effect on people.

Game

3 Play

Long list game: Write the names of famous buildings in English-speaking countries on the board. Before beginning, guess how many you think your class will find. The person whose guess is the closest wins.

The story of the Glasgow School of Art

Did you know?

Charles Rennie Mackintosh (1868-1928) built the iconic Glasgow School of Art in 1909. He and his wife Margaret Macdonald Mackintosh (1864-1933) were very influential on European design movements such as Art Nouveau (inspired by natural forms such as the curved lines of plants).

1 A loved building

Students in front of the Glasgow School of Art (The "Mack")

1. **Use** the photo and the *Did you know?* to say what you can about the building.
2. **Read** the text and **pick out** names of places. **Say** how they are linked to the narrator.
3. **Read** lines 1-20 and **pick out** words and expressions that reveal his feelings about the Mack.
4. **Read** the last paragraph and **compare** what he discovered with his previous impressions.
   ▶ *He used to think that… • As he'd never visited…*

My Mack. For a period in my early teenage years, I lived on Rose Street which is a block away from the Glasgow School of Art. As a child, the Mackintosh Building was exotic. A curious and intricate[1] building that was on my doorstep. I had never been inside it, I was 12. Why would I want to go in? What would I do? I would get chased by the Jannie[2]! But she was my neighbour and I was proud of that, and I didn't know why. I just knew that I found it interesting and different and that it was important. I loved her majesty on a backstreet in Garnethill.

Then, I didn't know much about her significance architecturally, her history or her civic importance. This was the period of Glasgow's Miles Better[3], and Charles Rennie Mackintosh merch[4] was only really becoming a thing that we lapped up[5]. In reflection, not because we overly wanted the tea-towel or the cuff links[6], but for me because we wanted to own a little bit of it. We coveted[7] the beauty and what it represented. But that is what merchandise is; the t-shirt from your favourite rock-star. From an architectural rock-star.

My secondary school took me and some classmates on a trip to the Glasgow School of Art to see the Degree Show[8] in 1987. I was inside the Glasgow School of Art. Finally, I'm in. But it wasn't a stuffy[9] museum. It was a working artist studio with all sorts of curiosities on display and hanging from its beams. It had paint stained[10] sinks[11] and smelt of warm turpentine.

Sean Murray, thedrum.com, June 17, 2018

1. intricate (adj.) = complex
2. Jannie = janitor (n.): *concierge*
3. Glasgow's Miles Better (1983) = campaign to promote the city
4. merch (n.) = merchandising
5. lap up (v.) = accept easily
6. cuff link (n.): *bouton de manchette*
7. covet (v.): *convoiter*
8. degree show (n.): *exposition des travaux des diplômés*
9. stuffy (adj.) = old-fashioned
10. paint stained (exp.): *taché(e) de peinture*
11. sink (n.): *évier*

2 Rising from the ashes

DOSSIER documentaire

The library of the Glasgow School of Art (GSofA) after the 2018 fire

1. **Describe** and comment on the picture. **Find** a picture of the library before the fire and **compare**.
2. Use the tweets to **explain** what happened. **Pick out** words that show how people felt.
3. **Read** the text and **find** arguments that echo those feelings.
   ▶ *People feel… • It was so unexpected that…*
4. **Find** information about the possible plans for the building (options – difficulties – opinions).

Mary Anderson @MaryMac - 16 June
Replying to @GSofA
I am speechless! This building is like a friend…
5

Ali @AliGhighfive - 15 June
Replying to @GSofA
Wait, the Mackintosh AGAIN??? That's horrible… and it happened around the same time of the year four years ago… I hope no one was hurt.
As a former student, it makes me feel terrible how different the campus will become.
16

It is hard to think, out of all the great and historic buildings in the British Isles that might be lost to fire, of any destruction more heartbreaking than that of Charles Rennie Mackintosh's Glasgow School of Art. (…)

What's gone is gone, said the architectural professor Alan Dunlop and the London design guru Stephen Bayley. Better to cart away[1] its surviving stonework[2]. Let some new Mackintosh demonstrate his or her talent. A new competition should be organised, said the professional competition organiser Malcolm Reading. (…)

Despite which arguments it is extremely welcome news that the school's director, Tom Inns, has announced: "We're going to rebuild the Mackintosh building… it is critically important that the building comes back as the Mackintosh building." The main, overwhelming reason is this: it was a wonder, so why wouldn't you want it back if you could? The hard question is, how do you actually achieve[3] this task?

Rowan Moore, *The Guardian*, Jul. 15, 2018

1. cart away (v.): *emporter*
2. stonework (n.) = parts made of stone
3. achieve (v.): *accomplir*

Need help?

- ashes = cinders
- creativity
- Glaswegian = from Glasgow
- landmark: *monument incontournable*
- rebirth: *renaissance*
- reconstruction = rebuilding
- affected = moved
- architectural
- attached to
- devastated = heartbroken
- fascinated = captivated
- heartbreaking
- historic
- iconic = emblematic
- impressed by
- luckily
- at a loss for words
- go up in flames: *s'embraser*

Prepare your project

Imagine one of your favourite buildings disappears: write a tweet about how you feel.

Lire • Écouter • Écrire

The story of the Red Road Flats

1 Hard-living conditions

The last occupants of a tenement, Glasgow, 1970

1. **Describe** the picture, **read** the caption and **imagine** what life must have been like in the tenements.
2. **Read** the text and check. Focus on numbers and places and **use** what you find to **sum up** the subject of the text.
3. **Make** a list of the problems mentioned then **divide** them into causes and consequences.
4. **Agree on** a list of suggestions to resolve the problems detailed in this text.

Pairwork

Throughout the 19th century and the first half of the 20th, Scotland's housing was generally cramped[1] and unsanitary – without access to the conveniences[2] we now take for granted. Whole families lived in just one or two rooms without basic amenities[3]. Large numbers of people shared toilets and cooking facilities and the lack of hygiene and severe overcrowding caused diseases such as cholera, typhus and tuberculosis, to spread.

Some of the worst conditions anywhere in the UK were in Glasgow, where it was not uncommon for four, six or even eight people to share a room. Often up to 30 people might share a toilet with 40 to a tap.

scotlandhousingcrisis.org.uk

1. cramped (adj.): *exigu* 2. conveniences (n.) = modern comfort
3. amenities (n.): *équipements*

2 A utopian dream

Classe 2 Pistes 46-47

1. **Imagine** you lived on the top floor of a high-rise tower. **Give** three things you would like and dislike.
   ▶ *I'd love the view because… • I'd be afraid of… • If I lived there I'd…*
2. **Listen** to the recording and focus on the peripheral elements (number of voices – sounds – mood). **Use** what you have noticed to **guess** what the recording is about.
3. **Listen** to the 1st part and **pick out** numbers and places.
   Use them to **sum up** the main message so far.
4. **Listen** to the 2nd part. **Note down** what you understand, focusing on stressed and repeated words. **Classify** your notes using the following categories: the project – reasons – amenities – cost.

Grammar

Le prétérit

– In the 1960s, many Glaswegians **lived** in crowded housings.

➥ *Grammar p. 167*

3 Life in the sky

1. **Read** the texts and **find out** what the people have in common.
2. Focus on numbers and **say** what they refer to.
3. **Pick out** references to life in the flats and **divide** them into three categories: factual – negative – positive.

"I was born and grew up at Red Road until I was 13 with my sister and friends. I loved every minute of it, it was like living in your own little world, fantastic memories, except when there were high winds and the building used to move – you could see the toilet water move in the pan!"

Pamela Gibson (Red Road 1980s)
Red Road Flats residents, *Red Road Stories, Volume 1*, March 2010

"My favourite memory was the sense of community throughout the student population between the two tower blocks. There were many parties. My worst memory has to be the fire alarms. Evacuating 30 floors of flats in the middle of a freezing winter evening, climbing down 19 flights of stairs, only to be told it was a "false alarm". Then having to walk up 19 flights of stairs, as the queue for the lift was far too long!"

Shirley King (Red Road 1992-1993)
Red Road Flats residents, *Red Road Stories, Volume 1*, March 2010

"My time at the flats was one of shock. (...) I was terrified of heights, and it was quite a depressing environment to live in, but a home nonetheless. (...) They almost seem like a Glasgow monument. But it will remain forever part of my memory; those flats. Boy was it an eye opener (...)!"

Scott McKay (Red Road 1991-1992)
Red Road Flats residents, *Red Road Stories, Volume 1*, March 2010

4 The end of an era

1. **Describe** the picture and **react**.
   ▶ *I think I recognise… • They're demolishing… • It's spectacular… • What a…*
2. **Read** the information box and find out what happened. **List** words and expressions referring to life in the flats and **divide** them into two groups: negative aspects – positive aspects.
3. **Imagine** you grew up in Red Road Flats. **Write** a short reaction (3-4 lines) for a local website after seeing the demolition.

Leslie Smith, *In Demolition*, 2015

By the time the Red Road Flats were demolished in 2015 they had become for many a symbol of social housing failure, characterised by anti-social behaviour and crime. Nonetheless, for other residents they held positive memories of family, childhood, community and friendship.

Need help?

- high-rise **buil**ding = **to**wer block
- mod-cons = **mo**dern con**ve**niences
- di**la**pidated = in bad con**di**tion
- **hope**ful ≠ **hope**less
- opti**mis**tic ≠ pessi**mis**tic
- over**crowd**ed = over**po**pulated
- de**mo**lish = knock down
- miss: *manquer*
- go down**hill** = de**te**riorate
- height of mo**der**nity

Mémoriser • Prononcer • Écrire

Words, words, words

➡ *Faire une carte mentale p. 234*
➡ *Mémoriser et enrichir son lexique p. 235*

Quizlet
quizlet.com/skysthelimit2e

Classe 2 Pistes 48-50 | 72 74

Créez votre propre carte mentale à partir de ce que vous avez vu en classe. Vous pourrez ensuite l'enrichir à l'aide de celle-ci. Écoutez les mots et répétez-les pour bien les prononcer. Écrivez-les aussi plusieurs fois pour mémoriser leur orthographe.

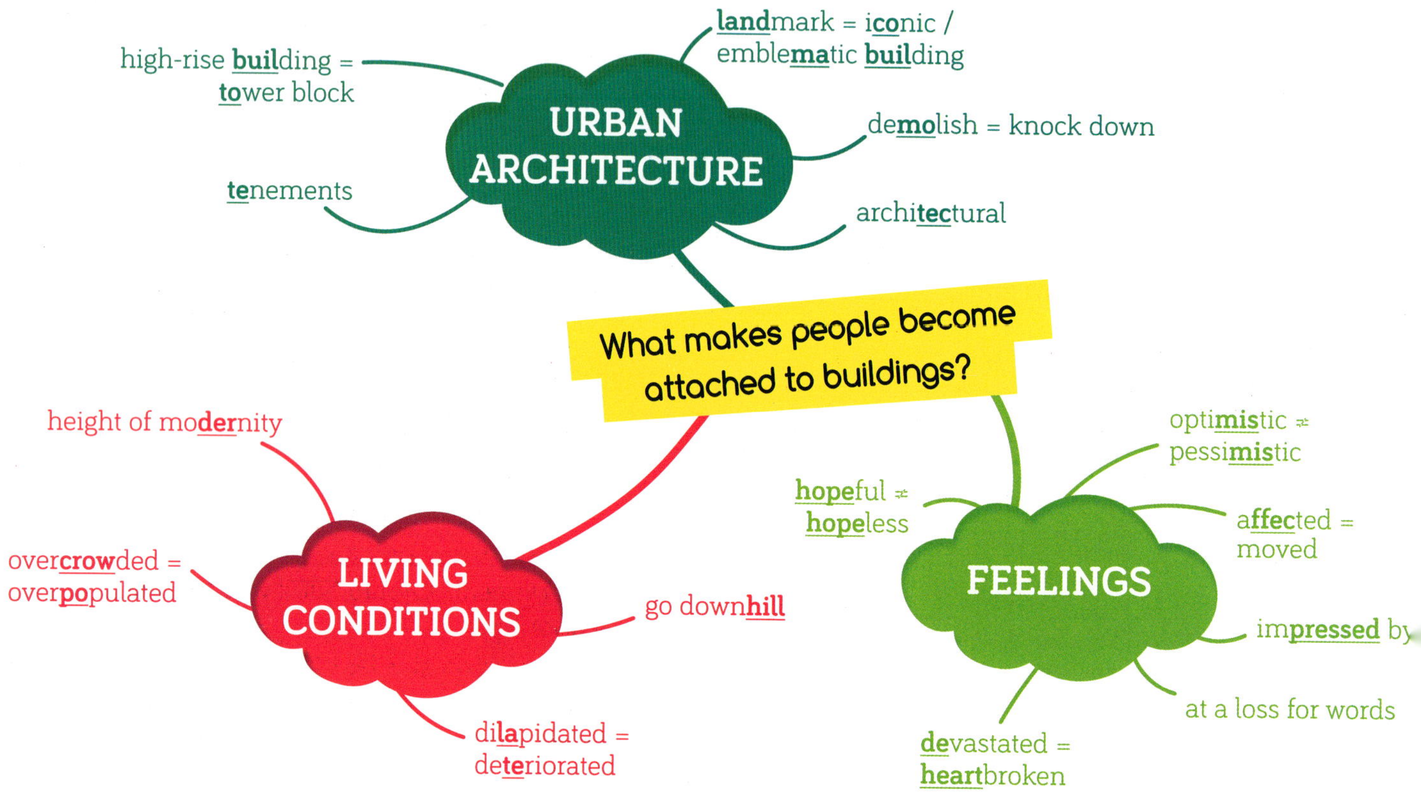

More words

Le lexique des sentiments

– Seeing the flats destroyed was **overwhelming**. I was **amazed** at how fast they came down.
– I **felt sorry for** the people who had such **shocking** living conditions.
– I am **in admiration** of the work of Mackintosh. It's **amazing**.

L'essentiel

• Il existe de nombreux mots et expressions pour **exprimer les sentiments** en anglais : *love, be passionate about, care very much for, feel deep affection for, hold very dear, adore, think the world of, dote on, cherish…*

• Enrichissez votre lexique à l'aide d'un dictionnaire (wordreference.com ou thesaurus.com) en vérifiant toujours l'utilisation des mots en contexte.

Attention : Les adjectifs en *-ed* décrivent une émotion / un état alors que les adjectifs en *-ing* décrivent la cause d'une émotion / d'un état.

1. Complétez le texte à l'aide des mots et expressions proposés.
speechless – delighted – homesick – missed – grew tired of heartbroken – close to their hearts – over-the-moon

Many Glaswegians held the Mack very (1 → *close to their hearts*). That's why they were (2) and (3) when it burnt down. Although residents were (4) when they first moved into the high-rise flats, they (5) them because of all the problems that developed. In the end, they were (6) to move out. However, former residents said they (7) their neighbours and sometimes felt (8).

Grammar

Le prétérit simple Repères, p. 249

- In the 1960s, many Glaswegians **lived** in crowded housings.
- Charles Rennie Mackintosh **built** the Glasgow School of Art in 1909.
- Back then, some people **didn't have** decent living conditions.
- They **used to live** in the old tenements but then they **moved** to the new high-rise flats.

L'essentiel

- Le **prétérit simple** (verbes réguliers : BV + *-ed* ; verbes irréguliers ➥ p. 264) permet de parler d'un fait passé, coupé du présent. On l'emploie pour raconter une suite d'événements (avec des marqueurs temporels comme *ago, when, last week / months, yesterday, in 2005*).
- À la forme négative, on emploie l'auxiliaire *do* au prétérit + BV.
- ***Used to*** est au prétérit et sert à parler de quelque chose qui était vrai autrefois mais qui ne l'est plus.

Attention : Ne confondez pas *used to* + BV et *be used to* + V-*ing* : *I* ***used to*** *live in Glasgow* (= passé révolu) et *I'm* ***used to*** *travel**ing*** (= habitude au présent).

1. Mettez les verbes au prétérit.

When (*you / visit*) Glasgow for the first time?
→ *When did you visit Glasgow for the first time?*

a. The residents (*not / want*) to move but they (*have*) no choice.
b. (*you / visit*) the School of Art when you (*go*) to Glasgow?
c. When he (*see*) the Red Road flats being demolished, he (*feel*) a pang.

2. Choisissez entre le prétérit simple ou *used to* + BV en vous appuyant sur le sens des phrases.

There (*be*) a library here, but it (*burn down*) in 2014.
→ *There used to be a library here, but it burnt down in 2014.*

a. I (*live*) in Glasgow from 2005 to 2010.
b. I (*live*) in Glasgow, but I don't live there anymore.
c. Many students (*study*) in the library before it (*burn*) down.
d. When he (*be*) young, he (*sit*) on the stairs of the GSofA for hours to watch the students come and go.

3. Traduisez les phrases.

À l'époque, les gens vivaient dans la misère.
→ *At that time, people used to live in poverty.*

a. Quand il était petit, il habitait dans un appartement. Aujourd'hui, il vit dans une maison.
b. Il a d'abord dessiné les plans (= *design*) du bâtiment, puis il l'a construit.
c. Lorsque l'école a brûlé, les étudiants ont été terriblement choqués.

Sounds, sounds, sounds

Was, were, had Repères, p. 246

L'essentiel

- ***Was***, ***were*** et ***had*** ont deux formes, une **forme pleine** : *was* [wɒz], *were* [wɜː], *had* [hæd] et une **forme réduite** : *was* [wəz], *were* [wə], *had* [həd].
- Lorsque la phrase est à la forme affirmative, *was / were* et *had* ne sont pas accentués.
- Lorsque l'auxiliaire est en début ou en fin de phrase, ou accompagné d'une négation, il prend sa forme pleine.

Classe 2 – Piste 51 – 75

1. Écoutez les phrases en vous concentrant sur les mots soulignés. Dites si le mot est accentué ou non.

When they <u>were</u> in Glasgow the weather <u>was</u> really warm. They <u>hadn't</u> brought summer clothes with them so they <u>weren't</u> really able to enjoy the sun. <u>Was</u> Glasgow a place they'd visit again? They said it definitely <u>was</u>.

Classe 2 – Piste 52 – 76

2. Lisez les phrases en accentuant *had* et *was / were* si nécessaire. Vérifiez à l'écoute.

a. He was sad to leave the flats.
b. He said it wasn't a problem for him but I could see that it was.
c. We were afraid of losing all the friends we had made.
d. Were you a friend of his?

STRATEGY | Écrire un texte personnel

Pour écrire un texte personnel, il faut :

1 ... réfléchir au contenu :

- Identifiez le **type d'écrit** demandé (lettre – récit d'expérience – journal intime...).
- Pensez aux **personnes qui liront votre texte** (professeur – camarades de classe – public en ligne, etc.).
- Définissez l'**objectif principal de votre texte** (partager – faire réfléchir – émouvoir – exprimer une émotion – faire rire, etc.).

2 ... écrire un brouillon :

- **Notez toutes vos idées** de façon spontanée **sans chercher à rédiger** dans un premier temps.
- Faites une **liste d'expressions utiles** (lexique des sentiments – synonymes ou antonymes...) pour nuancer et enrichir votre propos.

Pour élargir votre champ lexical, n'hésitez pas à vous servir d'un dictionnaire des synonymes (thesaurus.com).

- **Faites le tri** parmi vos idées pour ne garder que ce que vous souhaitez partager.
- **Organisez vos idées** pour **structurer votre récit** selon votre propre logique, il n'y a pas de plan type.

3 ... rédiger la version finale de votre texte :

- Trouvez le **ton** adapté à votre sujet et à votre destinataire.
- Adoptez un **style d'écriture** et un **point de vue** (1re personne pour un monologue intérieur – 2e personne si vous vous adressez à une personne réelle ou imaginaire – langue parlée ou soutenue).

Soyez original tout en soignant la qualité de votre texte.

- **Vérifiez** qu'il n'y a pas de **fautes de langue** (orthographe – grammaire – conjugaison).
- Veillez à ce que l'**enchaînement des idées** soit clair et utilisez des **mots de liaison** pour aider le lecteur à vous suivre : *However / And yet... • What's more... • On the other hand... • Since / As...*
- **Éliminez toute répétition** et réduisez les phrases trop longues.

Your project Write a text for a Memory Book

Bring a photo of a building that is special for you and write a short text for a "Special Places" Memory Book to explain why (memories, feelings, anecdotes).

Summer beach at the Riverside Museum, built by architect Zaha Hadid, first woman to receive the Pritzker Prize.

1 Choose a building.

- **Pick a building** that is important to you (famous building – home, etc.) and **choose an illustration**. You can take a photo or draw it or find a picture online.

2 Prepare your text.

- Open with a **short description** of the building (type – age – name – use – location…).
- **Think of a personal story** or anecdote that links you to this building.
- **Write down** ideas and keywords.
- Organise your notes into a **personal outline** (for example: building, anecdotes, feelings associated).
- **Remember** to think of **synonyms**, **antonyms**, verbs expressing **feelings** and **opinions.**

3 Write your text.

- **Develop your ideas** into a structured text.
- **Think of details** that will make it original and personal.
- **Add linkwords** (cause, consequence, condition…), **adjectives** and **adverbs.**

4 Correct your text.

- **Read over your text**. Make sure it's well written. Check the tenses, the vocabulary. Replace any repeated words with their synonyms.
- You can **read your text out loud** to someone in the class to test it. Ask them what they remember at the end and how it makes them feel.

5 Create your memory book.

- Find an **original way to present the illustration** with the text.
- **Share your contribution** with the class (blog, Padlet, scrapbook…).
- **Combine** all the contributions into a "Special Places" Memory Book.

Keys to success

Utilisez le vocabulaire du chapitre : architecture urbaine, conditions de vie, sentiments.
➥ *Words, words, words, p. 166*

Pensez à utiliser le lexique des sentiments.
➥ *More words, p. 166*

Pensez à utiliser le prétérit pour raconter un événement.
➥ *Grammar, p. 167*

Servez-vous des conseils pour écrire un texte personnel.
➥ *Strategy, p. 168*

12

Axe 6 : La création et le rapport aux arts

The power of words

1 Basics

List all the words that come to mind when you think about poetry. WORKSHEET 28

2 Discover

Classe 3 Piste 1

Listen and **pick out** references to poetry (people – activities – negative / positive opinions). Compare the speakers' opinions with your own.

Game 3 Play

The puzzle poem game: Write down the word of your choice vertically. **Brainstorm** as many words and phrases as you can think of to describe it. **Place** your words or phrases so that they fit the letter of each line. See if you can guess who wrote the poem.

Your project

Write a poem and perform it, *p. 179*
– Write a verse about your morning routine, *p. 174*

Keys to success

- **Strategy: mettre en voix un texte,** *p. 178*
- **Mind map:** poetry, themes, role, *p. 176*
- **Grammar:** mise en relief, *p. 177*
- **Sounds:** accentuation des mots à deux syllabes, *p. 177*

Solomon O.B. was crowned National Poetry Slam Champion at the Royal Albert Hall in London, 2016.

What role does poetry play today?

Écouter • Lire • Parler

Today's poets

1 Developing young voices

Classe 3 Piste 2

1. Listen and note down information about Youth Speaks.

2. Focus on the interview of Anvi, a 16-year-old teen poetry Youth Speaks finalist. Pick out stressed words and classify them (inspiration – theme(s) – feelings – parents' reaction).

3. Imagine you are taking part in a teen poetry slam contest. Say which topic you would like to discuss and the feelings you would like to express.

Did you know?

National Poetry Month is a celebration of poetry which takes place each April in the United States. It was introduced in 1996 to increase awareness and appreciation of poetry.

2 Verse goes viral

1. Look at the photo and guess the type of performance Kate Tempest is giving.

2. Read the text and find information about the new generation of poets (identity – themes – places to share poetry).

3. Compare with your perception of poets.
▶ *Usually, poets don't… • I imagine poets are rather…*

Pairwork
4. Agree on three positive adjectives to describe poetry.

British rapper, poet and playwright Kate Tempest performs during a music festival, 2015

In the UK, the young Somali-British poet Warsan Shire has shot to fame after featuring in Beyoncé's internet-breaking *Lemonade*. Tackling[1] issues of race, immigration, culture and relationships, Shire's poetry has commanded attention from a diverse audience, from her 50,000 Tumblr and Twitter followers to elite literary gatekeepers[2], who named Shire London's first-ever young poet laureate.

Over in London's south-east, the poet, rapper and performer Kate Tempest is unleashing[3] rapid-fire lyrical attacks on consumerism, inequality and injustice. From award-winning poetry collections, sellout hip-hop shows and YouTube spoken-word videos, to an opening slot[4] at this years' Sydney writers' festival, which itself commanded global attention, Tempest is as prolific as she is shapeshifting[5] – breaking down the boundaries[6] of what poetry is and can be in the current social order.

Rebecca Slater, *The Guardian*, Nov. 27, 2016

1. tackle (v.) = deal with
2. elite literary gatekeepers (exp.): *garants de l'élite littéraire*
3. unleash (v.): *déchaîner*
4. opening slot (exp.): *ouverture*
5. shapeshifting (adj.): *capable de changer de forme*
6. break down boundaries (exp.): *abattre les frontières*

3 Making poetry accessible

1. **Imagine** three questions you could ask a young poet.
2. **Read** the interview and **find** elements of everyday life that inspire Hollie McNish for her poetry.
   ▶ *What inspires Hollie McNish is… • Wherever she goes…*
3. **Pick out** words or expressions Hollie McNish uses to talk about the role of poetry.
4. **Use** the advice given in the last paragraph to **create** a list of things you should / shouldn't do if you want to be a poet.

Médiation

Hollie McNish (also known as Hollie Poetry), British poet, author and spoken word artist

What inspires you to write poetry?

I just find it a really lovely way to sort of condense my thoughts about things or work out roughly[1] how I'm feeling – so it can be anything, from a book I've read to something someone has said to a walk down the road. The more I read though, the more I do, the more I want to write. (…)

Do you think poetry is a useful vehicle for activism, feminism or otherwise?

I think it can be, but I don't think it needs to be. Like any art. Film, painting, whatever.

Some films are so politically motivating, other films just make you wee yourself laughing[2], and I think there's space for everything. I guess the wordiness[3] of poetry is pretty helpful as a tool. I think a lot of political speeches are intentionally poetic. (…)

Do you have any advice for aspiring young poets?

Enjoy it. Don't worry about "writer's block", just write when you want to write. And I guess the one thing I'd say is that if you don't want to share your writing, that's cool. If you do and you're nervous, that's fine too, but honestly sharing stuff is rarely as scary after as you thought it would be before. And finally, share it with actual live humans first, rather than online. I guess I don't mean this with poems shared on the page, more if you want to video yourself reading them. Join a reading group / poetry group / go to an open mic[4]. Don't start with YouTube basically, start with real humans because they are a lot more supportive often than random strangers online! I only put stuff online after I was asked by a teacher at a gig[5] if I could, but I think if I'd had the hate I got online before I'd ever done a gig, I might've never done one.

Chloe Scaling, palatinate.org.uk, Nov. 4, 2018

1. roughly (adv.) = approximately
2. wee oneself laughing (exp.): *exploser de rire*
3. wordiness (n.) = use of many words
4. open mic (n.) = an event in which amateurs may perform
5. gig (n.): *concert*

Need help?

- contest = competition
- gig = concert
- open mic [ˈmaɪk]: *soirée ouverte aux amateurs*
- poetry slam = competitive poetry
- social media
- appealing = attractive
- lively = energetic
- popular [ˈpɒpjʊlə] = appreciated
- successful: *qui a du succès*
- thriving [ˈθraɪvɪŋ]: *florissant*
- trendy = fashionable
- perform: *se produire*
- be on the rise = increasing
- go viral: *faire le buzz*
- on stage

Grammar

La mise en relief

– It was **Kate Tempest** who gave a fantastic performance in Glastonbury.

➥ *Grammar p. 177*

Écouter • Lire • Écrire

Poetry about everyday life

1 Morning routine

Classe 3 Piste 3

Pairwork

1. **Share** your morning routine with your classmate from the moment you get up until you arrive at school (what you do, see, hear, taste…).
▶ *Every morning I take… • Usually, I see… • Most of the time I hear…*

2. **Listen** to Hollie McNish reciting her poem. **Pick out** the stressed words. **Use** what you have understood to **make** a timeline of the speaker's morning routine (place – activity).

3. **Focus on** references to food and to advertising, then **deduce** the author's feelings about them.
▶ *She seems to think that… • What bothers her is… • What's not normal is…*

Médiation

4. **Sum up** the main message of the poem and **say** if you agree.

5. **Choose** an extract from the poem and copy it out. **Underline** stressed words and **use** a dictionary to help for pronunciation. **Practise reading** it out loud.

Ruth Israel, *Morning Routine*, 2008

Today I woke up, stretched, and stumbled out[1] of bed
Street lamps glared through the window
To start a fake light of day
I brushed my teeth, rinsed my mouth, splashed and washed my face
Still half asleep I heard the postman walk away
On the rug[2] below the letterbox a newspaper lay,
I sat down to browse it, like I do every day,
But as my eyes awakened I saw the words on the page weaken[3],
To see the truth wasn't always the same as what they'd say
My toast popped
As I search for a topping from the cupboard
I notice something wrong
There are no oranges in the ingredients of my carton of orange drink.
And my strawberry flavoured yoghurt has no actual strawberries in it
And my lunch box prawn[4] crackers contain no trace of fish
But there's animal fat in my cheese and onion crisps.
I put my lunch in my bag
I dash out[5] the door
I wait at the stop for bus number three
As the streets all go past me
I see adverts plaster me with fake scenes
Airbrushed faces advertising skin creams
Holiday adverts with fake families on photo-shopped beaches
And I'm wondering what it all means.

Hollie McNish, *Strawberry Yoghurt*, 2013

1. stumble out (v.): *sortir en trébuchant*
2. rug (n.) = carpet
3. weaken (v.): *s'affaiblir*
4. prawn (n.): *crevette*
5. dash out (v.) = leave in a hurry

Prepare your project

Write a 5 or 6-lined verse about your morning routine (feelings – actions – senses) and share with the class.

2 vidéo A helpful tool

1. **Recite** a few lines of something you know by heart in English (poem – song – play – quotation…).
2. **Watch** the poet performing live on the TV show *Blue Peter*. **Pick out** stressed words. **Classify** them into categories (school – poetry) then **explain** how the poet links these categories.
3. **List** the different pieces of advice given for writing poetry.
4. **Select** 4 lines from the poem. Try to **reproduce** the word stress, rhythm and intonation. **Practise** saying them out loud.
5. **Write** a 5-line text about your school homework (feelings – difficulties – tips) and **read** it to your classmate.

Pairwork

I've come to your favourite after school show[1]
To show you how to craft a cool flow[2].
The whole thing's pretty straightforward[3]:
You just write about things that occur to you.
You might want to rhyme, but you don't have to,
You just do whatever you'd prefer to do.
I like to rhyme 'cause it makes things easy to remember,
And that helps me learn.
I did it in school to summarise
Everything I'd learned in a subject,
And at the end of the term,
When I had exams I made revision poems,
And memorised all of them near the time. See,
Poetry, it can be a fun way to learn something new,
Relax and clear your mind.
For example, let me give you a sample:
This one's about how plants feed.
There's a few things that plants need:
Carbon dioxide, water and light,
The chemical symbols are shorter to write,
So: CO_2 + H_2O and sunlight, that's the way to go!
It's more than just gas and water still.
Leaves have this thing called chlorophyll.
But I suppose you can leave that for another time.
There's so many ways you could take it.
All you need is words in your mind,
'Cause poetry is what you make it.

George the Poet, *Untitled*, 2013

1. favourite after school show = *Blue Peter* is a British TV show
2. craft a cool flow (exp.) = to create a good rhythm
3. straightforward (adj.) = simple

British spoken word performer George the Poet

Need help?

- daily routine
- everyday life
- line: *vers*
- rhyme [raɪm]
- verse = stanza
- accessible
- creative = imaginative
- entertaining ≠ boring
- exceptional = unconventional
- helpful = useful
- monotonous
- ordinary = common
- school-related
- tedious = tiresome: *fatigant*
- come up with = imagine
- deal with
- get used to + V-ing
- inspire [ɪn'spaɪə]
- think about
- have fun = appreciate [ə'priːʃɪeɪt]

Mémoriser • Prononcer • Écrire

Words, words, words

➡ Faire une carte mentale p. 234
➡ Mémoriser et enrichir son lexique p. 235

Quizlet
quizlet.com/skysthelimit2e

Classe 3 – Pistes 4-6 – 77-79

Créez votre propre carte mentale à partir de ce que vous avez vu en classe. Vous pourrez ensuite l'enrichir à l'aide de celle-ci. Écoutez les mots et répétez-les pour bien les prononcer. Écrivez-les aussi plusieurs fois pour mémoriser leur orthographe.

More words

Les *phrasal verbs* Repères, p. 253

– Every morning when **I get up**, I hope (V. + particule) a cup of coffee will **wake me up**. (V. + pronom + particule)

L'essentiel
- Les ***phrasal verbs*** sont des verbes suivis d'une particule qui en change souvent le sens d'origine (*turn* = tourner – *turn off* = éteindre – *turn down* = refuser).
- Il faut s'appuyer sur le contexte et sur les mots qui suivent les verbes pour en déduire le sens.
- Lorsque le complément d'un *phrasal verb* est un pronom, ce dernier s'intercale entre le verbe et la particule (*find out* → *find* **it** *out*).

1. Sélectionnez la bonne particule pour chaque *phrasal verb*. Aidez-vous d'un dictionnaire si nécessaire.

I woke (*up / in / on*) this morning, remembering I had a test, I hope the teacher will put it (*on / off / out*) – yes, it would be best! What I see now is the school door, and I want to walk (*up / on / away*) but I need to move (*in / off / on*), and I'm glad I can meet (*up / down*) with my friends today. Next time, I will make (*out / up / on*) a good story, and I'll manage to run (*down / out / away*)!

2. Choisissez la particule adaptée au sens du verbe dans la phrase. Traduisez le verbe.

a. Please, come (*in / off*), the door is open.
b. She came (*up / down*) with a great idea for her poem.
c. Let's hope that something good will come (*in / out*) of this.
d. He came (*over / off*) and introduced himself.

Observer • Retenir • Appliquer

Grammar

La mise en relief

Kate Tempest gave a fantastic performance in Glastonbury.

– It was **Kate Tempest** who gave a fantastic performance in Glastonbury.

– It was **a fantastic performance** that Kate Tempest gave in Glastonbury.

– It was **in Glastonbury** that Kate Tempest gave a fantastic performance.

– What Kate Tempest gave was **a fantastic performance in Glastonbury**.

L'essentiel

• Lorsque l'on présente des **informations de manière neutre**, l'ordre des mots suit le schéma traditionnel : sujet + verbe + complément.

• Si l'on souhaite **mettre en avant des informations**, on peut réorganiser la phrase :
- *it* + *be* + information mise en relief + *who* / *that* + proposition ;
- *what* + proposition + *be* + information mise en relief.

1. Mettez en relief l'élément souligné.

He performed his poem in front of the class.
→ *It was in front of the class that he performed his poem.*

He performed his poem in front of the class.
→ *What he performed in front of the class was his poem.*

a. She is writing a poem. → What…

b. You wanted to participate in a slam poetry contest. → It…

c. I don't like to do my homework. → What…

d. Every morning when I get up, I hear the sound of the radio. → It…

e. Young poets can use social media. → What…

2. Mettez en relief un élément de votre choix.

I heard a performance yesterday. → *What I heard yesterday was a performance. / It was yesterday that I heard a performance. / It was a performance that I heard yesterday.*

a. Hollie McNish wrote a poem about morning routines.

b. The teacher suggests to write a poem on any topic.

c. We studied a sonnet in class.

d. My community doesn't understand my anger.

e. I recently discovered this successful artist.

f. I never hear my alarm clock in the morning.

Sounds, sounds, sounds

L'accentuation des mots à deux syllabes

Repères, p. 246

L'essentiel

• Le plus souvent, en anglais, **un mot à deux syllabes est accentué** sur la 1re syllabe si c'est un nom, mais sur la 2e si c'est un verbe.

• Certains mots ont la même orthographe, qu'ils soient des noms ou des verbes. À l'oral, on peut les distinguer grâce à l'accentuation.

Classe 3 – Piste 7 – 80

1. Écoutez et dites quand il s'agit d'un nom ou d'un verbe.

a. insult / insult – protest / protest – contrast / contrast – present / present

b. contract – survey – research – transfer – progress – rebel

Classe 3 – Piste 8 – 81

2. Lisez ces phrases à haute voix en faisant attention à l'accentuation des mots soulignés. Écoutez pour vérifier.

a. You are quite a rebel in the world of poetry but you rebel in a such poetic way!

b. Do you mind if I record your poem? It's just for the record.

c. The increase of poetry reading is spectacular among young American adults. And it will probably continue to increase.

STRATEGY — Mettre en voix un texte

Pour mettre en voix un texte, il faut :

1 … s'inspirer d'exemples de mise en voix :

→ **Visionnez des vidéos** de personnes **lisant des textes à haute voix** : **observez** leur gestuelle, prêtez attention au **rythme** qu'elles adoptent, à la manière avec laquelle elles **posent leur voix.**

2 … préparer son texte :

→ Assurez-vous d'**avoir bien compris** le texte que vous vous apprêtez à lire à haute voix.

→ **Lisez-le plusieurs fois** pour vous l'approprier.

→ **Réfléchissez à l'émotion** que votre texte vous inspire (espoir – tristesse – joie…).

3 … vérifier la prononciation des mots :

→ **Repérez les mots** dont vous n'êtes pas certain(e).

→ Entraînez-vous à les **répéter** isolément puis dans le contexte de la phrase.

Aidez-vous d'un dictionnaire en ligne (wordreference.com) et cliquez sur l'icône « haut-parleur » pour entendre le mot.

4 … annoter son texte :

→ Assurez-vous que **la police de caractères est assez grande** et **les interlignes larges.**

→ Notez la **prononciation et l'accentuation** sur votre script.

→ Indiquez les **pauses** et la **ponctuation.**

5 … lire de façon expressive :

→ **Ne lisez pas de manière linéaire :** parlez plus ou moins fort, réfléchissez aux **pauses**, aux **accélérations.**

→ Essayez d'**associer gestes, expression et voix.**

6 … s'entraîner à parler devant un public :

➥ S'exprimer devant un public, p. 233

→ **Enregistrez-vous, lisez devant un miroir** ou **devant un camarade** jusqu'à maîtriser parfaitement la lecture de votre texte.

→ **Échauffez-vous** avant de lire votre texte et **respirez** pour poser votre voix.

→ **Parlez** assez **fort**, pensez à **regarder le public.**

Tuto : Lire un texte littéraire : disponible avec FlashPAGE, sur lycee.editions-bordas.fr et dans le manuel numérique

Your project — Perform a poem

Write and perform a poem for a class poetry competition. Vote for the best poem in the different categories you have decided.

1 Choose a topic for your poem.

- It can deal with **everyday life** or **an issue** you would like to talk about.

2 Write your poem.

- Note down **ideas, images, feelings, moods**.
- **Organise your sentences**, make them short.
- You can make them **rhyme** but you don't have to.

3 Practise reading it out loud.

- **Practise** with a friend, in front of a mirror, or **record yourself**.
- Make sure you have written notes on your text to **indicate** the **rhythm** and the **pronunciation**.

4 Perform your poem in front of the class.

- You can read your text but don't forget to **make eye contact** with your audience.
- If you make a mistake, don't panic. Go back to the beginning of the line and say it again.

5 Vote for the best poem.

- You can **create categories** by **topic**, **type of poem** or **type of performance** as part of the contest.

Keys to success

- **Utilisez le vocabulaire du chapitre :** poésie, thèmes, rôle.
  ➥ *Words, words, words, p. 176*
- **Pensez à mettre en relief certains éléments de vos phrases.**
  ➥ *Grammar, p. 177*
- **Veillez à l'accentuation.**
  ➥ *Sounds, sounds, sounds, p. 177*
- **Servez-vous des conseils pour mettre en voix votre poème.**
  ➥ *Strategy, p. 178*
- **Servez-vous des conseils pour vous exprimer devant un public.**
  ➥ *Strategy, p. 233*

Entraînement aux épreuves communes

▶ **1re partie de l'épreuve 2 :** compréhension de l'écrit.
▶ **2e partie de l'épreuve 2 :** expression écrite : deux sujets au choix.

Compréhension de l'écrit

Sujet **Read the text entitled "My Life and my Poetry". Take notes on the narrator (family – environment – passion). Use your notes to sum up the text and explain the role poetry plays in the narrator's life.**

As usual, my mum wasn't home. (...) She works in the pediatric unit. The most consistent thing about seeing my mom is that you can count on her to look tired.

She left a note:

You can eat pasta or grilled cheese.
Your sheets are still in the dryer.
Please be in bed by ten p.m.

My mother's communications are becoming so spare[1], they are turning into poems. I edited the note to make it a haiku.

Pasta or grilled cheese.
Your sheets are in the dryer.
Bed by ten p.m.

(...) Grabbing some cold pasta from the fridge, I went down the hall to my room to check for email from Dorothea. I set the pasta down on my desk and forgot to eat any. (...)
Turning away from the computer, I flopped onto my bed and reached one hand into the cool, dark recesses[2] below my mattress. I like to think of my bed as a house and the space beneath it as the basement.
Down there in the cellar, nestling at the base of the nightstand where I left it, was my notebook. In the case of fire and a mad scramble to run from the flames, there is no contest among my possessions for the honor "item to be saved first". Poetry notebook wins. My only problem would be deciding which one. I have three notebooks full and am scribbling my way through number four. Most are standard composition books, their black-and-white-marbled covers eroded by stickers, traced Manga drawings, and quotes from famous people written in marker. My current notebook says, "Great things are not accomplished by those who yield[3] to trends and fads[4] and popular opinion. – Charles Kuralt."

I write poetry everyday. Sometimes people think poetry has to be obscure or complicated or spring forth directly from your soul with the magical force of nature. I think poetry is like music – you either like to make it or you don't.

I pulled out my notebook and wrote this poem:

I expected you to vanish
up and up into the tree,
a shake of the branches
and gone like you
had never happened.
But you came down
and handed me a leaf
"from seven limbs up,
already yellow," you said
and then you walked away
and you were still real.

I took the yellow leaf out of my hoodie pocket and pressed it between the pages of my notebook. Then I lay on my bed trying to read. It was two more hours until my heart slowed down enough to let me fall asleep.

Karen Finneyfrock, *The Sweet Revenge of Celia Door*, 2016

1. spare (adj.): *dépouillé(e)*
2. recess (n.): *recoin*
3. yield (v.): *céder*
4. fad (n.) = temporary fashion

▶ Les clés pour réussir

Avant la lecture.

– **Anticipez :** regardez les **informations autour du texte** (*title – source – date – illustration*).
– **Identifiez le type de texte** (*press article – literary extract – poem – play*).

La présentation (dialogue, poème, police de caractères) est une source d'information.

- **Imaginez le thème** de ce que vous allez lire.
- **Lisez la consigne** et **surlignez les mots-clés :** cela vous aidera à cibler votre lecture.

Pendant la lecture.

À la 1re lecture

- **Vérifiez vos hypothèses :** trouvez quelques éléments pour confirmer ou pas. Identifiez le sujet du document à partir de ces premiers éléments.
- **Annotez votre texte :** utilisez des couleurs différentes pour vous aider.
- **Repérez les éléments essentiels :** personnages (noms – pronoms – références à d'autres personnes), lieux, dates ou références temporelles (jours – mois – saisons…).

Au fur et à mesure des lectures

- **Concentrez-vous sur :** les champs lexicaux – les verbes – les termes descriptifs.
- **Analysez les personnages et les situations :** les relations entre les personnages – les lieux – l'époque…
- **Essayez de comprendre l'implicite :** ce qui n'est pas dit dans le texte (sentiments – émotions…).
- **Prenez des notes** en gardant la consigne à l'esprit.

Rédaction de votre compte-rendu

- **Organisez vos notes :** reformulez avec vos propres termes, sans recopier des passages du texte. Suivez votre propre plan en intégrant les mots-clés de la consigne.

Expression écrite

Sujet 1 **How important are poetry or music in your life?**

Sujet 2 **Think about a song, a poem, a book or a film you like. Tell the story of why it holds a special place in your heart (what – when – who – where – even it is linked to…).**

▶ Les clés pour réussir

Sujet 1 : Pensez à ce que vous avez étudié en cours sur l'axe 6 : La création et le rapport aux arts.

Sujet 2 : Écrire un texte personnel ➥ *p. 168*

Analysez le sujet que vous avez choisi.

- **Relevez les mots-clés du sujet :** listez toutes les idées qui vous viennent à l'esprit.
- **Lisez la consigne** et **surlignez les mots-clés :** les garder en tête vous aidera.

Organisez vos notes.

- **Faites un plan :** regroupez les idées et classez-les – pensez à ajouter des **exemples**.

Rédigez.

- **Préparez une introduction et une conclusion.**
- Utilisez des **phrases complexes** et variez le **lexique**.
- Faites des **transitions** avec des expressions pour relier vos idées.
- N'oubliez pas de **vous relire**.

Pour l'épreuve 1, rendez-vous ➥ p. 64-65 et 128-129.

Axe 7 : Sauver la planète,

penser les futurs possibles

13

Axe 7 : Sauver la planète, penser les futurs possibles

American green teens

1 Basics

List all the words that come to mind when you think about saving the planet (behaviour – society – dangers – solutions).

WORKSHEET 29

2 vidéo Discover

Watch the video and note down what you see (environment – people – actions).
Pick out stressed words and use them to explain the purpose of the video.
Agree on a list of three simple ideas you could propose to help protect your planet.

▶ *We could… • People should… • Whenever we see…*

Game 3 Play

Mystery words game: Choose five words linked to the environment. **Mix up** the letters of each word. The person who finds the words the fastest wins.

Your project

Participate in an environmental campaign on a social media, *p. 193*

- Post a message to convince young people to get involved, *p. 187*
- Write a tweet to give your opinion about the #NoDAPL movement, *p. 189*

Keys to success

- **Strategy: réagir à l'écrit,** *p. 192*
- **Mind map:** environmental problems, commited people, action, *p. 190*
- **Grammar:** expression du futur, *p. 191*

The "Zero Hour" March, Washington D.C., 2018. Zero Hour is an environmentally-focused movement created and led by teenagers in 2017.

How can we fight to protect the environment?

Écouter • Lire • Écrire

Teens taking it to the top

1 Kids in court

DOSSIER documentaire

Classe 3 Piste 9

1. **Use** the introduction, the photos and captions to **find** what these teens have in common.
2. **Listen** to Victoria Barrett, one of the 21 plaintiffs, interviewed in 2018. **Pick out** keywords to sum up the young people's actions.
3. **Read** the post and **pick out** expressions used to encourage people to fight for the cause. **Explain** the role that social media can play.

These three young people are among the group of 21 plaintiffs who have been suing (= poursuivre en justice) *the US government for the right to a stable climate since 2015 in the case Juliana v. The United States.*

Nathan Baring, 19, concerned about melting ice and warmer winters in Fairbanks, Alaska

28 **Events**

Calendar

Birthday

Discover

Our Future, Our Rights, march w MN Youth for a Fossil Free Future

Hosting

+ Create Event ▾

OCT 28 March w MN Youth for a Fossil Free Future
Sunday 28 October 2018
Public: hosted by Youth Climate Intervenors and 6 others

★ Interested | ✓ Going | Share ▾ | ...

On October 29, 2018, 21 youth will confront the federal government at the #TrialoftheCentury in open court.

Join us at the rally at the Supreme Court (sidewalk in front) on Monday October 29, 2018, from 12 p.m. to 2 p.m. to be a part of the #TrialoftheCentury and support these young climate warriors[1].
Our freedom depends on a climate system that will sustain human life. Let's show the government that it has a duty to prepare and implement[2] a Climate Recovery Plan to protect our basic and most fundamental rights!

For more information or to find the rally in a different state, visit www.youthgov.org/october29

To get email updates from Our Children's Trust, sign up here: www.youthgov.org/join

1. young climate warriors = the 21 young plaintiffs
2. implement (v.): *mettre en œuvre*

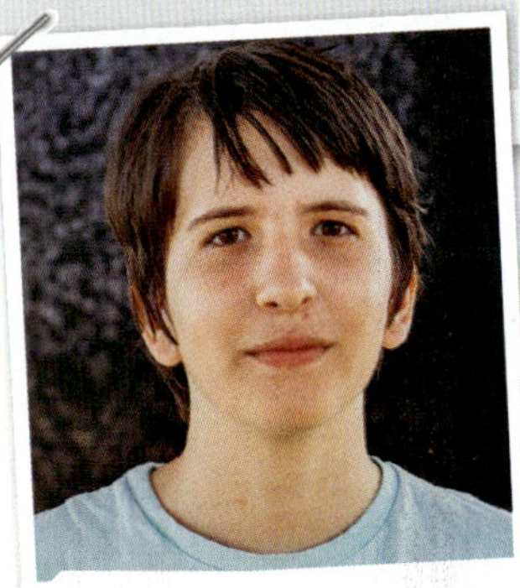

Jayden Foytlin, 15, of Rayne, Louisiana, alarmed about the increasing frequency of devastating storms in her region

Miko Vergun, 17, worried that her home country of the Marshall Islands is destined to go under the rising seas

2 How to be an activist

DOSSIER documentaire

Classe 3 Piste 10

1. **Use** the picture and the caption to **note down** information about the author of the text (name – age – activities).

2. **Listen** to X. Martinez speaking at the United Nations in 2015. **Pick out** information about him and his fight.
▶ *He started… • He has already… • He fights for…*

3. **Pick out** stressed and repeated words (environment – living conditions) and use them to **sum up** his message.

4. **Read** the text to find out more.

Médiation

5. Use everything you have found out in the two documents to **make** a list of the different forms of activism that teenagers get involved in.

Grammar

L'expression du futur

– The UN **is meeting** in February
be + V-ing
to discuss the problem.

➥ *Grammar p. 191*

Eco-warrior and hip-hop artist Xiuhtezcatl (pronounced "Shoe-Tez-Caht") Martinez speaking in Australia

Finding ways to make a difference by using your passion brings joy and purpose into your work. Break free from the traditional tactics of activism and evaluate your skill set[1], as well as the unique and fresh perspective you could bring to the movement. Ask yourself "What makes me feel alive?" Put your passion into a cause you want to put energy toward, and be creative with your solutions, meetings, events and projects.
However serious or mature I may appear to be in front of the UN or while giving a TedTalk[2], I'm still just a 17-year-old kid trying to make a difference, while having a hell of a[3] good time doing it. The events (…) people most want to be a part of are the ones that are different, outside the box[4], innovative, creative, and fun. Not everyone is an outspoken[5] leader, a frontline fighter wanting to risk arrest, or even a skilled organizer, but everyone has a part to play, no matter how small it is. We can all be leaders in our own ways. I've learned that no matter your age, you've got to have fun and be inspired by the work you do. Transforming your passion into action is one of the best ways I've found to avoid burnout and feeling overwhelmed[6] by the movement.
So write songs, design apps, build social media platforms, plant seeds, grow gardens, paint murals, and make the medicine the world needs. We need every piece and there is something special within you.

Xiuhtezcatl Martinez, Justin Spitzman, *We Rise*, 2017

1. skill set (n.) = competences
2. TedTalk (n.) = influential videos from expert speakers
3. hell of a (informal) (exp.) = really
4. outside the box (exp.) = very original
5. outspoken (adj.): *franc(he)*
6. overwhelmed (adj.): *dépassé(e)*

Need help?

- activist = campaigner
- committment = *engagement*
- global warming: *réchauffement de la planète*
- heatwave = very hot period
- lawsuit: *procès*
- plaintiff = accuser
- policy = strategy
- rally: *rassemblement*
- target = objective
- involved in = committed to
- sustainable: *durable*
- sue: *poursuivre en justice*
- sustain: *maintenir*
- tackle = deal with
- take legal action: *intenter un procès*

Prepare your project

Pairwork

Agree on a message to convince young people to get actively involved in an environmental cause (fighting electronic waste or air pollution – street litter (= *détritus*) – encouraging recycling…). Post it on the class blog or on Padlet.

Protecting Native American territory

Did you know?

Standing Rock: one of the largest Native American Reservations in the US. In September 2016, construction workers destroyed part of the Sioux tribe's sacred ground while building the North Dakota Pipeline.

1 Water protectors

DOSSIER documentaire — Classe 3 — Piste 11

1. Use the picture and the caption to imagine what is happening and why.
2. Read the tweet and guess the role of Tokata Iron Eyes.
3. Listen and check. Pick out keywords and classify them (people – places – actions – problems). Sum up what you have understood so far.
4. Read the text. Find information about Alexander, then focus on lexical fields (danger – future – responsibility). Sum up the message in your own words.
5. Médiation — Organise your notes to report what you understood (people involved – initial problem – fears – solutions – initiatives – social media).

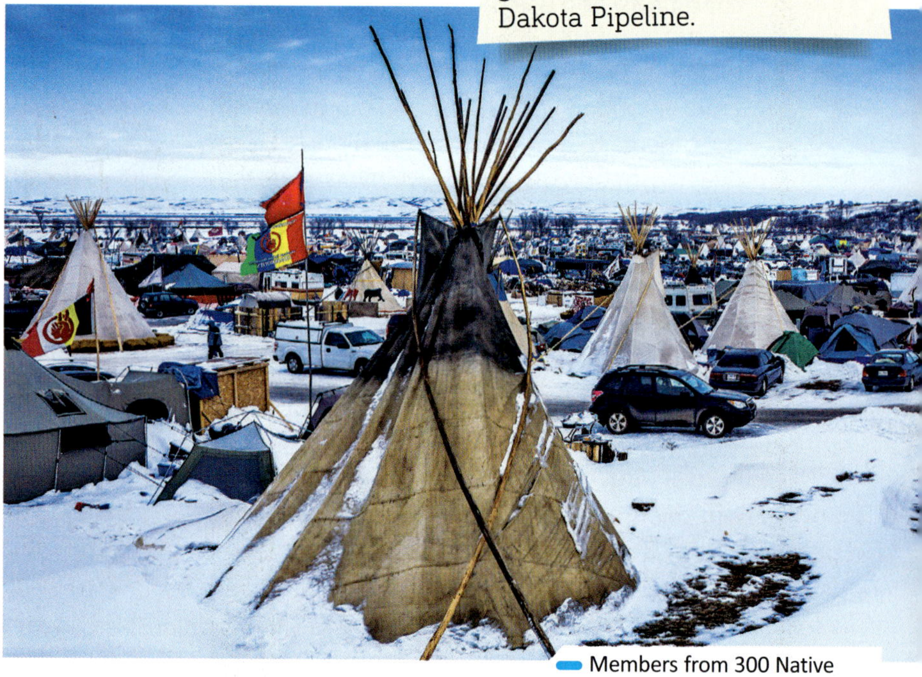

Members from 300 Native American Tribes came from all over the USA

Zero Hour @ThisisZeroHour — Follow

Meet Tokata Iron Eyes! – she is a teenage leader of the #NoDAPL[1] movement and a member of the Standing Rock tribe – we had the honor of having her speak at the DC #YouthClimateMarch. Tokata is a young #WaterProtector standing up to the #DAPL pipeline and fossil fuel[2] industry!

23:50 - 13 August 2018

1. NoDAPL = No Dakota Access Pipeline
2. fossil fuel (n.): *énergies fossiles*

International Indigenous Youth Council co-Founder, Alexander Howland, 21, from Dulce, New Mexico.

"I am scared of (…) the oil, it's not [if the pipeline] breaks, it's when it's going to break, because time erodes everything. We may not be dealing with it in our lifetime but our future generations (…) are going to be on the line because they don't have any clean water if we poison it all. It is extremely pitiful [that] we are looking for water in other worlds when we are so willing to poison our own here on Mother Earth. Everyone's number one fear is this pipeline is going to break. We['ve] got to think seven generations ahead just like our ancestors did. We've got to make sure our future generations have a healthy planet to live on, to inhabit, to survive, to adapt and evolve but we can't do that if the planet is dying because of mining companies, and fracking[1] and oil spills[2] and global warming."

madelinecottingham.com, 2016

1. fracking (n.): *fracturation hydraulique* 2. oil spill (n.): *marée noire*

#RezpectOurWater – #NoDAPL – #YouthClimateMarch – #DAP

2 vidéo Stars uniting for a community

1. **Watch** the video and focus on what you see (people – places – actions).

2. **Listen** to the lyrics of the song and take notes. **Use** what you have understood to **deduce** the theme(s) of the song.

3. **Read** the lyrics and **pick out** references to people: **divide** them into two groups and **define** each group.

4. **Focus on** repetitions and **guess** what they are for. **Sum up** the message of the song.

Pairwork

5. **List** famous people who have contributed to important causes. **Share** with the class.

Shailene Woodley at the Dakota Access Pipeline Protest rally, August 2016

[Verse 1: *Taboo*]
Stand up with the First Nations
A people that been livin' here for thousands of years (stand up)
We been fightin' for our freedoms since *the Niña* and *Pinta* and *the Santa Maria*[1] (stand up)
Like Geronimo, Sittin' Bull, Red Cloud, Crazy Horse[2], Leonard Peltier[3]
Now they poisonin' the waters for our sons and our daughters, so
We on the frontier (we one) one nation, one cause, one people, one tribe
Now it's us against the pipeline
Get on your feet for Standing Rock and we'll show you how strong we can be when we unify

[Chorus: *PJ Vegas*]
To all my native people
Recognize yourself, keep your head up
To all my tribal people
Recognize yourself, keep your head up
To all my native people, to all the original people, to all my indigenous people
Recognize yourself, keep your head up
Stand up, stand up (4x)
For Standin' Rock

Taboo, *Stand up, Stand n' Rock*, 2016

1. *The Niña, Pinta* and *the Santa Maria* = three ships of the Christopher Columbus expedition
2. Geronimo, Sittin' Bull, Red Cloud, Crazy Horse (n.) = Native American chiefs
3. Leonard Peltier (n.) = Native American activist

CULTURE QUEST

Find out information about the Native American chiefs mentioned in the song (dates – biography – events).
Keywords: Geronimo – Sitting Bull – Red Cloud – Crazy Horse chief.

Need help?

- campaign
- fossil fuel: *énergies fossiles*
- leader / leadership
- Native American: *Amérindien*
- convince = persuade
- launch = organise
- resist = oppose
- stand up against: *s'élever contre*
- threaten: *menacer*
- be affected
- make a decision
- raise awareness
- worth fighting for

Prepare your project

Write a tweet to give your opinion about the #NoDAPL movement.

#StandWithStandingRock – #WaterProtector

Mémoriser • Prononcer • Écrire

Words, words, words

➥ *Faire une carte mentale p. 234*
➥ *Mémoriser et enrichir son lexique p. 235*

Quizlet
quizlet.com/skysthelimit2e

Classe 3 – Pistes 12-14 – 82-84

Créez votre propre carte mentale à partir de ce que vous avez vu en classe. Vous pourrez ensuite l'enrichir à l'aide de celle-ci. Écoutez les mots et répétez-les pour bien les prononcer. Écrivez-les aussi plusieurs fois pour mémoriser leur orthographe.

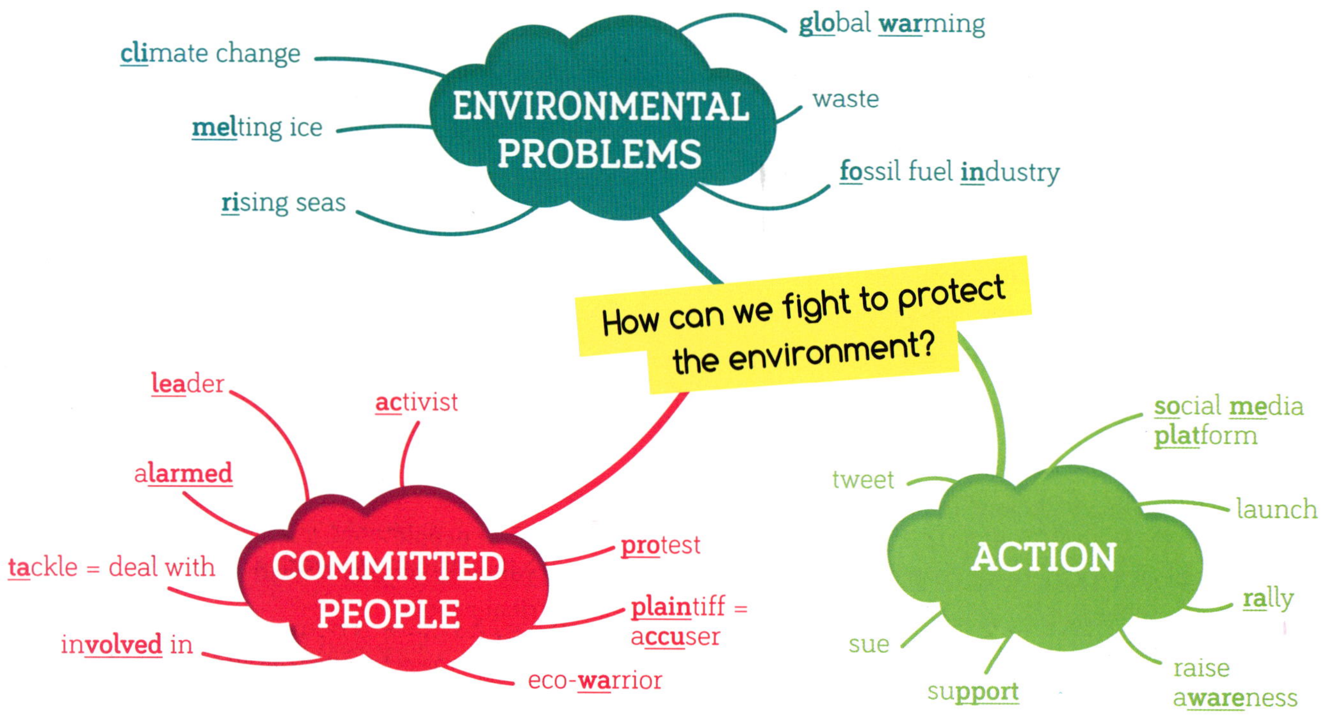

More words

Les composés en *-ever* et équivalents

Repères, p. 257

– **Whatever** the problem, there is always a solution.
– You will find interesting initiatives **wherever** you go.
– **However** serious he may seem, he is just a teenager who wants to have fun.
– **No matter how** old you are, you can get involved.

L'essentiel

• Les **composés en *-ever*** (pronom interrogatif + *-ever*) expriment un large choix, une absence de restriction (équivalents de « quel que soit », « quoi que », « où que », etc.).
• On peut les remplacer par l'expression : *No matter + wh- (why / what / where / when / who / how).*

1. Complétez avec *whatever* – *whoever* – *whenever* – *wherever* – *however* ou leur équivalent.

There is waste (?) you go.
→ *There is waste wherever you go. / No matter where you go, there is waste.*

a. (?) you decide, I will help you organise it.
b. You can hire (?) you want for this project.
c. He tells me about his new project (?) I see him.
d. They will do (?) they can to solve the problem.
e. (?) interesting this project is, I don't have time to get involved.
f. They organise meetings about environmental protection (?) they go.

Grammar

L'expression du futur

Repères, p. 250

- We **won't** manage to save our planet unless we work together.
- It **is going** to rain tomorrow.
- I'**m about to** send off this letter to the president!
- The protest march **begins** at 4 pm. I **am leaving** school early so that I don't miss it.
- I'**m participating** in the Science Fair next year.
- The UN **is meeting** in February to discuss the problem.

L'essentiel

En anglais, pour exprimer le futur, on peut employer :
- le **modal *will*** (forme réduite *'ll* et forme négative *won't*) ;
- ***be going to*** qui exprime une conviction ou une intention ;
- ***be about to*** qui exprime un futur très proche ;
- le **présent simple** associé à un repère temporel précis ;
- le **présent en *be* + V-*ing*** pour évoquer des événements projetés quasi sûrs ou une volonté forte (souvent avec un repère temporel).

1. Réécrivez les phrases avec *will* ou *be about to*. Faites les changements nécessaires.

When I leave school, I (?) become an eco-warrior.

→ *When I leave school, I will become an eco-warrior.*

a. It's almost time! X. Martinez's speech (?) start!

b. Bob has opened a recycling shop and he's optimistic that he (?) have lots of work.

c. If you need help to set up an association we (?) give you some advice.

d. Some politicians (?) only think about ecology when it helps them win votes.

e. We (?) leave, but you can call us back tomorrow for more information.

f. He (?) tell me about his commitment when you interrupted us.

2. Complétez avec *be* + V-*ing* ou le présent simple.

He (*arrive*) in San Francisco tonight. In fact I think his plane (*land*) at 7 pm.

→ *He is arriving in San Francisco tonight. In fact I think his plane lands at 7 pm.*

We (*attend*) the Science Fair next month. It (*start*) at 9 am and (*end*) at 5 pm. My parents (*come*) because they are so proud of the work we have done.

3. Complétez les phrases pour exprimer le futur. Faites les changements nécessaires.

I'm sure it (*rain*) tomorrow. That's why I (*not / go*) to the charity concert as it's outdoors, but I (*visit*) the exhibition they have set up about climate change. What about you? (*you / go*) to the concert? It (*start*) at 7 in the evening.

Sounds, sounds, sounds

Voyelles brèves et voyelles longues

Repères, p. 245

L'essentiel

• Certaines voyelles sont **courtes** (*hill*), d'autres sont **longues** (*heal*).

• Une voyelle longue est notée dans la transcription phonétique avec le signe [ː] (*green teens* [iː]). En cas de doute, servez-vous d'un dictionnaire.

Attention : Certaines lettres se prononcent différemment selon le mot (*decide* [ɪ] – *recent* [iː] ou *heavy* [e] – *heat* [iː]).

Classe 3 – 85 – Piste 15

1. Écoutez les paires de mots et identifiez les voyelles longues et courtes. Puis répétez-les.

green / grim – chat / chart – hit / heat – dirt / dot – meet / met – full / fool – keep / kit – pack / park

Classe 3 – 86 – Piste 16

2. Lisez les phrases en veillant à bien prononcer les mots soulignés. Enregistrez-vous, puis écoutez.

a. Australia was hit by a terrible heat wave.

b. I met him thanks to a chat about environmental issues.

c. The future doesn't look grim to me: a green future is possible!

d. They can sit in their teepees if it rains.

STRATEGY RÉAGIR À L'ÉCRIT

Pour réagir à l'écrit, il faut :

1 ... s'assurer qu'on a compris l'échange en cours :

→ **Lire tous les messages** pour savoir de quoi il s'agit.

2 ... oser s'insérer dans le fil de discussion :

→ Commencez la discussion avec une **formule de politesse**.

Hello there! • Welcome to everyone. • Let's begin!

→ **Votre avis compte !** N'ayez pas peur d'être jugé(e), votre opinion peut faire avancer les choses.

3 ... utiliser des expressions adaptées :

→ Montrez que vous vous appuyez sur le message précédent et que vous prenez en compte ce qui a été dit :

– soit parce que **vous rejoignez** ce qui vient d'être dit ;

Absolutely! • I couldn't agree more. • As you say…

– soit parce que **vous vous opposez**, en restant toujours poli(e) et mesuré(e) ;

Are we certain that…? • I'm not sure this is always true…

– soit parce que **vous souhaitez nuancer**.

We should also take into account… • Shouldn't we also think about… ? • Sometimes it's rather…

Soyez spontané(e) : utilisez des formulations qui vous viennent naturellement. Sinon vous risquez de perdre votre place dans l'échange.

4 ... apporter votre touche personnelle :

→ Usez d'expressions qui montrent qu'il s'agit de **votre opinion personnelle**.

I (strongly) believe… • I think…

→ N'hésitez pas à **interpeller vos lecteurs** pour les inviter à réagir.

Don't you agree… • Isn't it true that…? • Who has never… • It's undeniable, isn't it?

Inutile de trop rédiger : un langage proche de l'oral est souvent utilisé dans les échanges écrits (contractions, abréviations, question-tags, etc.).

Your project

Participate in an environmental campaign on social media

Groupwork

Your class has set up a social media page to share ideas to improve the environment. Exchange messages on the wall.

#ProtectWater Campaign, WWF, 2018

1 Identify a problem.

- **Agree** on a problem that needs solving (electronic waste – air or sea pollution – litter – lack of recycling…).
- **List the causes** of the problem (lack of awareness – lack of services – different priorities…).
- Think of all the **risks** the problem you have identified is creating.
- Try to **define the subject** in one sentence so that anyone can understand it.

2 Imagine the solutions to the problem.

- **Come to an agreement** on your short-term and long-term objectives.
- **List** the solutions your group proposes.
- Imagine **forms of action** you could use to **defend your cause** (social media campaign – protest march – petition – awareness posters…).

3 Prepare a text to defend your cause.

- Make it **short** and **to the point**.
- Choose the **best ideas and arguments** your group has come up with.
- Find the right words to **be convincing**.
- Do not hesitate to **address your readers** directly.

4 Set up your page.

- **Decide on a social media** you will use (class forum – Padlet – interactive blog, etc.).
- **Illustrate it** with a striking photo and add smileys, icons, etc.

5 React to the other groups' messages.

- **Write** at least one answer to the other problems posted. **Suggest a solution**, provide them with an **example** to illustrate and / or give your opinion and justify.

Keys to success

- **Utilisez le vocabulaire du chapitre :** problèmes environnementaux, personnes engagées, action.
  ➥ *Words, words, words, p. 190*
- **Faites des phrases au futur.**
  ➥ *Grammar, p. 191*
- **Vous pouvez intégrer des composés en *-ever*.**
  ➥ *More words, p. 190*
- **Servez-vous des conseils pour réagir à l'écrit.**
  ➥ *Strategy, p. 192*
- **Servez-vous des conseils pour le travail en groupe.**
  ➥ *Strategy, p. 237*

14

Axe 7 : Sauver la planète, penser les futurs possibles

Feed our future

1 Basics

List all the words that come to mind when you think about the future of food and the environment (possible problems – solutions).

WORKSHEET 30

2 Discover

Classe 3 Piste 17

Listen and **pick out** words related to the future of food (food – environment – future).

3 Play

Game

Invention game: Imagine a new type of food that doesn't exist today (taste – size – shape – colour – health benefits).
Create an ID card of your invention.
Share with the class. Then **make** your own futuristic menus from the different food inventions of the class.

Your project

Groupwork Médiation

Conduct a food enquiry to help improve the environment and write a report about food choices, *p. 203*
– Interview your classmates about meat, *p. 197*

Keys to success

- **Strategy: synthétiser des informations à partir de plusieurs documents,** *p. 202*
- **Mind map:** food, environment, solutions, *p. 200*
- **Grammar:** auxiliaires modaux (sens 2), *p. 201*

How can we both feed a growing population and protect our planet?

Maze Runner: The Scorch Trials, by Wes Ball, 2015

Lire • Écouter • Échanger

Eat meat or not eat meat?

1 Cheeseburgers are out

Veggie burger ad from Lightlife – the veggie cow

1. **Describe** and **comment on** the poster. **Guess** what the text is about.
2. **Read** and check. **Pick out** numbers and **say** what they correspond to.
3. **Scan** the text for lexical fields (population – food consumption – environment).
4. Médiation – Use them to **identify** the main problem and **write** a list of possible solutions.
5. Pairwork – **Exchange** about your eating habits and **come up** with a list of three things you would agree to change.

Recycling or taking the bus rather than driving to work has its place, but scientists are increasingly pointing to a deeper lifestyle change that would be the single biggest way to help the planet: eating far less meat. A swathe of[1] research released over the past year has laid bare[2] the hefty[3] impact that eating meat, especially beef and pork, has upon the environment by fueling climate change and polluting landscapes and waterways.

Industrialized agriculture and the onset[4] of the worst species extinction crisis since the demise[5] of the dinosaurs means that livestock and humans now make up 96% of all mammals. But despite consuming the vast majority of farmland, meat and dairy accounts for just 18% of all food calories and around a third of protein.

The mighty hoofprint[6] of farmed meat isn't just inefficient. Deforestation to make way for livestock, along with methane emissions from cows and fertilizer use, creates as much greenhouse gas emissions as all the world's cars, trucks and airplanes. Meat rearing[7] practices risk mass extinctions of other animals, as well as spawn[8] significant pollution of streams, rivers and, ultimately, the ocean.

In October, scientists warned that huge reductions in meat eating are required if the world is to stave off[9] dangerous climate change, with beef consumption in western countries needing to drop by 90%, replaced by five times more beans and pulses[10].

Consumption of pork, milk and eggs will also need to decline sharply, all as the world's population balloons by an extra 2 billion people by 2050. Researchers said there will need to be a global shift to a "flexitarian" diet to help keep the global temperature increase from breaching a 2° limit agreed by governments.

Oliver Milman, *The Guardian*, Dec. 21, 2018

1. a swathe of (exp.): *une série de*
2. lay bare (exp.) = reveal
3. hefty (adj.) = massive
4. onset (n.) = beginning
5. demise (n.): *disparition*
6. hoofprint (n.): *empreinte*
7. rearing (n.): *élevage*
8. spawn (v.) = generate
9. stave off (v.) = avoid
10. beans and pulses (exp.): *légumes secs*

2 vidéo You'll be eating crickets soon!

1. **Look** at the photo and read the caption. **Guess** the content of the video.
2. **Watch** the 1st minute of the video without the sound and check. **List** the words that you think you will hear, then **listen** and check.
3. **Watch** the whole video with the sound. **Write down** keywords and **classify** them (animals – environmental problems – solutions).
4. Pairwork — **Imagine** a future where meat is no longer available. **Exchange** with your partner.
   ▶ *If I had to… • I would… • I think I could…*
5. **Write** a short text to promote insect-based food using what you understood.
   ▶ *We should / could… • Why don't we…*

The Cadesky Brothers are betting we'll turn to crickets for protein in the future, Toronto, 2016.

3 vidéo "Clean" meat

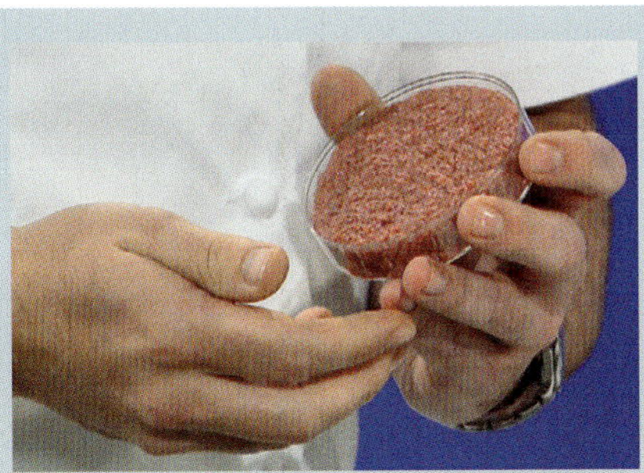

Lab-grown meat

1. **Look** at the photo and the caption and **say** if you would be ready to eat this.
2. **Watch** the video and **list** the different people you see and hear.
3. **Note down** arguments in favour of this new invention.
4. Pairwork — **Come up** with a list of three other ideas to help feed our growing population in a more environmentally-friendly way.

Need help?

- carbon footprint: *empreinte carbone*
- hatchling = newborn animal
- insect farming
- livestock: *bétail*
- chemical: *chimique*
- disgusting
- eco-friendly
- environmentally friendly: *respectueux de l'environnement*
- (un)ethical
- free range: *élevé(e) en plein air*
- lab-grown: *cultivé(e) en laboratoire*
- meat-free: *sans viande*
- organic: *biologique*
- scarce = rare
- sustainable: *durable*
- harvest: *récolter*
- process = transform
- slaughter = massacre
- make the most of something = profit from
- release greenhouse gases
- see the bigger picture: *voir la situation dans son ensemble*
- the greater good: *l'intérêt général*

CULTURE QUEST

Watch a comic sketch about trying to be environmentally aware.

Keywords: Portlandia – Is this chicken local – Vimeo.

Prepare your project

Pairwork — Interview your classmates about meat (daily meat eater? vegetarian? ready to taste insects? / lab meat? etc.). Analyse the answers and report to the class.

Écouter • Lire • Échanger

The problem of food waste

1 A massive issue

Classe 3 Piste 18

The Compost Cats, a University of Arizona student organisation, Tucson, Arizona, USA

1. **Look** at the photo and **guess** what the audio will be about.
   ▶ *It must be… • I suppose… • It may be about…*
2. **Listen** to Mr Sandjayan, a scientist talking about food waste. **Remember** as many words as you can and **classify** them into different categories (numbers – countries – environmental problems, etc.).
3. **Sum up** what you have understood about food waste in America. (Médiation)

2 Ugly can be delicious

Classe 3 Piste 19

1. **Look** at the infographics and **identify** the main subject. **Pick out** words used to describe the produce.
2. **Comment on** the figures.
   ▶ *Almost half of… • A vast majority… • I can't believe… • It's incredible that people should…*
3. **Listen** to Anthony Bourdain, a famous chef. **Pick out** stressed and repeated words, and use them to **identify** the solutions he proposes.
4. **Pick out** repeated words at the end of the interview and **say** what it shows about his message.
5. **Write** a list of very concrete solutions based on what you understood.

The *Ugly Produce is Beautiful* Educational Campaign was started in January, 2016.

1. bruised (adj.): *abîmé*

Did you know?

In 2018, a 17-year-old Canadian called **Justin Kulik** got over 160,000 signatures for his petition to end food waste. He took it to the Canadian Minister for Agriculture, asking for a law that would force supermarkets to donate any food they can't sell to charities.

3 Waste-killing inventions

1. **Look** at the picture and read the caption. **Imagine** the subject of the text.

2. **Read** the text and check. **Pick out** references to people, places and numbers. **Use** them to **explain** the problem and the solutions proposed.

Groupwork

3. **Exchange** to imagine a new device to fight food waste. Share with the class and **vote** for the best ideas.
▶ *People could start with… • It might be a good idea to…*

CULTURE QUEST

Discover Lawrence Okettayot's invention.
Keywords: Uganda – Lawrence Okettayot – BBC – food waste warrior.

Two low-tech innovations could help reduce waste in a continent where millions are hungry.

Food waste in Africa is a serious issue. Half of all the fruit and vegetables produced there are thrown away, even though millions of people across the continent are going hungry.

Intermittent power supplies and poor storage facilities mean that staple[1] foods – among them cereals, roots and tubers – are too often lost after being harvested[2], and before they arrive at market. According to the UN, if food wasted in Africa was saved instead, it could feed about 300 million people.

Entrepreneur Nnaemeka Ikegwuonu, 35, is hoping his innovation will address the problem in his country, Nigeria. (…)

"Nigeria is a very large country, with 90 million smallholder[3] farmers who do not have access to any form of cold storage[4]," says Ikegwuonu. "(…) So we came up with solar-powered, walk-in cold rooms which can extend the life of food up to 21 days, and my goal is to push these hubs[5] to all developing countries." (…)

In Uganda, meanwhile, engineering graduate Lawrence Okettayot, 23, is seeking to address food waste in his country.

Okettayot's farming family has suffered from heavy economic losses due to food waste over the past few decades, and his solution comes in the form of dehydration rather than cold storage.

The "Sparky Dryer", as he and his colleagues call it, runs on biofuel from a farmer's garden, which burns with zero-carbon emissions to dehydrate the farmer's chosen produce, be it mangoes, guavas, pineapples or even cereals such as maize and sorghum.

Kate Hodal, *The Guardian,* Dec. 28, 2017

The "Sparky Dryer" is one of a number of inventions aimed at solving the problem of food waste in Africa.

1. staple (adj.) = principal
2. harvest (v.): *récolter*
3. smallholder (n.): *petit cultivateur*
4. storage (n.): *conservation*
5. hub (n.) = centre

Grammar

Les auxiliaires modaux (sens 2)

– The document **must be** about food waste.
modal + BV

➥ *Grammar p. 201*

Need help?

- amount = quantity
- environmental impact
- food industry
- leftovers: *restes*
- ressources
- storage: *rangement*
- warrior = fighter
- waste: *gaspillage*
- shocked = appalled
- address = deal with
- challenge: *mettre à l'épreuve*
- contribute to
- grow: *faire pousser*
- reduce = lower
- solve: *résoudre*
- sort: *trier*
- throw away: *jeter*
- pay attention to

Mémoriser • Prononcer • Écrire

Words, words, words

➡ *Faire une carte mentale p. 234*
➡ *Mémoriser et enrichir son lexique p. 235*

Quizlet
quizlet.com/skysthelimit2e

Classe 3 — Pistes 20-22 — 87-89

Créez votre propre carte mentale à partir de ce que vous avez vu en classe. Vous pourrez ensuite l'enrichir à l'aide de celle-ci. Écoutez les mots et répétez-les pour bien les prononcer. Écrivez-les aussi plusieurs fois pour mémoriser leur orthographe.

How can we both feed a growing population and protect our planet?

ENVIRONMENT
- release greenhouse gases
- environmental impact
- carbon footprint
- sustainable
- scarce
- throw away
- environmentally friendly

FOOD
- leftovers
- abundance
- waste
- free range
- lab-grown
- organic
- meat-free

SOLUTIONS
- insect farming
- sort
- pay attention to
- storage
- contribute to
- ethical
- address = deal with
- reduce = lower

More words

La dérivation Repères, p. 260

- **Hopelessness** is a feeling that develops when we do nothing.
- **Feeding** the **population** of the world isn't **impossible**.
- We need to **rationalise** food **production**.

L'essentiel

- La **dérivation** permet de modifier le sens d'un mot grâce à un préfixe et / ou un suffixe placé avant ou après le mot-racine. On peut combiner plusieurs suffixes / préfixes.
- La catégorie grammaticale du mot est en fonction du suffixe : ***-ate***, ***-ify***, ***-ise*** = verbe ; ***-ion***, ***-ism***, ***-ity***, ***-ing***, ***-ness*** = nom ; ***-able***, ***-al***, ***-ible***, ***-ic***, ***-less*** = adjectif et ***-ly*** = adverbe.

Attention : L'ajout d'un suffixe peut changer la catégorie grammaticale du mot-racine.

1. Créez au moins dix mots à partir des éléments du tableau. Vérifiez le mot et sa catégorie dans un dictionnaire.

Préfixe		Mot-racine	Suffixe		
un- dis-	mis- im-	real – scarce – hope – courage – environment – sustain – success – inform – waste – perfect – nature – aware	-ity -ful -ness	-ing -al	-ly -less

Observer • Retenir • Appliquer

Grammar

Les auxiliaires modaux (sens 2)

Repères, p. 253

– The document **must be** about food waste.
modal + BV

– People **may have** to eat insects one day.
modal + BV

– The food is gone: they **must have eaten** it all.
modal + *have* + part. passé

– She didn't come: she **might not have wanted** to see the film.
modal (*not*) + *have* + part. passé

– They **may be having** a meeting.
modal + *be* + V-*ing*

L'essentiel

CAN'T (almost) impossible 10 %	MIGHT/COULD not really sure 25 %	MAY maybe/ perhaps 50 %	MUST (almost) sure 80 %

• Les **auxiliaires modaux** (sens 2) indiquent le degré de probabilité d'un événement présent, passé ou futur.

• Ils sont toujours suivis d'une BV (*may* ***go*** / *may* ***be*** *going*). Pour un événement passé, on utilise : modal (*not*) + *have* + participe passé (*may* ***have gone***). ➥ *Verbes irréguliers, p. 264*

Attention : Deux modaux ne se suivent jamais.

• Certains adverbes et expressions (*it's possible that, perhaps, maybe, probably*…) expriment aussi la probabilité.

1. Complétez les phrases avec les modaux appropriés.

may – must – might have – must have – can't have

People (?) become more aware over time. (*perhaps*)
→ *People may become more aware over time.*

a. I (?) buy local from now on. (*perhaps*)
b. Organic food (?) be good for you. (*sure*)
c. The bin is still full: you (?) emptied it! (*impossible*)
d. There's no one here. They (?) forgotten about the meeting. (*sure*)
e. I know it's raining, but she (?) decided to come by bike anyway. (*not sure*)

2. Reformulez en introduisant des modaux. Faites les changements nécessaires.

She's going to stop eating meat. (Well, maybe…)
→ She…
→ *She may be going to stop eating meat.*

a. The invention saves a lot of energy. (I'm almost sure.) → The invention…
b. They are unaware of the problem. (I think this is impossible.) → They…
c. They made the documentary to inform consumers. (Maybe this is true.) → They…
d. People are beginning to change their behaviour. (I think it's possible.) → People…

Sounds, sounds, sounds

Formes fortes et faibles des mots grammaticaux

Repères, p. 247

L'essentiel

• Les **mots grammaticaux** à une syllabe ont une forme forte (*for* [fə]) et une forme faible (*for* [fɔː]).

• La **forme faible** est en général utilisée, sauf si le mot grammatical est en fin de phrase ou s'il porte un accent contrastif : *I* ***do*** *believe that…*

➥ *L'accent contrastif, p. 61*

Classe 3 Piste 23 — 90

1. Écoutez et répétez en vous concentrant sur les mots soulignés.

a. What <u>is</u> the device <u>for</u>?
b. I went <u>for</u> a vegetarian meal.
c. They <u>were</u> surprised to see me eat insects.
d. I know because they told me they <u>were</u>.

Classe 3 Piste 24 — 91

2. Dites si les mots soulignés prennent la forme faible ou la forme forte. Écoutez pour vérifier.

a. I want <u>to</u> be more aware.
b. That <u>is</u> the environmental radio programme I listened <u>to</u>.
c. He <u>had</u> heard about the problem.
d. I told him I <u>would</u> give him what leftover food I <u>had</u>.

STRATEGY

SYNTHÉTISER DES INFORMATIONS À PARTIR DE DOCUMENTS DIVERS Médiation

Pour faire la synthèse d'informations à partir de plusieurs documents, il faut :

1 ... identifier le destinataire et l'objet de la synthèse :

- Assurez-vous d'avoir bien compris l'**objectif de la synthèse** demandée : pour qui ? dans quel but ?
- Formulez une question à laquelle vous allez répondre.

2 ... faire des recherches en variant les sources :

- Ciblez vos **recherches** pour répondre à la question que vous vous posez. Prenez des **notes** synthétiques et organisées.

Gardez des traces (sources, photos, copies…) de vos recherches pour avoir des preuves de ce que vous avancez.

3 ... adapter votre méthode à chaque support :

- Identifiez la **source** et le **type de document**.
  Audios et vidéos : appuyez-vous sur la **bande-son** (mots accentués – intonations – voix) et sur les **images**. *Strategy, p. 30*
  Textes : pensez à regarder le **paratexte** (titre – auteur – date). *Strategy, p. 140*
- Repérez les **données factuelles** (chiffres – noms – dates – lieux).
- Isolez les **chiffres importants** en notant les dates et références des supports utilisés, en particulier pour des **sources** telles que statistiques – enquêtes – rapports.
- Les **documents visuels** (affiches – photos – graphiques) servent pour **trouver des informations** ou pour **illustrer un propos**.

4 ... organiser vos notes et faire des sélections :

- **Relisez vos notes** à la lumière de la question posée.
- Ne gardez que ce qui sera utile pour **répondre à votre question**.
- Faites un **plan cohérent et structuré**.
- Prévoyez une **introduction** et une **conclusion**.

5 ... rédiger votre synthèse :

- Veillez à **choisir le lexique** et les **structures** adaptés, soyez **concis** et mettez bien en évidence les **éléments importants**.
- Vous pouvez mettre en annexe la **liste de vos sources**.

Restez le plus neutre possible, ne prenez pas parti.

Your project Write a report about food choices

Groupwork
Médiation

You have been asked to conduct a food enquiry[1] to help improve the environment. Write a short report to make recommendations.

1 Decide where and when you will conduct your investigation.

- Choose the **places** (school canteen – home…) and **times** for observation.
- Think of a **question** you would like to answer with your report.

2 Prepare your investigation.

- Make a **list** of **people** (your family – friends…) to interview and **questions** to ask.
- List other possible **sources of information** (canteen menus – shopping lists, etc.).
- **Gather** the **material** you need (camera – voice recorder – notebook…).

3 Conduct your investigation.

- You can ask your questions in English or in French.
- Gather as much **information** as you can (type – quantity – origin of meat – treatment of waste, etc.).
- Take **notes**, **photos**.

4 Select the information you have found.

- Choose the most **relevant information** from your different sources.
- Analyse the **results** of the interview (common points – hypotheses – differences).

5 Write your report.

- Decide on an **outline**.
- Use the **appropriate vocabulary** (food – environment…) and **linkwords**.
- In your own words, rephrase the **essential points** of your enquiry.
- Include a **list of recommendations** based on your observations.
- **Illustrate** your report. Don't forget to add a **short explanation** for your visuals.
- Check your **report** for spelling mistakes. Make sure it is **short**, **precise** and **illustrated**.

Keys to success

- **Utilisez le vocabulaire du chapitre :** nourriture, environnement, solutions.
  ➥ *Words, words, words, p. 200*
- **Utilisez la dérivation.**
  ➥ *More words, p. 200*
- **Utilisez les auxilaires modaux (sens 2).**
  ➥ *Grammar, p. 201*
- **Servez-vous des conseils pour faire la synthèse des informations issues de documents divers.**
  ➥ *Strategy, p. 202*
- **Servez-vous des conseils pour le travail en groupe.**
  ➥ *Strategy, p. 237*

Axe 8 : Le passé

dans le présent

Axe 8 : Le passé dans le présent

15 Notting Hill's Caribbean Carnival

Your project

Create a poster to promote a cultural event, *p. 215*

– Write a paragraph to promote the next Notting Hill Carnival, *p. 211*

Keys to success

- **Strategy: communiquer une information par écrit**, *p. 214*
- **Mind map:** migration, community, celebration, *p. 212*
- **Grammar:** proposition infinitive, *p. 213*

How can a carnival help connect the past and the present?

London's Notting Hill Carnival was originally led by members of the local West Indian community, especially those from Trinidad and Tobago

1 Basics

List all the words that come to mind when you think of cultural celebrations (names – places – activities – atmospheres). WORKSHEET 31

2 Discover

Classe 3 – Piste 25

Listen and **pick out** references to Notting Hill Carnival (people – places – music – food – costumes).

▶ *Teens go to the carnival to…*

Game 3 Play

Name game: Name as many Caribbean islands as you can in 30 seconds. **Check** your answers using a map, then **find** the classmate who named the most.

Écouter • Lire • Parler

The origins of the carnival

1 vidéo From the West Indies to London

Did you know?

The **West Indies** are Caribbean islands colonised by Europeans (16th-17th centuries).
After WWII, Britain asked the West Indians to come and help in vital fields such as building and nursing.

1. Watch the 1st part without the sound, and say what you see (people – places – attitudes).

2. Watch the 1st part again with the sound and pick out key information.

3. Watch the 2nd part. Find details about the people you see (family situation – job – living conditions).

Médiation **4.** Use what you have understood to report on the immigrants' experiences.

The ship *SS Empire Windrush* arrived in 1948 with people from the West Indies.

2 The realities of a new life

Classe 3 Piste 26

1. Read the poem and pick out references to places and people. Use them to describe what happened.

2. Focus on stanza 1. Find references to the media. Guess what people saw in the news.

▶ *There must have been… • The media probably showed…*

3. Read stanza 2. Pick out information about the Jamaicans and say how they reacted.

4. Listen then practise reading the poem out loud.

1. de = the (Jamaican accent) 2. an = and
3. settle down (v.) = make a home
4. Teddy Boy (n.) = a British underground culture associated with rock'n'roll music
5. steadfast (adj.) = determined
6. Commonwealth (n.): *association d'États issus de l'ancien Empire britannique*
7. wid = with

In late summer 1958, several hundred white youths attacked the local West Indian residents, leading to over 140 arrests.

Race riots in Notting Hill Gate said de[1] headline
De cameras were there as de flames burnt about,
De fighters for race were establishing front lines
As de great British welcome just seemed to fall out,
Race riots in Nottingham City an[2] Bristol
Race riots in Cardiff an sweet Camden Town,
De newspapers said it was dreadful and shameful
But the men from Jamaica were settling down[3].

The men from Jamaica would not die in silence
The men from Jamaica just got radical,
To counter de negative Teddy Boy[4] violence
They created blues dances an carnival,
The men from Jamaica were steadfast[5] and growing
Despite Commonwealth[6] immigration controls,
They learnt a few lessons an soon they were knowing
That there were no streets paved wid[7] silver or gold.

Benjamin Zephaniah, "The Men from Jamaica are Settling Down", *Too Black, Too Strong*, 2001

3 Creating the carnival spirit

DOSSIER documentaire

Classe 3 Piste 27

A carnival-goer gets a lift from a police officer at Notting Hill Carnival in 1980.

Grammar

La proposition infinitive

– The Jamaicans **expected to find** a better life. *to + BV*

➥ *Grammar p. 213*

1. **Look** at the photo and **read** the caption. **Describe** what you see and **react**.
   ► *It's unusual to see… • You don't expect… • That must have been…*

2. **Read** the text and **pick out** information about the carnival (people – places – dates – cause – aim). **Describe** how the carnival began.

3. **Listen** to the recording and **pick out** stressed words. **Classify** them into two groups: information about Claudia Jones (origins – occupation – activism) and the carnival.

4. Médiation **Use** what you have understood to **compare** the beginning of the carnival with today.
   ► *The first ever London carnival helped to… • It encouraged different communities to…*

As of late 1958, the WIG[1] had assembled and worked with an organising Carnival Committee to stage a joyous event that at once echoed the carnival festivals of the Caribbean and served to bring British Caribbeans and their non-Caribbean friends together in a spirit of defiance against the kinds of division that had marked the riots of the summer of 1958.

They could not have known then that they were founding what was to come to be described in the 1990s as the largest street event in all Europe. (…) In 1959 Claudia had reached out to the friends she held dear[2] in artistic circles to stage an event that would symbolise a spirit of bouncing back[3] after the saddening street rioting events of Nottingham and Notting Hill in the summer of 1958.

Marika Sherwood, *Claudia Jones. A Life in Exile*, 2000

1. WIG (n.) = *West Indian Gazette*, Britain's first major black newspaper
2. hold dear (v.) = love
3. bounce back (v.) : *rebondir*

A postage stamp honouring Claudia Jones issued 50 years after the riots (2008) to commemorate her community reconciliation initiative.

Need help?

- manual labour: *travail manuel*
- passenger ship
- riot: *émeute*
- shortage ['ʃɔːtɪdʒ] of workers = lack of workers
- apprehensive = nervous
- crowded
- growing = increasing
- overqualified: *surqualifié*
- settle down: *s'installer*
- ease tensions = reduce conflict
- second-class citizen: *citoyen de seconde zone*
- seek a new beginning = search for a new life

Lire • Écouter • Écrire

The carnival today

Did you know?

The **British colonies** in the Caribbean included The Bahamas, Barbados, Guyana, Jamaica, Trinidad and Tobago.

1 Remembering the past

DOSSIER documentaire

Classe 3 Piste 28

At Notting Hill Carnival, masks often include representations of the devil.

1. **Describe** and compare the two pictures.
   ▶ *In both pictures… • Contrary to… • What is very similar is that… • They all seem to want to…*
2. **Read** the text and find references to people, slavery and carnival. **Imagine** why people wear masks at carnival.
3. **Listen** and check. **Pick out** stressed words and **classify** them (slavery – masks – people and places).
4. **Sum up** the significance of masks in Caribbean culture. (Médiation)

The carnival in Port of Spain, the capital of Trinidad and Tobago, 1888

Dawn-Maria France is a journalist and broadcaster who has written about the history of Notting Hill Carnival. She says that the carnival tradition emanates from the struggle[1] of the Caribbean people.

"Upon emancipation, freed African slaves from the Caribbean transformed the old European festival tradition forever, with their mix of African and Caribbean culture," she explains.

"It was a celebration of the end of slavery – the rejoicing in the freedom of enslaved Africans liberated from the evils[2] of forced human labour."

The Caribbean and African take on carnival eventually spread across various countries, including the UK. During the late 50s and early 60s, Notting Hill had one of the most concentrated populations of West Indians in the country.

Georgia Chambers, *The Evening Standard*, August 24, 2018

1. struggle (n.): *combat*
2. evil (n.) = misery

2 vidéo Coming together DOSSIER documentaire

1. **Describe** the picture and **react**.

2. **Read** the text and **focus on** references to people, numbers, activities and time. Use them to **make** a short description of the event.

3. **Watch** the 1st minute of the video. **Find** information about the speaker (name – job – experience of carnival – passion). **List** the music styles he mentions.

4. **Watch** the whole video. Try to **remember** as many words as you can related to music.
Explain what changed.

5. **Watch** the last minute again and focus on repetitions. **Explain** what carnival represents for the speaker.

00:00

At first a simple celebration of Caribbean culture, with a parade of steel drum bands through West London, Notting Hill Carnival has become so popular that it now attracts over 1 million people.

Carnival is a mass of artistry, creativity, the result of the people who make it happen. The artists, performers, musicians, dancers, chefs, merchants and all the people who attend are contributors to its massive size and effect. In the weeks leading up to the August bank holiday[1], the glazing[2] and doorways of shops and houses are fortified with timber panels[3] ready for the onslaught[4]. After the first day, refuse services patrol into the early hours, only for the streets to become covered with assorted carnival detritus on the Monday again.

Two million people – roughly equivalent to the entire population of Slovenia, Gabon or Latvia – crammed into a small area is not a challenge to underestimate. Surely successfully hosting such an event is something to be proud of.

Ishmahil Blagrove, *The Guardian*, July 12, 2017

1. August bank holiday (n.): *dernier lundi d'août férié*
2. glazing (n.) = windows
3. timber panels (n.) = wood barricades
4. onslaught (n.) = arrival of lots of people

Need help?

- beat = rhythm
- creed = religion
- devil = Satan
- entertainment
- dedicated = devoted
- digital: *numérique*
- modern ≠ old-fashioned
- export ≠ import
- pay homage [ˈhɒmɪdʒ] to = show respect for

Prepare your project

Use what you have learnt to write a paragraph to promote the next Notting Hill Carnival (where – when – things to do and see – where it comes from).

▶ *Come and see…! • It celebrates… • It's the greatest… • It originated in…*

Mémoriser • Prononcer • Écrire

Words, words, words

➡ *Faire une carte mentale p. 234*
➡ *Mémoriser et enrichir son lexique p. 235*

Quizlet
quizlet.com/skysthelimit2e

Classe 3 Pistes 29-31 — 92-94

Créez votre propre carte mentale à partir de ce que vous avez vu en classe. Vous pourrez ensuite l'enrichir à l'aide de celle-ci. Écoutez les mots et répétez-les pour bien les prononcer. Écrivez-les aussi plusieurs fois pour mémoriser leur orthographe.

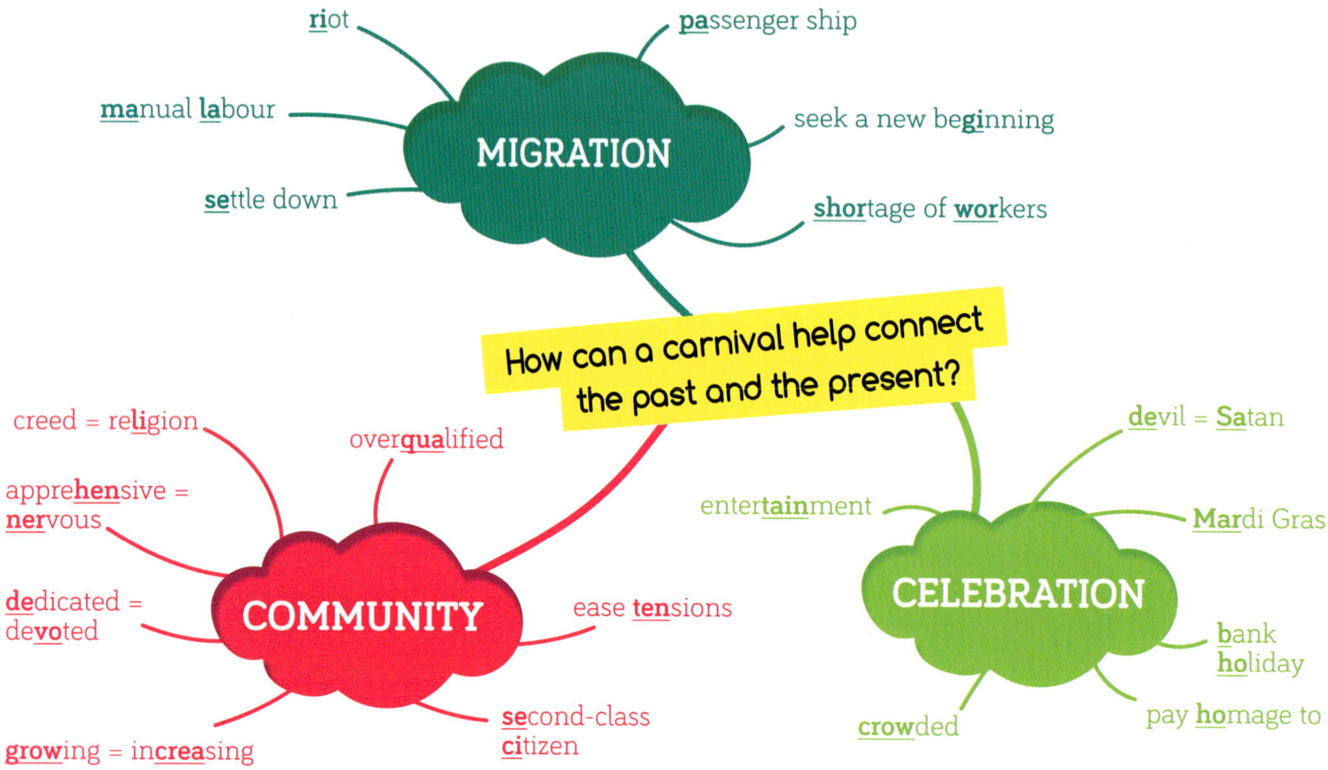

More words

Les *gap fillers*

– **So**, what did you think of the band we saw this weekend?
– **Well**, **actually** I thought the music was... **basically** rubbish. **I guess** you don't agree?
– **No way!** I thought it was excellent! **Seriously!** A real heavy beat. **You know what I mean?**
– Yeah... **I mean**, **sure**, there were some parts that were, **like**, okay.

L'essentiel
• Les *gap fillers* permettent au locuteur de marquer une pause. Ils sont aussi utilisés pour accentuer ou nuancer une idée, ou pour inclure quelqu'un dans la conversation.

1. Complétez les phrases avec un des *gap fillers* entre parenthèses.

Where's my homework? (?), my dog ate it! (actually – I mean – totally) → Actually, my dog ate it!

a. (?), let's see whether we have packed everything. (*basically – right – no way*)

b. (?), come on, man! I didn't mean to lose your stuff! (*I mean – you see – actually*)

c. We were going to eat out, but (?) we can go back home. (*seriously – well – I guess*)

d. I really liked that DJ, (?)? (*like – you know what I mean – basically*)

Grammar

La proposition infinitive Repères, p. 261

– The Jamaicans **expected to find** a better life.
– We **need to understand** our history.
– They **invited** **the police officers** **to dance**.
– He **asked** him **not to go** to the Carnival.

L'essentiel

• La **proposition infinitive** (introduite par *to* + BV) s'utilise après des verbes exprimant une demande, une requête, un conseil, etc. (*want, hope, would like, advise, ask*…).

• Elle sert de complément et on peut la remplacer par *something* ou *this* : *She would like something / this.* → *She would like them (not) to go.*

Attention : Contrairement au français, quand il y a deux sujets, le 2e est un pronom complément : Elle voulait qu'ils s'entendent. → *She wanted them to get along.*

1. Formez une phrase avec le verbe entre parenthèses.
The dancers were ready. (*seem*) → *The dancers seemed to be ready.*
a. The carnival music crews are in place. (*seem*)
b. Carnival remind us of the past. (*aim*)
c. The Caribbean carnivals in the past were influenced by Europe's Mardi Gras. (*tend*)
d. Some carnival participants mimicked former slave masters. (*try*)
e. Today, carnival has expanded into a huge Caribbean-themed street party. (*appear*)

2. Réunissez les deux phrases en une seule.
The Jamaicans wanted this: people were welcoming.
→ *The Jamaicans wanted people to be welcoming.*
a. The hospitals asked this: West Indian nurses worked for them.
b. I expect this: he will drive me to Notting Hill Carnival.
c. She encouraged this: they got along together.
d. They have decided this: they will invite more people next year.

3. Reformulez les phrases en utilisant les amorces.
Mum said I could add sequins to my costume. (*Mum allowed…*)
→ *Mum allowed me to add sequins to my costume.*
a. Our dad said I should take my brother to carnival. (*Our dad persuaded...*)
b. If we get this bus, we'll get there early. (*Getting this bus will enable...*)
c. My friends said I must try the chicken. (*My friends advised...*)
d. Make sure we take lots of photos and videos. (*Let's remember...*)
e. Our parents said that we shouldn't stay out late. (*Our parents warned...*)
f. We were disappointed because carnival ended early. (*We didn't expect...*)

Sounds, sounds, sounds

Les liaisons Repères, p. 247

L'essentiel

En anglais comme en français, on fait **une liaison** entre la consonne en fin de mot et la voyelle au début du mot suivant. Cela vaut également pour les mots qui se terminent par un *r* muet.

Classe 3 – Piste 32 – 95

1. Écoutez et répétez en insistant sur les liaisons.
sing and dance – a group of artists – more and more – the drums are loud – such an event – what a crowd!

Classe 3 – Piste 33 – 96

2. Lisez le texte et faites les liaisons. Écoutez pour vérifier.
Carnival takes place over two days and features a parade and lots of fantastic music including reggae, dub and salsa. There are also steel bands and a lot of singing and dancing!

STRATEGY — COMMUNIQUER UNE INFORMATION PAR ÉCRIT

Pour communiquer une information par écrit, il faut :

1 … s'interroger sur l'objectif du document :

- **Quel est l'événement** sur lequel je dois communiquer (événement culturel – rencontre sportive – réunion…) ?
- **Qui est le destinataire** (la classe – le lycée – le quartier…) ?
- **Quel but** a ce document (faire venir le public – demander de l'aide – apporter des idées…) ?

2 … se préparer à la rédaction du document :

- **Listez les informations essentielles** (date – lieu – contenu – prix – personnes à contacter…).
- Pensez à mettre en valeur **les mots-clés**.
- **Décidez** du **type de support** (affiche – dépliant…).

3 … rédiger le document :

- **Adaptez le vocabulaire** et **le ton** au sujet.
- Choisissez **un titre parlant**.
- Inventez une **phrase d'accroche** qui attire l'attention.

4 … faire la mise en page :

- Veillez à **aérer le document :** ajoutez des tirets (ou « puces ») pour améliorer la lisibilité d'une liste.
- **Mettez en valeur les éléments importants** (police de caractères plus grande, couleurs, etc.).

Faites une lecture critique de la version finale : votre message est-il immédiatement compréhensible ? Le document contient-il toutes les informations essentielles ?

Your project

Create a poster to promote a cultural event

Create a poster to convince your classmates to vote for your cultural event.

1 Choose the basis for your cultural event.

- **Agree on** a **local**, **regional** or **national culture** that you would like to make your class discover and celebrate.
- Decide **how** you will **celebrate** it: fashion show – photographic exhibition – party – poetry contest…
- List **interesting aspects of the culture** you have chosen: traditional recipes – clothes – music – history…

2 Decide on what you need to inform the class about.

- Think about the **organisation of the event** (number of people – what they will do – where they will do it) and work out **how to explain your event** to the class.
- Find **photographs** (past or present) or create drawings to **illustrate** your ideas.
- Think of a **catchphrase** to attract the viewer's attention.

3 Write a short text containing the information you want to share.

- Include all the **important details** (time – place – information).
- Make sure people can understand what makes your event **special**.
- Use sentences to address the people of your school directly.
- Identify the **keywords** and make sure that they are immediately **noticeable**.
- **Organise the information** in a logical and eye-catching (= *accrocheur*) manner.

4 Display your poster and present it to the class.

- During your presentation, **refer to the poster** and be ready to **answer questions.**
- At the end of the presentations, the class can **vote** to decide **which cultural event will be organised** in the class.

Keys to success

- **Utilisez le vocabulaire du chapitre :** migration, communauté, célébration.
  ➡ *Words, words, words, p. 212*
- **Utilisez des *gap fillers* pour vous exprimer à l'oral.**
  ➡ *More words, p. 212*
- **Utilisez la proposition infinitive.**
  ➡ *Grammar, p. 213*
- **Faites les liaisons nécessaires pour votre présentation orale.**
  ➡ *Sounds, sounds, sounds, p. 213*
- **Servez-vous des conseils pour communiquer une information par écrit.**
  ➡ *Strategy, p. 214*

Axe 8 : Le passé dans le présent

16 Shaking up fairy tales

1 Basics

List the words that come to mind when you think of fairy tales.

WORKSHEET 32

2 Discover

Classe3 Piste 34

Listen to teenagers talking about their favourite fairy tales.
Pick out the tales they like and their reasons for liking them.

3 Play

Game

Guess who game: Ask five yes / no questions to your classmates to guess who their favourite fairy tale character is.

▶ *Does the character…? • Has the character got…? • Is he / she…?*

Your project

Write your own fairy tale, *p. 231*
- Create a twisted tale, *p. 221*
- Imagine the starting point of a new fairy tale, *p. 223*
- Write the beginning of a reinvented fairy tale, *p. 225*

Keys to success

- **Strategy: écrire une histoire,** *p. 230*
- **Mind map:** traditional tales, characters, reinvented fairy tales, *p. 226*
- **Grammar:** prétérit simple et *past perfect*, prétérit en *be* + V-*ing*, hypothèses en *if*, *p. 228*

ABC fantasy-drama *Once Upon a Time*, 7th season, 2017

How can fairy tales be reinvented?

Lire • Écouter • Écrire

Traditional tales

Once upon a time…

Contents

- The Gingerbread Man
- The Three Little Pigs
- Goldilocks and the Three Bears
- Jack and the Beanstalk
- Snow White and the Seven Dwarfs

A

B

1 "Fee-fi-fo-fum,
I smell the blood of an Englishman,
Be he alive, or be he dead
I'll grind his bones to make my bread."

2 "Run, run as fast as you can, you can't catch me…" "I ran from a husband, I ran from a wife, I ran from a butcher with a carving knife and I'll run from you too, I can, I can."

E

3 "This porridge is too hot!" she exclaimed.
So, she tasted the porridge from the second bowl.
"This porridge is too cold," she said.
So, she tasted the last bowl of porridge.
"Ahhh, this porridge is just right," she said happily and she ate it all up.

4 "Mirror, mirror, on the wall,
Who is the fairest of them all?"
The looking-glass answered,
"Thou, o Queen, art the fairest of all."

C

"Let me in, let me in (...) or I'll huff and I'll puff and I'll blow your house in!"
"Not by the hair of my chinny chin chin!"

5

D

1. Match each quote with the corresponding title and picture.
▶ *Picture X may / must illustrate quote Y… and is from… • I guess / think that… because…*

2. Listen. Classe 3 Pistes 35-39
Practise saying the refrains and **act** them **out** in front of the class.
Vote for the best performance.

3. Select one of these tales and **list** all you can remember about it (characters – opening situation – events – problem – resolution).
Check and **complete** your findings. **Write** a 5-line version of it.
Groupwork
WORKSHEET 33

They lived happily ever after…

Need help?

- **e**vil ['iːv(ə)l] **step**mother: *marâtre*
- **god**mother: *marraine*
- **king**dom: *royaume*
- knight [naɪt]: *chevalier*
- **ma**gic wand: *baguette magique*
- **o**gre
- **vi**llain ≠ **he**ro
- witch: *sorcière*
- **fright**ening = **sca**ry
- huge [hjuːdʒ] = e**nor**mous
- **jea**lous ['dʒeləs] = **en**vious
- un**for**tunately = un**luck**ily
- **res**cue ['reskjuː] = save
- run a**way** = es**cape**
- by **ma**gic: *par magie*
- cast a spell: *jeter un sort*

Grammar

Le prétérit simple et le *past perfect*

– She **had** already **fallen** asleep when the prince **arrived**.
action antérieure à l'action passée — action passée

➥ *Grammar p. 228*

Lire • Écrire • Parler

A classic tale... with a twist

DOSSIER documentaire

1. **Read** the classic tale and **complete** a table with the following elements: initial situation (characters, place, etc.) – problem – events – resolution.

2. **Do** the same with the second text. **List** the similarities and the differences between the two versions.
▶ *Like / Unlike… • Both the stories… • On the one hand… on the other hand… • X is the same as / different from…*

Pairwork

3. **Decide** what the message of each story is and **write** it down in a short sentence.
▶ *In my opinion… • It means… • It conveys a message of… • The moral could be…*

The Princess and the Pea

Once there was a Prince who wanted to marry a Princess. Only a real one would do. So he traveled through all the world to find her and everywhere things went wrong. There were Princesses aplenty[1], but how was he to know whether they were real Princesses? (...) So he came home again and was unhappy, because he did so want to have a real Princess.

One evening a terrible storm blew up. (...) In the midst of it all came a knocking at the town gate. The old King went to open it. Who should be standing outside but a Princess, and what a sight she was in all that rain and wind. (...) Yet she claimed to be a real Princess.

"We'll soon find that out," the old Queen thought to herself. Without saying a word about it she went to the bedchamber, stripped back the bedclothes, and just put one pea in the bottom of the bed. Then she took twenty mattresses and piled them on the pea. Then she took twenty eiderdown feather beds[2] and piled them on the mattresses. Up on top of all these the Princess was to spend the night.

In the morning they asked her, "Did you sleep well?"

"Oh!" said the Princess. "No, I scarcely slept at all. Heaven knows what's in that bed. I lay on something so hard that I'm black and blue all over. It was simply terrible."

They could see she was a real Princess and no question about it, now that she had felt one pea all the way through twenty mattresses and twenty more feather beds. Nobody but a Princess could be so delicate. So the Prince made haste[3] to marry her, because he knew he had found a real Princess.

Hans Christian Andersen, *Tales Told for Children*, 1835, English edition, 1846

1. aplenty (adv.): *à profusion* 2. eiderdown feather bed (n.): *édredon* 3. make haste (exp.) = hurry

Need help?

- **thick**ness: *épaisseur*
- ab**surd** [əbˈzɜːd]
- **del**icate = **sen**sitive
- dis**ho**nest
- **im**moral ≠ **mo**ral
- **i**ronic
- domi**neer**ing = con**trol**ling
- **sche**ming [ˈskiːmɪŋ] = ma**ni**pulative
- **twis**ted: *tordu*
- de**ceive** = trick: *tromper*
- de**fy**
- a**chieve** one's aims = get what one wants
- hard to please = **ne**ver **sa**tisfied

Grammar

Le prétérit en *be* + V-*ing*

– When the king **saw** her, she **was standing** in the rain.

action passée ponctuelle — circonstance

➡ *Grammar p. 229*

The Princess and the Bowling Ball

Once upon a time there was a Prince. And this Prince's dad and mom (the King and Queen) somehow got it into their royal heads that no Princess would be good enough for their boy unless she could feel a pea through one hundred mattresses.

So it should come as no surprise that the Prince had a very hard time finding a Princess. Every time he met a nice girl, his mom and dad would pile one hundred mattresses on top of a pea and then invite her to sleep over.

When the Princess came down for breakfast, the Queen would ask, "How did you sleep, dear?"

The Princess would politely say, "Fine, thank you."

And the King would show her the door.

Now this went on for three years. And of course nobody ever felt the pea under one hundred mattresses. Then one day the Prince met the girl of his dreams. He decided he better do something about it. That night, before the Princess went to bed, the Prince slipped his bowling ball under the one hundred mattresses. When the Princess came down for breakfast the next morning, the Queen asked, "How did you sleep, dear?"

"This might sound odd," said the Princess. "But I think you need another mattress. I felt like I was sleeping on a lump[1] as big as a bowling ball."

The King and Queen were satisfied.

The Prince and Princess were married.

And everyone lived happily, though maybe not completely honestly, ever after.

The End.

Jon Scieszka & Lane Smith, *The Stinky Cheese Man and Other Fairly Stupid Tales*, 1992

1. lump (n.): *bosse*

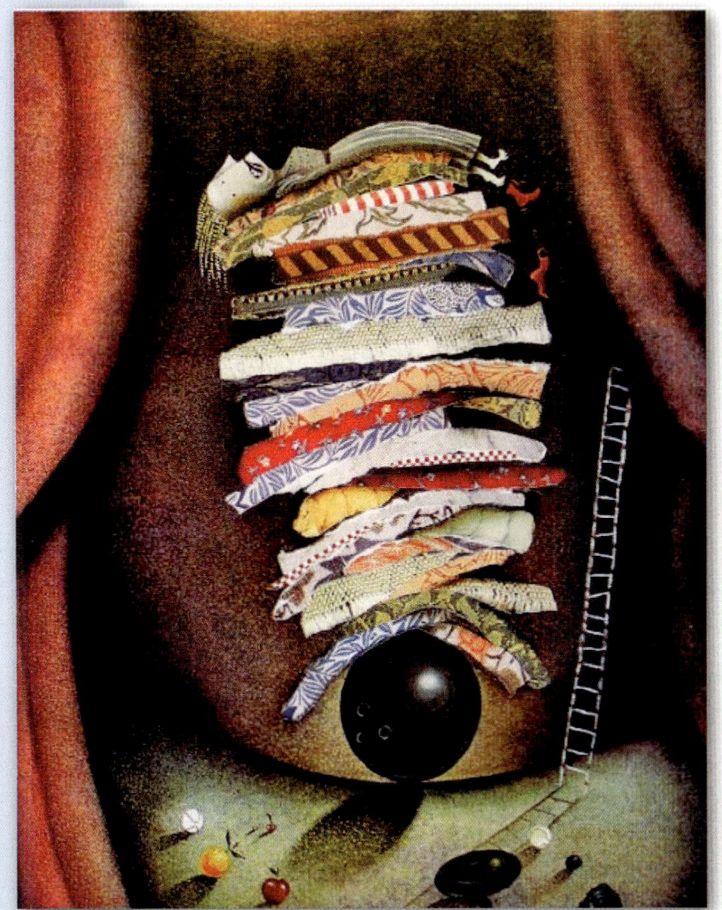

Prepare your project

Create a twisted fairy tale. Choose a classic, think of a twist, then draw a table with the essential elements: initial situation (characters, place, etc.) – problem – events – resolution. Practise telling your story. You can record yourself.

Rewriting the classics

1 Impertinent tale(s)

1. Describe the picture and find elements that are unusual.
▶ *Instead of… • Usually… • Whereas… • You would expect… • What's surprising is that…*

2. Read the text and pick out elements about the characters. Deduce which fairy tale has been rewritten.

3. List the similarities and differences with the original story (characters – events – tone – form).
WORKSHEET 34

4. Imagine the continuation of the original story. Write down your ideas and share them with the class.

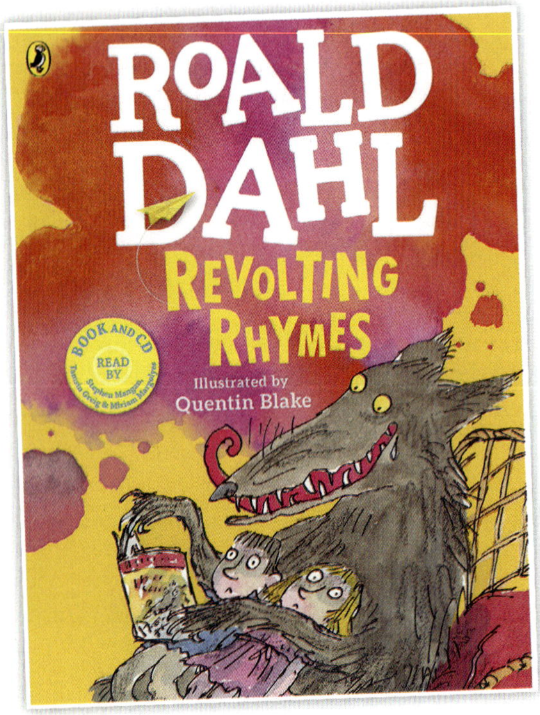

The hero tells his mum about seeing the Giant for the first time.

"Oh mum!" he gasped. "Believe you me
"There's something nasty[1] up our tree!
"I saw him, mum! My gizzard[2] froze!
"A Giant with a clever nose!
"*A clever nose!*" his mother hissed.
"You must be going round the twist[3]!"

"He smelled me out, I swear it, mum!
"He said he *smelled* an Englishman!"
The mother said, "And well he might!
"I've told you every single night
"To take a bath because you smell,
"But would you do it? Would you hell!
"You even make your mother shrink[4]
"Because of your unholy stink[5]!"
Jack answered, "Well, if you're so clean
"Why don't you climb the crazy bean."

Roald Dahl, *Revolting Rhymes*, 1982

1. nasty (adj.) = bad or unpleasant
2. gizzard (n.) = stomach
3. be going round the twist (exp.) = have lost your mind
4. shrink (v.) = move back suddenly, as in horror
5. unholy stink (exp.) = unpleasant smell

CULTURE QUEST

Discover the videos of Roald Dahl's *Revolting Rhymes*.
Keywords: *Revolting Rhymes* - BBC / CSW - *Cinderella / Little Red Riding Hood / Jack and the Beanstalk.*

Need help?

- bedtime story
- verse = rhyming line
- humorous = comical
- rude = not polite
- unexpected = surprising
- answer back = reply impertinently
- criticise sb for = blame sb for
- eat up = devour
- mix up: *mélanger*
- refer to = be a reference to
- switch = reverse
- make fun of = laugh at
- turn sth upside down: *renverser*

2 Crossover tales

Bill Watterson, *Calvin and Hobbes*, 1990

1. hold it (exp.) = wait
2. untimely demise (exp.): *mort prématurée*

1. **Read** and **identify** the characters then **pick out** the fairy tales that are mentioned.
2. **Use** the cartoon to **explain** what a "crossover story" is.
3. **Develop** the story the little boy wants to hear.
   ▶ *Once upon a time…* • *All of a sudden…* • *When, unexpectedly…* • *So, who could believe…*
4. **Imagine** a pitch for your own crossover using characters from fairy tales that you know (for example: Fairy Godmother – Tom Thumb – The Little Mermaid – Rapunzel – The Ugly Duckling). Share with the class and **vote** for the most original ideas.

Did you know?

Many **popular films** based on fairy tales use crossovers to create new stories: *Into the Woods* (2014), *Hoodwinked* (2005), *Shrek* (2001-2010).

Prepare your project

What if the Big Bad Wolf married Sleeping Beauty?

What if Hansel and Gretel met Little Red Riding Hood when walking in the deep dark woods?

Write a "what if" question for a crossover tale.
Pairwork: Give it to your partner who has to make up a story orally.
Then do the same with your partner's "what if" question.

Grammar

Les hypothèses en *if*

– **If** I **were** very rich, I **would buy** a big castle.
if + prét. modal — *would* + BV

➥ *Grammar p. 229*

Écouter • Lire • Partager • Écrire

New figures for our times

Différenciation

You are going to learn about modern fairy tales.
Work on **one of these topics** to discover different types of rewritings.

Step 1: Pick out information and take notes (main strategy – similarities / differences with original fairy tales – reasons for creating such stories).

Médiation **Step 2:** GROUPWORK Share your findings. WORKSHEET 38

TOPIC 1 vidéo Changing points of view

WORKSHEET 35

1. **Look** at the picture and **list** the elements you know about the film (characters – original fairy tale – point of view).
2. **Watch** and **find out** more about the retold story and the message.
3. Use what you have found to **sum up** what was changed in the story and **give** the reasons.

Angelina Jolie playing an evil fairy in Disney's 2014 film *Maleficent*

"Like that?"

TOPIC 2 Changing roles

Classe Piste 4

WORKSHEET 36

1. **Look** at the cartoon and **write** a short paragraph to give your opinion.
   ▶ *It is quite surprising / unusual to see... • I really like the fact that...*
2. **Listen** to Jeanette Winterson and **find out** more about the subject.
3. **Use** what you have found to **write** notes explaining the role fairy tales can have today.

CULTURE QUEST

Watch the video (from 00:00 to 1:29).
Keywords: *If Cinderella were a guy – rebelgirls.*

TOPIC 3 A real-life fairy tale WORKSHEET 37

1. Look at the picture and write down your impressions about the people represented.

2. Read the text to find out information about the main character.

3. Use what you have found to prepare notes explaining what real-life fairy tales are.

Rosa Parks (1913-2005), an illustration by Matthew Land

Once upon a time, Montgomery, Alabama was a segregated city. Black people and white people went to different schools, prayed in different churches, shopped in different stores, rode different elevators, and drank from different drinking fountains. Everyone rode the same buses, but they had to sit in different areas: white people up front, black people at the back. Rosa Parks grew up in this black-and-white world. It was hard for black people, and many were angry and sad because of segregation, but if they protested, they were thrown in jail.

One day, forty-two-year-old Rosa was sitting in the back of a bus on her way home from work. It was crowded, and there were not enough seats in the front section (the one reserved for whites), so the driver told Rosa to give up her seat so a white person could sit down.

Rosa said no.

She spent the night in jail, but this one brave act showed people that it was possible to say no to injustice.

Rosa's friends declared a boycott. They asked every single black person not to use any of the buses in the city until the law was changed. The word spread fast and wide. The boycott lasted for 381 days. It ended when bus segregation was declared unconstitutional by the U.S. Supreme Court. It took ten years for segregation to be banned in any other state, but it happened finally, thanks to Rosa's first, brave, "No".

Elena Favili and Francesca Cavallo, *Good Night Stories for Rebel Girls*, 2017

Prepare your project

Select one of the types of reinvented tales you've discovered and write the beginning of your own story.

Need help?

- role **mo**del = **i**dol
- sword [sɔːd]

- **help**less = de**fense**less
- re**be**llious = diso**be**dient
- self-su**ffi**cient = self-re**li**ant
- **ste**reotyped
- sub**mi**ssive = o**be**dient

- de**feat** = **van**quish
- **iden**tify with
- slay = kill

- be dis**cri**minated against
- fend for oneself: *se débrouiller seul(e)*
- strength of **cha**racter
- take re**venge** on sb

Mémoriser • Prononcer • Écrire

Words, words, words

➥ Faire une carte mentale p. 234
➥ Mémoriser et enrichir son lexique p. 235

Quizlet
quizlet.com/skysthelimit2e

Classe 3 – Pistes 41-49 – 97 105

Créez votre propre carte mentale à partir de ce que vous avez vu en classe. Vous pourrez ensuite l'enrichir à l'aide de celle-ci. Écoutez les mots et répétez-les pour bien les prononcer. Écrivez-les aussi plusieurs fois pour mémoriser leur orthographe.

How can fairy tales be reinvented?

CHARACTERS

- **Roles**
  - big bad wolf
  - giant
  - knight
  - witch
  - evil stepmother
  - godmother
  - ogre
  - prince charming
  - villain ≠ hero

TRADITIONAL TALES

- **Action**
  - climb up / climb down
  - rescue
  - run away
  - eat up = devour
  - cast a spell
  - slay = kill
  - defeat = vanquish
- **Context**
  - castle = palace
  - kingdom
  - deep dark woods
  - sword
  - magic wand
- **Narrative elements**
  - once upon a time
  - happily ever after
  - bedtime story
  - all of a sudden
  - unexpectedly

REINVENTED FAIRY TALES

- **(Impertinent) behaviour**
  - answer back = reply impertinently
  - rebellious = disobedient
  - rude = not polite
  - make fun of = laugh at
  - take revenge on sb
  - deceive = trick

Attitude
- manipulative
- delicate = sensitive
- dishonest
- controlling
- helpless = defenseless
- submissive

Role models
- self-sufficient = self-reliant
- identify with
- fend for oneself
- strength of character

Interpretation
- immoral ≠ moral
- absurd
- criticise sb for = blame sb for
- ironic
- humorous = comical
- refer to

Changes
- point of view
- rewriting
- crossover (story / tale)
- twist (a story)
- switch = reverse
- mix up

More words

Les connecteurs et les marqueurs de temps

Repères, p. 252

Once upon a time there was an old king who had no children. **One day**, he decided to ask a witch for help. She gave him three little peas and told him to plant them in the castle garden. **The day after**, three little babies appeared where the king had sown the magical peas. **Then** the babies grew up and became three beautiful princesses. The king was **finally** reassured and lived happily **ever after**.

L'essentiel

Les connecteurs et les marqueurs de temps permettent de rendre les étapes d'une histoire claires pour le lecteur.

- **Les connecteurs :**
Pour indiquer **l'ordre des actions**, on peut utiliser par exemple : *once (upon a time) – first – then – later – in the end – eventually – finally – ever after – while – meanwhile – in the meantime.*

Attention aux faux amis : *eventually* signifie « finalement » !

- **Les marqueurs de temps :**
Pour indiquer quand une action a eu lieu, on utilise des marqueurs temporels, comme : *a long time ago – on a stormy night – on a bright morning – on a snowy day – the day before – the day after – ten years earlier – a hundred years before – on a cold winter's day.*

1. Choisissez parmi les marqueurs de temps ceux qui permettent de compléter les phrases.

in the end – one day – a long time ago – some time later – while

(1), in a magical kingdom far far away, lived a fearless little girl. (2), she decided it was time to kill the wicked witch who terrorised her village. (3) she was away, the villagers started to believe the little girl was dead. But (4), she returned to the village and the witch was never seen again. (5), she was honoured as a heroine for the rest of her life.

2. Remettez dans l'ordre les phrases et ajoutez des connecteurs et marqueurs temporels quand c'est nécessaire.

a. The little pig ran home and closed the door just in time.
b. His mother told him never to go to this dangerous place.
c. The wolf tried to catch the pig but he was old and weak from hunger.
d. His mother was really worried.
e. A hungry old wolf was hiding in the forest.
f. The little pig did not believe his mother and decided to go look for mushrooms.
g. There was a little pig who wanted to explore the deep dark woods.
h. The little pig promised never to go into the woods again.
i. The mother could not find her son anywhere.

Grammar

Le prétérit simple et le *past perfect* Repères, p. 249-250

» Le prétérit simple

– The prince **entered** the cave and **killed** the dragon.
V + *-ed* ... V + *-ed*

– The witch **didn't like** the young boy.
did + *not* + BV

– **Did** the second little pig **build** a solid house?
did ... + BV

» Le *past perfect*

– She **had** already **fallen** asleep when the prince **arrived**.
action antérieure à l'action passée ... action passée

– The little boy **tried** to remember everything the magic frog **had told** him.
action passée ... action antérieure à action passée

L'essentiel

Pour relater des faits passés, on peut utiliser soit le prétérit simple, soit le *past perfect*.

• Le **prétérit** sert à raconter des faits passés, coupés du présent. C'est le temps qu'on utilise dans les récits. Il se forme ainsi pour les verbes réguliers : V + *-ed*.

• Le ***past perfect*** permet d'exprimer une action antérieure à une action passée. Il se forme ainsi : *had* + participe passé (V + *-ed* pour les verbes réguliers).

Attention : Beaucoup de verbes sont irréguliers ; il faut les connaître par cœur !

➥ *Verbes irréguliers p. 264*

1. Réécrivez les phrases en mettant le verbe à la forme qui convient.

Why the witch (*poison*) Snow White?
→ *Why did the witch poison Snow White?*

a. The dragon (*not – enjoy*) kidnapping princesses.
b. The giant (*already – rescue*) the princess, when the prince (*arrive*).
c. Why Hansel and Gretel (*walk*) through the woods alone?
d. When they (*get lost*) in the woods, they (*realise*) their parents (trap) them.
e. The evil queen (*feel*) jealous of her beauty.
f. The little pigs (*not – listen*) to their mother.
g. Before Snow White (*come*) to see her, the witch (*already – poison*) the apple.

2. Pour chaque phrase, faites une frise chronologique sur laquelle vous indiquerez l'ordre dans lequel les actions se déroulent.

The brother and sister **arrived** (A) at the witch's house and **started** (B) eating it after their parents **had abandoned** (C) them in the woods.

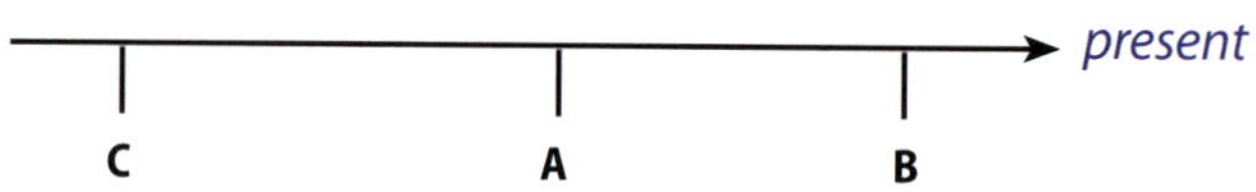

a. She **had heard** (A) of fairies a long time ago but **she did not believe** (B) in them anymore.
b. The dwarves **were** (A) very **surprised** when they **found** (B) the young princess who **had fallen** (C) asleep on one of their beds.
c. The frog **had told** (A) the princess to kiss him but she **had refused** (B).

Le prétérit en *be* + V-*ing* Repères, p. 250

– When the king **saw** her, she **was standing** in the rain.
(saw: action passée ponctuelle; was standing: circonstance)

– The moon **was shining**. The prince **looked up and saw** the princess at her window.
(was shining: circonstance; looked up and saw: actions passées ponctuelles)

L'essentiel
- Pour décrire les circonstances d'une action dans un récit au passé, on utilise le **prétérit en *be* + V-*ing*** (*was / were* + V-*ing*).

3. Mettez les verbes entre parenthèses à la forme qui convient (prétérit simple ou prétérit en *be* + V-*ing*).

The ogre (*have*) breakfast when the little boy (*arrive*).
→ *The ogre was having breakfast when the little boy arrived.*

a. As he (*walk*) towards the enchanted forest, he (*hear*) a call for help.
b. The wicked witch (*prepare*) her potion when her glasses (*fall*) in the cauldron.
c. The princess (*brush*) her long hair and (*sing*) when Prince Charming (*hear*) her beautiful voice.

4. Faites des phrases au prétérit simple ou au prétérit en *be* + V-*ing*. Faites les changements nécessaires.

prepare – The Three Little Pigs – the wolf – the fire – arrive
→ *The Three Little Pigs were preparing the fire when the wolf arrived.*

a. Snow White – the house – the witch – clean – arrive – when
b. the wolf – pick flowers – her – Little Red Riding Hood – surprise – when
c. celebrate – Maleficent – their daughter's birth – The king and queen – when – appear

Les hypothèses en *if* Repères, p. 262

– **If** I **were** very rich, I **would buy** a big castle.
(If ... were: *if* + prét. modal; would buy: *would* + BV)

– **If** she **lived** in the Bahamas, she **wouldn't be** able to build an ice castle.
(If ... lived: *if* + prét. modal; wouldn't be: *would* + *not* + BV)

L'essentiel
- Pour exprimer une hypothèse, on utilise *if* + prétérit modal puis *would* + BV pour exprimer la conséquence de cette condition.

Attention : Pour le verbe *be*, on utilise *were* à toutes les personnes.

5. Remettez les groupes de mots dans l'ordre.

listened – If – to the wolf. – she – Little Red Riding Hood – wouldn't talk – to her mother
→ *If Little Red Riding Hood listened to her mother, she wouldn't talk to the wolf.*

a. saw – would – the wicked witch – If – you – she – eat you up.
b. herself. – did not come – If – the princess – the dragon – the prince – would have to kill
c. the bears – would be – If – made – happy. – Goldilocks – a cake

Sounds, sounds, sounds

La terminaison en *-ed* Repères, p. 246

L'essentiel
- La prononciation de la **terminaison en *-ed*** varie en fonction du dernier son de la base verbale :
  - quand le dernier son est [k], [p], [s], [ʃ], [f], [tʃ] ou [θ] → le *-ed* se prononce [t] : *stopped, locked* ;
  - quand le dernier son de la base verbale est [t] ou [d] → le *-ed* se prononce [ɪd] : *added, arrested* ;
  - pour les autres bases verbales → le *-ed* se prononce [d] : *stayed, rained.*

Classe 3 – Piste 50 – 106

1. Écoutez et classez les verbes en fonction de la prononciation de leur terminaison en *-ed*.

carried – changed – transformed – selected – asked – answered – trapped – played – followed

Classe 3 – Piste 51 – 107

2. Lisez à voix haute les verbes en *-ed* de l'exercice 2 en veillant à bien prononcer la terminaison. Écoutez pour vérifier.

STRATEGY ÉCRIRE UNE HISTOIRE

Pour réussir à rédiger une histoire, il faut savoir...

AU BROUILLON

1 ... préparer son récit :

- **Définissez la situation initiale :** qui ? quoi ? quand ? où ? comment ?
- **Planifiez les étapes du récit :** situation initiale – élément perturbateur – péripéties – dénouement.
- **Choisissez le ton :** optimiste ? tragique ? critique ? humoristique ?

AU PROPRE

2 ... rédiger son histoire en respectant les règles du récit :

- **Utilisez les temps du récit :**

  prétérit simple | prétérit en *be* + V-*ing* | *past perfect*

- **Utilisez des marqueurs de temps** pour montrer la chronologie des événements et les **connecteurs** pour relier les idées entre elles :

  → *Once upon a time • a long time ago • then • X years / days later • at the same time • while • meanwhile • as*

- **Respectez la ponctuation** (guillemets – points d'interrogation – d'exclamation) et **allez à la ligne** pour le changement de locuteur.

  "What are you doing, good old woman?" asked the princess.
  "I am spinning, my pretty child."

- **Variez les verbes introducteurs** pour les dialogues :

  say • explain • ask • agree • answer • insist • laugh • scream • exclaim • whisper

- **Utilisez des adjectifs** pour enrichir la description du décor et des personnages :

  Jack was a giddy, thoughtless boy, but very kind-hearted and affectionate.

- **Relisez-vous** une fois la rédaction terminée !

Your project | Write a fairy tale

Groupwork

Su Blackwell, *Once Upon a Time*, 2016

Your are participating in a writing competition: write your own fairy tale.

1 Choose the style of your story.

- **Rewriting** of a classic fairy tale, **crossover**, **twisted** fairy tale, **modern** fairy tale or a mix of different styles.

2 Agree on the basic elements.

- Initial situation (characters – setting – time and place), problem(s), events, resolution.

3 Develop the characters and decide on the tone.

- **Physical appearance**, personality of the main characters, how they interact, their role in the story…
- **Tone**: humorous, tragic, overdramatic.

4 Assign tasks for each member of your group.

- **Share** the different parts of the story and / or write collaboratively (you can use an online platform).

5 Proof-read your story.

- Make sure your story is **coherent** from beginning to end.
- **Check** the verb forms, the spelling and the punctuation (especially for the dialogues). Practise reading it aloud.

6 Read or listen to your classmates' stories.

- **Vote** for the best story, most original / inspiring story or (re)writing, funniest adaptation, best crossover, etc.

Keys to success

- **Utilisez le vocabulaire du chapitre :** contes traditionnels, personnages, contes revisités.
  ➥ *Words, words, words, p. 226*
- **Utilisez des connecteurs et des marqueurs de temps pour construire votre récit.**
  ➥ *More words, p. 227*
- **Pensez à utiliser correctement les temps du récit (prétérit simple et en *be* + V-*ing*, *past perfect*).**
  ➥ *Grammar, p. 228*
- **Appliquez les conseils pour écrire une histoire.**
  ➥ *Strategy, p. 230*
- **Utilisez les conseils pour travailler en groupe.**
  ➥ *Strategy, p. 237*

Outils pour réussir et gagner en autonomie en 2de

Stratégies transversales

MP3, repères et banque d'exercices

▶ Lexique et phonologie

▶ Grammaire

Corrigés disponibles sur **lycee.editions-bordas.fr**

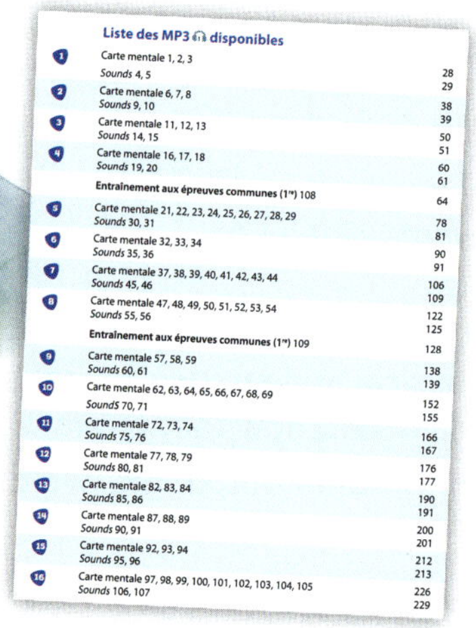

Liste des MP3 disponibles

1	Carte mentale 1, 2, 3	28
	Sounds 4, 5	29
2	Carte mentale 6, 7, 8	38
	Sounds 9, 10	39
3	Carte mentale 11, 12, 13	50
	Sounds 14, 15	51
4	Carte mentale 16, 17, 18	60
	Sounds 19, 20	61
	Entraînement aux épreuves communes (1re) 108	64
5	Carte mentale 21, 22, 23, 24, 25, 26, 27, 28, 29	78
	Sounds 30, 31	81
6	Carte mentale 32, 33, 34	90
	Sounds 35, 36	91
7	Carte mentale 37, 38, 39, 40, 41, 42, 43, 44	106
	Sounds 45, 46	109
8	Carte mentale 47, 48, 49, 50, 51, 52, 53, 54	122
	Sounds 55, 56	125
	Entraînement aux épreuves communes (1re) 109	128
9	Carte mentale 57, 58, 59	138
	Sounds 60, 61	139
10	Carte mentale 62, 63, 64, 65, 66, 67, 68, 69	152
	SoundS 70, 71	155
11	Carte mentale 72, 73, 74	166
	Sounds 75, 76	167
12	Carte mentale 77, 78, 79	176
	Sounds 80, 81	177
13	Carte mentale 82, 83, 84	190
	Sounds 85, 86	191
14	Carte mentale 87, 88, 89	200
	Sounds 90, 91	201
15	Carte mentale 92, 93, 94	212
	Sounds 95, 96	213
16	Carte mentale 97, 98, 99, 100, 101, 102, 103, 104, 105	226
	Sounds 106, 107	229

Et aussi des entraînements numériques

▶ Activités *Quizlet* pour réviser le lexique de la séquence

▶ Banque d'exercices grammaticaux autocorrectifs

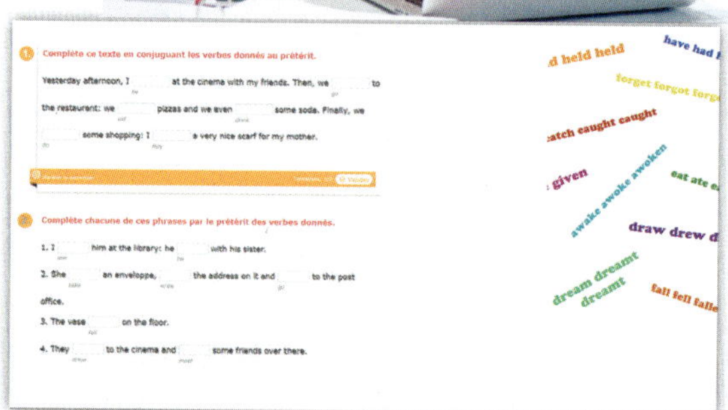

1 Complète ce texte en conjuguant les verbes donnés au prétérit.

Yesterday afternoon, I ____ at the cinema with my friends. Then, we ____ to the restaurant: we ____ pizzas and we even ____ some soda. Finally, we ____ some shopping: I ____ a very nice scarf for my mother.

2 Complète chacune de ces phrases par le prétérit des verbes donnés.

1. I ____ him at the library: he ____ with his sister.
2. She ____ an envelope, ____ the address on it and ____ to the post office.
3. The vase ____ on the floor.
4. They ____ to the cinema and ____ some friends over there.

STRATÉGIE S'EXPRIMER DEVANT UN PUBLIC

Pour s'exprimer devant un public, il faut :

1 ... adopter la bonne posture :

- **Tenez-vous droit(e)** sans être raide, la tête haute et de préférence **debout**.
- **Prenez une posture synonyme de confiance et de disponibilité :** ne croisez pas les bras, ne mettez pas les mains dans les poches et ne vous cachez pas derrière votre feuille.

2 ... regarder votre auditoire :

- **Appuyez-vous** sur votre **auditoire**. Commencez par identifier une personne qui vous semble **bienveillante** et focalisez-vous sur elle. Puis, quand vous aurez pris **confiance**, élargissez votre champ visuel.
- **Établissez** un **contact visuel** pour capter l'attention et savoir si vous devez ralentir ou reformuler un point.

3 ... soigner votre gestuelle :

- **Utilisez vos mains** pour accompagner votre discours.
- Adaptez vos gestes et votre ton **à l'esprit de votre message** : si le sujet est léger, pensez à sourire ; si vous voulez convaincre votre auditoire, soyez enthousiaste et cherchez son approbation.

__Si vous avez la possibilité, faites filmer__ votre prestation pour l'analyser et l'améliorer.

4 ... vous assurer d'être compréhensible :

- **Parlez suffisamment fort :** tout le monde dans la salle doit pouvoir **vous entendre** sans difficulté.
- **Parlez lentement :** prenez votre temps et articulez pour que le message soit le plus clair possible.

5 ... utiliser un langage propre à l'oral :

- Faites des phrases **courtes et simples.** Utilisez du vocabulaire connu de tous. **Accentuez les mots-clés** de la phrase pour les faire ressortir.
- Utilisez des ***gap-fillers*** (*well... • actually... • you know... • how can I put it...*) pour prendre le temps de réfléchir à la suite de votre message.

Ne craignez pas de faire des erreurs ! L'important est de s'exprimer de manière naturelle, quitte à en faire quelques-unes.

STRATÉGIE | FAIRE UNE CARTE MENTALE

À QUOI SERT UNE CARTE MENTALE ?

- Répondre à une question centrale
- Réviser un sujet
- Créer un visuel synthétique
- Réviser son vocabulaire

Pour réussir à faire une carte mentale, il faut :

1 … préparer la structure générale en amont :

→ Notez le **thème**, la **question centrale** au milieu.

→ Ajoutez les **branches principales** correspondant aux sous-thèmes.

Vous pouvez utiliser une couleur par branche.

2 … faire un *brainstorming* et classer ses idées :

→ Notez tous les **mots** qui vous viennent **spontanément** à l'esprit, dans le désordre. Faites des associations d'idées.

Laissez libre cours à votre créativité, ne vous censurez pas.

→ Essayez d'**ordonner** vos idées.

3 … remplir sa carte :

→ Vous pouvez créer une carte mentale seul(e) ou en groupe.

→ Il n'y a pas de bonne ou mauvaise carte.

→ Créez des **sous-branches**. Vous les remplirez **intégralement** avant de passer à une autre ou vous les compléterez **simultanément**.

4 … la faire évoluer au fil de la réflexion :

→ **Mettez votre carte de côté** et regardez-la à nouveau.

→ **Enrichissez-la**. Soulignez les mots-clés.

→ Établissez des **liens** entre les mots / idées.

5 … la finaliser :

→ Mettez votre carte mentale **au propre**.

Vous pouvez la réaliser sur une feuille de papier ou en numérique : Framindmap, Xmind8, Popplet, Mindnode, Vocabulary Box pour tablettes.

→ **Illustrez-la** en intégrant des dessins, des photos. Cela vous aidera à la mémoriser.

STRATÉGIE — MÉMORISER ET ENRICHIR SON LEXIQUE

Quizlet
quizlet.com/skysthelimit2e

Pour mémoriser et enrichir son lexique, il faut :

1 ... utiliser sa mémoire de manière efficace :

- **Associez** les **éléments** à apprendre soit de manière **visuelle** (en associant une image mentale ou réelle), **auditive** (en écoutant et répétant les mots) ou **corporelle** (en écrivant les mots ou en associant un geste).
- **Jouez pour mémoriser :** créez vos propres jeux, testez les jeux proposés par différentes plateformes (*British Council* ou *Quizlet*).
- **Revoyez le lexique nouveau** 24 heures, puis 1 semaine et enfin 1 mois après la première leçon pour optimiser la mémorisation.

2 ... classer le lexique :

- **Regroupez les mots** selon la logique qui vous convient : champs lexicaux, ressemblance phonétique, associations d'idées...
- Créez vos propres **listes** ou **cartes mentales.**
  ➥ *Faire une carte mentale p. 234*

Vous pouvez enrichir ces listes au fur et à mesure de l'année scolaire et même tout au long de votre vie !

3 ... créer des liens :

- Appuyez-vous sur la **dérivation** et la **composition** pour enrichir votre lexique. ➥ *Repères grammaticaux p. 257 et 260*
- **Apprenez les mots associés** en même temps qu'un nouveau terme. Exemple : avec *time* : *waste time / spend some time / free time / dead on time...*
- Cherchez des **synonymes** et des **antonymes**.

Le dictionnaire en ligne wordreference.com contient des rubriques pour les associations de mots et les synonymes, testez-les.

4 ... se servir du lexique :

- **Multipliez les occasions** d'utiliser le lexique nouveau : il faut utiliser un terme nouveau environ 10 fois pour bien le mémoriser.
- Créez des **énoncés**, des **histoires** ou même des **chansons** dans lesquelles vous réinvestissez le lexique nouveau.

Testez le lexique nouveau en participant en classe et utilisez-le en dehors du lycée. ➥ ***English is everywhere** p. 14*

STRATÉGIE | APPRENDRE SA LEÇON

Pour bien apprendre sa leçon, il faut :

1. ... être dans de **bonnes conditions** : travailler au fur et à mesure ; seul(e), en binôme ou en groupe (en fonction de la tâche à effectuer).

2. **... lire / écouter plusieurs fois** le(s) document(s) (textes, images, graphiques, audios ou vidéos) vus en cours et **relire** la leçon.

3. ... utiliser des **couleurs** pour souligner ce qui est à retenir (lexique, structures, temps, etc.).

4. ... vérifier dans un **dictionnaire le sens** et la **prononciation** des mots que vous ne connaissez pas. Recopiez-les plusieurs fois pour bien les mémoriser. Écoutez leur prononciation sur les dictionnaires en ligne.
➥ *Utiliser un dictionnaire p. 238*

5. ... relire les pages ***Language in use*** de chaque séquence, **utiliser** les **Repères grammaticaux** et **phonologiques** du manuel pour revoir un point dont vous ne vous souvenez pas ou que vous avez besoin d'approfondir. N'hésitez pas à faire quelques exercices de grammaire ➥ *p. 266* ou dans votre manuel numérique.

6. **... lire** votre leçon à haute voix ou l'écrire plusieurs fois pour vous aider à la **mémoriser**.

7. **... restituer** votre leçon par écrit puis vérifier que votre restitution est correcte en relisant la leçon.

8. ... vous entraîner à **créer des phrases personnelles** à partir des éléments retenus.

9. ... vous entraîner à **enchaîner des phrases** sans vous interrompre en vous enregistrant.

10. **... vous auto-évaluer :** imaginer les questions qu'on peut vous poser et tenter d'y répondre à l'oral ou à l'écrit.

STRATÉGIE | TRAVAILLER EN GROUPE

1
Définir en équipe les objectifs du projet

Un travail en équipe implique une **participation active** de chacun (chef de projet – responsable recherches / mise en pages / prise de notes, etc.). Au moment de l'attribution des tâches, pensez à valoriser les compétences de chacun.

Indiquez les **moyens à mettre en œuvre** pour atteindre vos objectifs. Identifiez les **forces** de votre équipe et les **zones de risque** de votre projet.

2
Donner un rôle à chaque membre de l'équipe

3
Se mettre d'accord sur le planning et les dates limites pour chaque tâche

Partez de la date finale de rendu pour **établir un planning** en intégrant des étapes de validation intermédiaires. Attention, la création des ressources peut prendre beaucoup de temps.

4
Réaliser votre travail

Faites le point régulièrement avec les autres membres de l'équipe pour vous assurer que vous êtes dans les temps.

5
Finaliser le projet.

→ **Congrats! Good teamwork!**

STRATÉGIE | UTILISER UN DICTIONNAIRE

It's raining cats and dogs.

Pour bien utiliser un dictionnaire, il faut :

1 ... sélectionner le bon outil :

- **Utilisez les dictionnaires** (papier ou en ligne) plutôt que les traducteurs automatiques en ligne qui ne tiennent pas toujours compte du contexte dans lequel le mot est employé.
- Choisissez le **dictionnaire qui correspond à vos besoins** : traduction, prononciation, expressions en contexte, synonymes...

Assurez-vous que l'orthographe du mot que vous recherchez est correcte, faites attention aux homonymes.

2 ... faire attention au contexte :

- **Lisez les exemples en contexte** que les dictionnaires vous donnent pour vous assurer que la traduction correspond à ce que vous voulez dire ou au sens que vous recherchez.

Pour être sûr(e) que vous avez choisi la bonne traduction, vérifiez-la dans la section anglais-français de votre dictionnaire.

- **Choisissez le sens approprié :** un même mot, en anglais comme en français, peut avoir plusieurs sens. Exemple : le mot *chip* peut se traduire par « frite », « jeton », « puce électronique » ou « copeau ».

Les expressions idiomatiques sont souvent très différentes en anglais et en français. Exemple : It's raining cats and dogs. → *Il pleut des cordes.*

3 ... apprendre à décrypter les signes :

- Soyez attentif(ve) aux **abréviations** qui vous donnent des informations sur la nature des mots (n., adj., adv., v.).
- **Vérifiez la classe grammaticale du mot** en fonction du contexte : un même mot peut être un nom, un adjectif, un verbe...

De nombreux dictionnaires en ligne proposent aussi un enregistrement du mot. Il suffit de cliquer sur le 🔊 pour écouter sa prononciation.

Quelques dictionnaires en ligne :

- Traduction : wordreference.com/fr – dictionary.cambridge.org
- Synonymes : thesaurus.com
- Prononciation : dictionary.cambridge.org ou merriam-webster.com
- Expressions en contexte : linguee.fr
- Définitions simples : learnersdictionary.com

STRATÉGIE FAIRE DES RECHERCHES EN LIGNE

Pour faire des recherches en ligne, il faut :

1 ... définir ce que l'on recherche :

- Posez-vous les **questions** suivantes : qu'est-ce que je cherche ? et pour quoi faire ?
- Dressez une **liste de mots-clés** liés au sujet de votre recherche.
- Précisez dans les paramètres de recherche avancée le **type de contenu** recherché : **image** ou **vidéo**, **pays de publication**, **format** du fichier...

Saisissez uniquement les mots-clés dans la boîte de recherche : les mots tels que a, an, the, is, and *ne sont pas pris en compte.*

2 ... vérifier la nature du site :

- Regardez les lettres à la fin d'une adresse : elles indiquent la **nature du site**.

Sources généralement sûres : .gov – .org – .edu (site éducatif). Site commercial : .com (attention aux publicités).

- N'oubliez pas que les auteurs de **blogs**, **vidéos YouTube**, **pages Facebook**, etc., donnent leur opinion, ce qui ne constitue pas forcément une information fiable.

3 ... évaluer la fiabilité des sites :

- Assurez-vous que l'**orthographe** et la **grammaire** sont correctes.
- Vérifiez que l'**auteur** et les **sources** sont identifiables.

Remarque : *Bien que Wikipedia puisse être utile pour commencer des recherches et trouver des liens vers d'autres ressources, ce site ne constitue pas toujours une source fiable.*

4 ... s'assurer de la précision des informations :

- Remontez toujours à la **source** d'une information : lorsqu'une autre source est mentionnée sur un site, allez directement à cette source.
- **Croisez les différentes informations** que vous trouvez.

5 ... classer les informations :

- Enregistrez les pages intéressantes.
- **Classez** et / ou **renommez** les pages enregistrées pour les retrouver plus facilement.

N'oubliez jamais de citer vos sources (nom de l'auteur, date de la publication, titre de l'article, adresse du site).

STRATÉGIE | DÉCRYPTER UNE IMAGE FIXE

Pour décrypter une image fixe, il faut :

1 ... identifier les éléments essentiels du document :

- **Nature :** *painting – cartoon – drawing – screenshot – photo.*
- **Auteur :** *photographer – artist – advertising agency.*
- **Sujet :** *landscape – historical event – everyday life.*
- **Contexte** (pays, époque, artiste, sujet, exposition) : *It comes from...* • *It was taken in...* • *It was drawn / painted by...* • *It's entitled...*
- **Destinataire :** *customers – magazine readers – general public.*

2 ... analyser le document :

➥ *Analyser une image p. 123*

Joshua Reynolds, *George Clive and his Family with Indian Maid*, 1765.

- **Ce que l'on voit, l'explicite :**

It's composed of... | *It shows / represents / depicts...* | *He / She looks...* | *As far as I can see, they...*

  - personnages – objets – contexte – positionnement des éléments – point de vue des personnages ;
  - plans : *in the foreground – background – middle – center ;*
  - composition (diagonales – angles de vue – horizons – point focal) ;
  - couleurs, ombres, lumières.

- **Ce à quoi cela nous fait penser, l'implicite :**
  - les personnages / la situation : ce qui vient de se passer, ce qui va se passer après, ce que pensent les personnages ;
  - ce que l'image évoque pour vous.

It makes me feel... | *I can't help thinking about...* | *It's thought-provoking...* | *It's actually quite funny...*

- **Ce à quoi l'auteur a peut-être pensé** (un thème, un événement historique ou culturel).
- **L'objectif que l'auteur avait en tête :** *persuade – convince – inform – move – attract – appeal to – denounce – shock – warn.*

3 ... interpréter :

- **Concluez sur le sens véhiculé** par l'image selon vous.

What the author probably wants to highlight... | *He aims at -V-ing...* | *He may want to make us + BV...*

- **Donnez votre avis** (avez-vous aimé ? avez-vous été ému ?...).

I find it + adj. | *What I find + adj. is that ...*

L'analyse d'une image répond à des codes, mais peut garder une part personnelle.

STRATÉGIE DÉCRYPTER UNE IMAGE MOBILE

Pour décrypter une image mobile, il faut :

1 ... identifier le document :

→ **Nature :** *film / movie (adventure – musical – science fiction – comedy – cartoon – horror film – fantasy film...) – advert – documentary – trailer.*

→ **Auteur :** *film director – journalist – advertiser – YouTuber.*

→ **Sujet** et **contexte** (pays, époque, exposition).

2 ... analyser le document :

The movie *The Birds*, by Alfred Hitchcock, 1963

→ **Ce que l'on voit, l'explicite :**

- → les mouvements de caméra : *long shot* (plan d'ensemble) – *full shot* (plan moyen) – *medium shot* (plan américain) – *close-up* (gros plan) ;
- → le cadrage et les angles de prise de vue : *high-angle shot* (plongée) – *low-angle shot* (contre-plongée) – *zoom in / on ;*
- → le cadre : *set* (décors) – *special effects – shoot in the studio / on location* (en extérieur) ;
- → les effets de caméra : *fade* (fondu) – *sharpness* (netteté) – *freeze frame* (arrêt sur image) – *in daylight – speed* (vitesse) ;
- → le montage *(editing).*

The editing gives the impression that…

The quick sequencing of the images…

The fast / slow motion emphasizes the impression that…

→ **Ce à quoi cela nous fait penser, l'implicite :** les impressions générées par le rythme, l'enchaînement des images, les associations.

3 ... interpréter :

→ **Concluez sur le sens véhiculé** par les choix du réalisateur.

The director probably intended to…

It illustrates…

The creator of the video obviously intended to…

→ **Donnez votre avis** (avez-vous aimé ? été ému ?...).

To me… In my opinion…

It reminds me of…

L'analyse d'une vidéo répond à des codes, mais peut garder une part personnelle.

STRATÉGIE — RENDRE COMPTE D'UN TEXTE À L'ÉCRIT

Pour rendre compte d'un texte à l'écrit, il faut :

1 ... comprendre les grandes lignes du document :

- Relevez les **éléments périphériques pertinents** (nature du document – titre – date – auteur – année).
- Suite à la première lecture, notez les **points essentiels** (narrateur – personnages – sujet principal – idée centrale de chaque paragraphe).

2 ... procéder à une lecture détaillée :

- **Approfondissez votre compréhension** grâce à plusieurs relectures.
- **Prenez des notes** au fur et à mesure : ce qui n'est pas écrit mais **sous-entendu** – ce qui suscite une **émotion** en vous – la répétition de tel ou tel mot – les **champs lexicaux** dominants.

3 ... organiser vos notes :

- Entourez les **mots** et **expressions** qui vous semblent clés.
- Établissez des **liens** : cause – conséquence – exemple – contre-exemple.
- Regroupez les points qui serviront à **introduire** le document (auteur – date – lieu – nature – objectif – sujet principal).
- Allez du **plus évident** et **descriptif** au **moins évident** et **analytique**.

4 .... faire le tri de tout ce que vous avez compris :

- Privilégiez les **idées principales**, puis enrichissez-les des éléments qui permettent d'avoir une compréhension plus fine.
- Mettez de côté pour l'instant ce qui est redondant, isolé ou anecdotique.

Conservez votre brouillon pour compléter ou enrichir votre résumé.

5 .... rédiger en vous appropriant le sujet :

- Piochez dans tout ce que vous avez noté pour **préparer votre compte-rendu**.
- Faites un **plan** et rédigez une **introduction**.

Ne suivez pas de façon linéaire le texte d'origine mais trouvez une logique personnelle d'organisation.

- Rédigez ensuite les parties : une **idée par paragraphe**.
- Utilisez des **phrases de transition** entre les différentes parties de votre plan.
- Incluez des **phrases complexes** et variez le **lexique**.

6 ... vous relire :

- Relisez votre compte-rendu pour vérifier la **cohérence** de votre texte.
- Corrigez les **erreurs** (orthographe – grammaire – conjugaison) et remplacez les mots répétés par des **synonymes**.
- Vérifiez que vous avez le nombre de mots demandé (± 10 %).

STRATÉGIE RENDRE COMPTE D'UN TEXTE À L'ORAL

Pour rendre compte d'un texte à l'oral, il faut :

1 ... comprendre les grandes lignes du document :

- Relevez les **éléments périphériques pertinents** (nature du document – titre – date – auteur – année).
- Suite à la première lecture, notez les **points essentiels** (narrateur – personnages – sujet principal – idée centrale de chaque paragraphe).

2 ... procéder à une lecture détaillée :

- **Approfondissez votre compréhension** grâce à plusieurs relectures.
- **Prenez des notes** au fur et à mesure : ce qui n'est pas écrit mais **sous-entendu** – ce qui suscite une **émotion** en vous – la répétition de tel ou tel mot – les **champs lexicaux** dominants.

3 ... organiser vos notes :

- Entourez les **mots** et **expressions** qui vous semblent clés.
- Établissez des **liens** : cause – conséquence – exemple – contre-exemple.
- Regroupez les points qui serviront à **introduire** le document (auteur – date – lieu – nature – objectif – sujet principal).
- Allez du **plus évident** et **descriptif** au **moins évident** et **analytique**.

4 .... faire le tri de tout ce que vous avez compris :

- Privilégiez les **idées principales**, puis enrichissez-les des éléments qui permettent d'avoir une compréhension plus fine.
- Mettez de côté pour l'instant ce qui est redondant, isolé ou anecdotique.

Conservez votre brouillon pour compléter ou enrichir votre résumé.

5 ... préparer votre compte-rendu :

- Piochez dans tout ce que vous avez noté pour **préparer votre compte-rendu.**
- Notez les **mots-clés** de chaque partie, de l'**introduction** et de la **conclusion**.

Ne rédigez pas des phrases complètes, vous seriez tenté(e) de les lire et votre présentation orale serait moins naturelle. Optez pour la prise de notes !
➥ Parler à partir de notes p. 82

- **Vérifiez** dans un dictionnaire en ligne la **prononciation** des mots inconnus.
- **Entraînez-vous à voix haute** et **enregistrez-vous. Réécoutez.** Identifiez les mots ou expressions qui posent problème et répétez-les avant de vous entraîner à nouveau.

6 ... présenter votre compte-rendu :

- **Regardez** votre **public** pendant votre prise de parole.
- Ne **lisez pas vos notes** sauf si vous avez un trou de mémoire : *Sorry, where was I? • Just a second, please.*
- **Articulez** et adaptez votre **débit** à votre public. Soignez votre **intonation**.
- Utilisez des ***gap-fillers*** si vous hésitez.

➥ S'exprimer devant un public p. 233

Index phonologique

Symboles phonétiques

Voyelles simples

/ɑː/	car	/æ/	cat
/e/	bed	/ɜː/	bird
/ɪ/	fish	/iː/	tree
/ɒ/	dog	/ɔː/	door
/ʊ/	cook	/uː/	blue
/ʌ/	bus	/ə/	banana

Diphtongues

/eɪ/	cake	/aɪ/	bike
/ɔɪ/	boy	/əʊ/	ghost
/aʊ/	house	/ɪə/	ear
/eə/	bear	/ʊə/	tourist

Triphtongues

/aɪə/	fire	/aʊə/	shower
/ɔɪə/	royal		

Consonnes

/h/	hat	/t/	two
/k/	kangaroo	/ʃ/	shoe
/θ/	three	/ð/	mother
/ʒ/	garage	/tʃ/	chocolate
/r/	rabbit	/ŋ/	sing
/p/	pony	/j/	yellow
/dʒ/	jump		

Les sons

Graphie-phonie : la lettre *h*

La lettre ***h*** est presque toujours prononcée (= aspirée [h]) : *here*, *house*, *home*, *heritage*, *inhale*, mais aussi *whole*), sauf pour les mots suivants : *hour*, *honour*, *honest*, *heir* (« héritier »), *exhibit*, *exhausted*... et leurs dérivés.

Graphie-phonie : la lettre *k*

Quand un mot commence par *kn-*, la lettre ***k*** est muette : *know*, *knot*, *knees*...

Graphie-phonie : les consonnes

1. Il y a souvent plusieurs prononciations possibles pour une même graphie. Les lettres ***th*** peuvent se prononcer [θ], [d] ou encore [t]. Les lettres ***ch*** peuvent se prononcer [tʃ] ou [k].
2. Les sons [tʃ] et [dʒ] se ressemblent un peu. Il faut s'entraîner à les prononcer pour les maîtriser.

Différences graphie-phonie

1. La syllabe ***ea*** peut être prononcée de plusieurs façons : *seat* [iː], *great* [eɪ], *dread* [e], *heard* [ɜː], *hear* [ɪə], *pear* [eə].
2. Inversement, deux orthographes différentes peuvent être prononcées de la même manière : *great* / *hate* [eɪ], *head* / *bed* [e], *pear* / *pair* [eə].
3. En cas de doute, cherchez dans un dictionnaire en ligne où vous pouvez écouter la prononciation du mot.

La phonie [uː] et la graphie *ou*

1. Les lettres ***ou*** peuvent être prononcées de plusieurs façons : [uː] (*group*), mais aussi [aʊ] (*mount*), [əʊ] (*shoulder*), [ɔː] (*brought*), [ʊ] (*could*) et [ʌ] (*country*).
2. Le son [uː] peut s'écrire de différentes façons : ***oo*** (*food*), ***ew*** (*new*), ***ue*** (*blue*), ***ui*** (*fruit*), ***eu*** (*queue*), ***oe*** (*shoe*), ***o*** (*lose*), mais aussi ***ou*** (*group*).

Les sons proches

1. En anglais, certains sons peuvent avoir une prononciation très proche : la différence entre voyelle courte et diphtongue (*got* / *goat*), voyelle courte ou longue (*ship* / *sheep*) ou encore deux sons ressemblants (*but* / *bat*) est parfois subtile.
2. Si on peut parfois se servir du contexte pour différencier des mots dont la prononciation est proche, il faut aussi s'entraîner à écouter et à répéter ces mots afin de savoir les reconnaître et les prononcer sans aide contextuelle.

Voyelles brèves et voyelles longues

1. La transcription phonétique d'une voyelle longue se reconnaît au signe [ː] → *youth* [juːθ].
2. Une voyelle qui porte l'accent principal d'un mot est généralement brève si elle est suivie soit d'une consonne unique (*kid*), soit de deux consonnes (*rock*). Attention aux exceptions : *class* (GB [klɑːs] / US [klas]).
3. Il y a plusieurs façons d'écrire les sons voyelles. Le son [ɪ] par exemple peut s'écrire *rip* – *crazy* – *decide*. Le son [iː] peut s'écrire *recent* – *upheaval* – *street* – *key*.
4. Une voyelle suivie de la lettre *-r* en position finale est parfois longue et le *-r* devient « silencieux » en anglais britannique : *door* [dɔː] – *guitar* [gɪˈtɑː].

Les diphtongues et les triphtongues

1. La diphtongue est composée de deux sons voyelles qui s'enchaînent en une seule syllabe.

   Pour un même son, l'orthographe peut être différente (*pane* / *pain*) et pour une même orthographe, les sons peuvent être différents (*low* [əʊ] / *cow* [aʊ]).
2. Les triphtongues sont des diphtongues auxquelles on ajoute le son « schwa » [ə] : *lie* [aɪ], *liar* [aɪə].
3. L'ajout d'un *-e* peut changer un son voyelle simple en diphtongue (*scrap* [a] / *scrape* [eɪ]), mais il y a des exceptions (*come* / *done* se prononcent [ʌ]).

Les mots

La prononciation des mots en *-ate*

1. La terminaison *-ate* a deux prononciations : [eɪt] lorsqu'il s'agit d'un verbe et [ət] lorsqu'il s'agit d'un nom ou d'un adjectif.
2. Il y a des exceptions telles que *debate* et *mate* qui se prononcent toujours [eɪt], quelle que soit la nature du mot.
3. Il est important de bien analyser le contexte pour déterminer la nature du mot et le prononcer correctement.
4. Pour les mots de plus de deux syllabes, l'accent tonique n'est jamais placé sur la terminaison en *-ate*.

Les homophones

Les homophones sont des mots qui ont la même prononciation mais, des significations et / ou des orthographes différentes : *right / write* [raɪt], *see / sea* [siː], *hair / hare* [heə].

Différencier V-*ing* et V-*en*

Certaines terminaisons inaccentuées comme *-ing* ou *-en* peuvent être difficiles à différencier à l'écoute.

1. Associées à l'auxiliaire *be*, cela peut entraîner des confusions : *He was eating / He was eaten*. Vous devez donc vous fier au contexte pour faire la différence : *He was eating chips / He was eaten with remorse*.
2. Veillez à ne pas accentuer les terminaisons *-ing* et *-en* (*eating*, *broken*, *sitting*).

La prononciation du *-s* final

1. Au présent simple, les verbes à la 3e personne du singulier prennent un *-s* à l'écrit.
2. À l'oral, ce *-s* s'entend toujours, mais la prononciation est différente en fonction du dernier son de la dernière syllabe de la base verbale : [s], [z], [ɪz].

La prononciation de la terminaison *-ed*

Il y a trois prononciations possibles de la terminaison *-ed*, en fonction du dernier son de la base verbale.

1. Quand le dernier son de la base verbale est [k], [p], [s], [ʃ], [f], [tʃ] ou [θ], la terminaison *-ed* se prononce [t] : *talked*, *slipped*, *missed*.
2. Quand le dernier son de la base verbale est [t] ou [d], la terminaison *-ed* se prononce [ɪd] : *decided*, *wanted*.
3. Pour les autres bases verbales, la terminaison *-ed* se prononce [d] : *played*, *called*, *named*.

L'effacement des voyelles

1. En anglais, certains mots peuvent sembler avoir plus de syllabes à l'écrit qu'ils n'en ont quand ils sont prononcés : *chocolate* = *cho(co)late* ['tʃɔklət] (deux syllabes).
2. Sans avoir entendu le mot, il peut être difficile de savoir le nombre exact de syllabes à prononcer. Il faut toujours vérifier la prononciation de nouveaux mots, à l'aide d'un dictionnaire en ligne, par exemple : dictionary.cambridge.org.

La prononciation de *had*, *was* et *were*

1. Lorsque la phrase est à la forme affirmative, les auxiliaires *was* / *were* et *had* ne sont pas accentués. Ce sont les mots porteurs de sens qui sont accentués. Seul le contexte permettra de faire la différence entre ***she****'d* ***met*** *him* et ***she met*** *him* ou ***they*** *were* ***hun****gry* / ***they****'re* ***hun****gry*.
2. Lorsque l'auxiliaire est en début ou en fin de phrase, ou accompagné d'une négation, il prend sa forme pleine. ***Had*** *he ever heard of South Africa? That's where I* ***was***.

L'article *the*

L'article ***the*** se prononce [ðə] quand le premier son du mot qui le suit est une consonne et [ði] quand le premier son du mot qui le suit est une voyelle.

the Native Americans [ðə 'neɪtɪv ə'merɪkənz]
the Aborigines [ði,abə'rɪdʒəniz]

L'accent de mot (l'accent tonique)

1. Dans la langue anglaise, lorsqu'un mot comporte plus d'une syllabe, l'une d'entre elles est forcément accentuée : c'est l'accent principal. À l'oral, il faut insister sur cette syllabe accentuée.
2. Le dictionnaire permet également de trouver la transcription phonétique des mots. Le site bbc.co.uk/worldservice/learningenglish/grammar/pron/ vous aide à pratiquer et améliorer votre prononciation.

L'accentuation des mots à deux syllabes

1. Le plus souvent, en anglais, un mot à deux syllabes est accentué sur la première syllabe si le mot est un nom, mais sur la deuxième si c'est un verbe.
2. Certains mots ont la même orthographe, qu'ils soient des noms ou des verbes. À l'oral, on peut les distinguer grâce à la différence d'accent de mot.

La règle de *-ion*

1. L'accentuation des mots se terminant par *-ion* porte sur la syllabe qui précède cette terminaison : *tele****vi****sion*, *delibe****ra****tion*.
2. Cette règle s'applique par extension à d'autres terminaisons commençant par un *i* suivi d'une ou deux voyelles et éventuellement d'une ou deux consonnes (*-ious*, *-ian*, *-ial*…) : *con****scien****tious*.

L'accentuation des nombres

1. Les nombres qui se terminent par *-y* sont accentués sur la première syllabe : ***twen****ty*, ***thir****ty*, ***for****ty*.
2. Le plus souvent, les nombres se terminant par *-teen* sont accentués sur la dernière syllabe : *fif****teen***, *six****teen***, *seven****teen***.

3. **Attention !** Les nombres se terminant par *-teen* sont accentués sur la première syllabe quand ils sont suivis d'un nom : *There were **fif**teen chairs in the room.*

Les formes fortes et faibles

1. Les mots grammaticaux à une syllabe ont une forme forte et une forme faible : *to* = [tə] → forme faible et [tuː] → forme forte ; *for* = [fə] → forme faible et [fɔː] → forme forte.
2. La forme faible est en général utilisée sauf si le mot grammatical est en fin de phrase ou s'il porte un accent contrastif. *Who is this for* [fɔː]*? It's for* [fə] *me.*

L'accentuation des mots composés

1. Bon nombre de mots composés sont accentués sur la première partie : ***paint**brush*, ***street** art*.
2. La deuxième partie d'un mot composé est souvent accentuée en plus de la première lorsqu'il ne s'agit pas d'un nom. Par exemple, lorsque c'est un adjectif : *This is a **well-paint**ed mural* (OOo).
3. Si un nom composé désigne un objet et si son premier élément correspond à la matière de cet objet, alors les deux parties du nom composé sont accentuées : ***brick wall*** (OO) (*the wall is made of bricks*).

Suffixes neutres et suffixes forts

1. La place de l'accent principal d'un mot dérivé n'est pas nécessairement la même que celle du mot-racine dont il est issu.
2. Les suffixes forts (*-ity*, *-ion*, *-ic*) changent la place de l'accent, alors que les suffixes neutres (*-ed*, *-ly*, *-able*, etc.) n'influencent pas la place de l'accent.
3. Plusieurs suffixes peuvent se combiner : *sus**tain*** ; *sus**tain**able* ; *sustaina**bil**ity*.

La phrase

L'accent de mot et de phrase

1. Dans une phrase, les mots accentués sont les mots porteurs de sens (noms, verbes, adjectifs).
   *I **loved** the **street art** in **Mumbai**.*
2. Les mots grammaticaux (articles, pronoms, etc.) sont, quant à eux, inaccentués en général.
   *The **artists went** to the **exhibition**.*

L'accent contrastif

1. Pour insister sur un mot, en anglais, on utilise l'accentuation : *What you do is **your** responsibility.* → C'est **ta** responsabilité (et pas celle de quelqu'un d'autre).
2. L'accentuation peut porter sur n'importe quel mot de la phrase : *She uses **her** website to give her opinions.* → **Son** site web, et pas un autre.

Attention ! Évitez de traduire littéralement du français (« c'est moi qui / c'est lui qui ») et pensez à l'accentuation : C'est lui qui a posté la photo. = ***He** posted the photo.*

Les liaisons

1. En anglais comme en français, on fait une liaison entre la consonne en fin de mot et la voyelle au début du mot suivant : *find a way – came out*. Cela vaut également pour les mots qui se terminent par un *r* muet : *more* [mɔː] mais *more* [r] *about*.
2. Lorsque les mots se terminent et commencent par des voyelles, si le premier se termine en :
   - [iː], [eɪ], [aɪ] ou [ɔɪ], on ajoute un [j] entre les deux mots : *the key* [j] *of success* ;
   - [aʊ], [əʊ] ou [ʊə], on ajoute un [w] entre les deux mots : *go* [w] *away*.

L'intonation

1. En anglais, on utilise une intonation descendante pour les phrases déclaratives : *I like kilts* ; les questions ouvertes : *What's his name?* ; et pour une phrase avec un *question-tag* si l'énonciateur est sûr de la réponse : *You know him, don't you?* → Je sais que tu le connais.
2. L'intonation montante est utilisée dans les questions fermées : *Is it far?* ; les phrases avec *question-tag* si la réponse n'est pas sûre : *You're not serious, are you?* → J'ai du mal à le croire ; et pour énumérer : *one* ↗, *two* ↗, *three* ↗…

   Si l'énumération est terminée, l'intonation descend : *Jack* ↗, *Marie* ↗, *Andrew* ↗ *and Joan* ↘.

L'intonation des questions

1. De façon générale, l'intonation est montante dans les questions introduites par un auxiliaire et auxquelles on répond par oui ou par non (questions fermées) : *Did you like the game?* ↗
2. Elle est descendante dans les questions qui commencent par un mot interrogatif (questions ouvertes) : *What was the score?* ↘

L'intonation des *question-tags*

L'intonation des *question-tags* varie en fonction de l'intention de celui qui parle.

1. Si la personne qui parle n'est pas sûre d'elle et cherche une réponse précise, l'intonation monte.
2. Si la personne qui parle est sûre d'elle et ne cherche pas de réponse particulière, l'intonation descend.

Index grammatical

Autour du verbe

Le présent simple (*Formation* ➤ *tableau p. 251*)

1. Le présent simple sert à exprimer les **goûts** : *He **loves** nature* ; les **opinions** : *I **agree** with you* ; les **vérités générales** : *Lots of teenagers **send** text messages* et les **habitudes** : *Most American teenagers **send** text messages every day.*
2. À la forme affirmative, il n'y a **pas d'auxiliaire**.
3. À la forme négative et interrogative, on utilise l'**auxiliaire *do / does***.
   *He **doesn't want** to take selfies.*
   ***Do** you **think** that people often forget the essential?*

Attention ! N'oubliez pas le -s à la 3e personne du singulier !
Le -s entraîne certaines modifications orthographiques :
- -y précédé d'une consonne ➝ ***-ies***
  study ➝ he studies
- ***-ch*** et ***-sh*** ➝ ***-ches*** et ***-shes***
  fetch ➝ she fetches
  flash ➝ it flashes
- ***-o*** ➝ ***-oes***
  do ➝ she does

Le présent en *be* + V-*ing*

(*Formation* ➤ *tableau p. 251*)

Le présent en *be* + V-*ing* sert à **exprimer une action en cours**, à **décrire quelque chose**, à **évoquer un événement temporaire** et à **exprimer une intention**.

On utilise l'auxiliaire *be* à toutes les formes (*am / is / are*).

*Everyone in the class **is working** hard this year.*
*What **are** you **doing**? I'**m updating** my profile.*
*That's it! I'**m not using** technology anymore!*

Attention ! Les verbes d'état (*be, have, belong, seem*, etc.), d'opinion (*agree, think, believe*, etc.) et de goût / d'envie (*love, want*, etc.) ne s'emploient que très rarement à la forme *be* + V-*ing*.

Le *present perfect* simple

(*Formation* ➤ *tableau p. 251*)

1. Le *present perfect* simple sert à exprimer un **constat** ou un **bilan dans le présent**.
2. Avec le *present perfect* simple, on met l'accent sur le **résultat de l'action**.
   *My car **has broken down**. I have to call a mechanic.* ➝ Ma voiture est tombée en panne : je dois la faire réparer.
   *I **have lived** in California for three years now and I love it!* ➝ Maintenant, au bout de trois ans, je fais le bilan : je peux dire que j'aime la Californie.
3. Le *present perfect* s'utilise donc souvent avec des **précisions temporelles** qui expriment un **bilan effectué au moment où on parle**, telles que : *so far, up to now, lately, recently, never, ever, already, since, not… yet*.
   *She **hasn't visited** London **yet**. She **has already been** to Cardiff.*
4. Le *present perfect* peut évoquer **un événement qui a commencé dans le passé et qui continue aujourd'hui.** Dans ce cas on traduit par le présent en français.
   *They **have lived** here for five years.* ➝ Ils habitent ici depuis cinq ans.
5. Les verbes exprimant un **état**, des **goûts**, la **possession**… (*be, seem, like, love, have, own*…) ainsi que les verbes qui expriment une **action brève** sont quasiment toujours à la **forme simple**.

Attention ! ***For*** introduit une **durée** (*for three years*) alors qu'avec ***since*** on indique un **point de départ** (*since yesterday*).

Attention ! On ne peut pas utiliser le *present perfect* avec les compléments de temps qui placent l'événement entièrement dans le passé : *last year, two months ago, yesterday*…

Le *present perfect* en *be* + V-*ing*

(*Formation* ➤ *tableau p. 251*)

1. Comme pour le *present perfect* simple, le *present perfect* en *be* + V-*ing* établit un **lien entre la situation présente et le passé**.
   *They'**re so tired** because they **have been playing** football for two hours.* ➝ Je vois qu'ils sont fatigués car ils jouent depuis deux heures.
2. Avec le *present perfect* en *be* + V-*ing*, on se concentre sur **l'événement** et / ou sur le **sujet de l'énoncé**.
   *What's wrong? You'**ve been crying**.* ➝ Je vois que vous avez les yeux rouges, donc je sais que vous avez pleuré.
   *They'**re** really **excited** because they **have been waiting** for the new season of that series for months!* ➝ Cela fait des mois qu'ils attendent la nouvelle saison de cette série.

Le prétérit simple (*Formation* ➤ *tableau p. 251*)

1. Le prétérit simple sert à parler d'un **événement** ou **fait passé, coupé du présent**. Il est le temps du récit car il permet de raconter les différentes étapes d'une histoire.
   *First, she **knocked** on the door, then she **went** inside. A few minutes later, she **saw** the ogre…*
2. Le prétérit simple s'emploie avec des **expressions qui situent l'événement dans le passé** : *ago, when, last week / month, yesterday, in 2005*…
   *The princess **grew up** in a castle far away from civilisation.*
   *She **didn't have** wifi so she **used** carrier pigeons to communicate with the outside world.*

Le prétérit en *be* + V-*ing* (Formation ➤ tableau p. 251)

1. Le prétérit en *be* + V-*ing* permet d'évoquer un **événement en cours de déroulement à un moment précis dans le passé.**

*He **was smoking** when she came in. Jimmy **was driving** to work when he heard on the radio about the factory closing down.*

2. Le prétérit en *be* + V-*ing* peut servir de **cadre**, de décor, à un **autre événement dans le passé.**

*The girl awoke and looked around her. The sun **was shining** and the leaves **were turning** green.*

Le *past perfect* simple (Formation ➤ tableau p. 251)

1. Le *past perfect* simple permet de parler des **événements situés dans le passé.** Il permet d'évoquer un **événement qui se situe avant un autre événement passé.**

*The party **had** already **started** when they arrived.*

2. Le *past perfect* joue le même rôle que le *present perfect* : il permet de **faire le bilan à un moment précis dans le passé.**

*He knew his way around Dublin as he **had been** there before.*

Le *past perfect* en *be* + V-*ing*

(Formation ➤ tableau p. 251)

En ajoutant *be* + V-*ing* au *past perfect*, on met l'accent sur l'**action** ou sur le **sujet de l'action** plus que sur le résultat.

*I could tell that he **had been playing** football as he was wearing his football boots.*

Attention ! On traduit le *past perfect* en *be* + V-*ing* par l'imparfait en français si la durée de l'événement est indiquée.
They had been walking for three hours when it started to rain. → Ils marchaient depuis trois heures lorsqu'il a commencé à pleuvoir.

L'impératif (Formation ➤ tableau p. 251)

On utilise l'impératif pour donner :

- un **ordre simple** :
  ***Listen** to me!* → Écoute-moi !
  ***Don't forget** to call her!* → N'oubliez pas de l'appeler !
- une **instruction** (recette de cuisine, manuel d'utilisation, signalisation) :
  ***Add** the sugar and mix.* → Ajoutez le sucre et mélangez.
- une **invitation** :
  ***Have** another apple!* → Prends une autre pomme !

Remarque : Si la **personne qui parle s'inclut dans l'action** on utilise *let's* (= *let us*) ou *let's not* (= *let us not*).

- à la forme affirmative : *let* + pronom + BV
  ***Let's think** about our soldiers!* → Pensons à nos soldats !
- à la forme négative : *let* + pronom + *not* + BV
  ***Let's not** forget our soldiers!* → N'oublions pas nos soldats !

Les différents types de verbes et auxiliaires en anglais

À RETENIR

Verbes lexicaux	Auxiliaires de conjugaison	Auxiliaires modaux
eat, sleep, make…	*be, do, have*	*must, can, may, will, shall, could, might, should, would*

Conjugaisons de *have*

À RETENIR

Présent simple	*I / you have* *he / she / it has* *we / you / they have*
Présent en *be* + V-*ing*	*be* au présent + *having*
Prétérit simple	*I / he / she / it / we / you / they had*
Prétérit en *be* + V-*ing*	*be* au prétérit + *having*
***Present perfect* simple**	*have* au présent + *been*
***Past perfect* simple**	*have* au prétérit + *been*
Impératif	*Have. / Let's have.*

Conjugaisons de *be*

À RETENIR

Présent simple	*I am* *you are* *he / she / it is* *we / you / they are*
Présent en *be* + V-*ing*	*be* au présent + *being*
Prétérit simple	*I / he / she / it was* *we / you / they were*
Prétérit en *be* + V-*ing*	*be* au prétérit + *being*
***Present perfect* simple**	*have* au présent + *been*
***Past perfect* simple**	*have* au prétérit + *been*
Impératif	*Be. / Let's be.*

Les formes verbales en anglais

(Voir tableau p. 251)

L'expression du futur

En anglais, il n'existe pas un temps unique pour exprimer le futur.

1. Les **modaux**, en particulier ***will*** (forme réduite = *'ll* ; forme négative = *won't*), peuvent servir à évoquer le futur.

*I'm sure they**'ll enjoy** their trip to Scotland.*

2. ***Be going to*** permet d'évoquer une **conviction** ou une **intention.**

*It's **going to** be hot in Mumbai this afternoon.* → J'en suis convaincu(e).

*I'm **going to** read that book.* → C'est mon intention.

À RETENIR

	Forme affirmative	Forme négative	Forme interrogative
Présent simple	BV à toutes les personnes, sauf BV + *-s* à la 3e personne singulier *She **plays** football every weekend.*	*Do* + *not* (*don't*) à toutes les personnes, sauf *does* + *not* (*doesn't*) à la 3e personne singulier *She **doesn't play** football on Wednesdays*	*Do* à toutes les personnes, sauf *does* à la 3e personne singulier + sujet + BV ***Does she play** basketball?*
Présent en *be* + V-*ing*	*Be* au présent + BV + *-ing* *He **is playing** video games at the moment.*	*Be* au présent + *not* + BV + *-ing* *They **aren't reading.***	*Be* au présent + sujet + BV + *-ing* *What **are they doing?***
Prétérit simple	BV + *-ed* à toutes les personnes pour verbes réguliers Verbes irréguliers : voir p. 264 *People **loved** Mandela.*	*Did* + *not* (*didn't*) à toutes les personnes + BV *I **didn't** see the film.*	*Did* + sujet + BV à toutes les personnes *Why **did you say** that?*
Prétérit en *be* + V-*ing*	*Be* au prétérit + BV + *-ing* *I **was reading** a book.*	*Be* au prétérit + *not* + BV + *-ing* *The sun **wasn't shining.***	*Be* au prétérit + sujet + BV + *-ing* *Who **was he talking to**?*
***Present perfect* simple**	*Have* au présent + participe passé (V-*en*) (du verbe) *I **have seen** him twice since last week.*	*Have* au présent + *not* + participe passé (V-*en*) du verbe *He **hasn't arrived** yet.*	*Have* au présent + sujet + participe passé (V-*en*) du verbe *Where **have you been**?*
Present perfect* en *be* + V-*ing	*Have* au présent + participe passé de *be* + BV + *-ing* *She **has been working** all week on the project.*	*Have* au présent + participe passé de *be* + *not* + BV + *-ing* *They **haven't been walking** for long.*	*Have* au présent + sujet + participe passé de *be* + BV + *-ing* *How long **have you been playing** the guitar?*
***Past perfect* simple**	*Had* + participe passé (V-*en*) du verbe *The party **had** already **finished.***	*Had* + *not* + part. passé (V-*en*) du verbe *He **hadn't forgotten** to buy a present.*	*Had* + sujet + part. passé (V-*en*) du verbe ***Had they remembered** to call?*
Past perfect* en *be* + V-*ing	*Had been* + BV + *-ing* *I **had been walking** all day.*	*Had been* + *not* + BV + *-ing* ***Had he been watching** the film?*	*Had been* + sujet + BV + *-ing* *What film **had he been watching**?*
Impératif	***Go** now! **Let's go** now!*	***Don't go.***	

▲ **Les formes verbales en anglais**

3. Pour exprimer un **futur très proche**, on peut avoir recours à ***be about to***.
*The film **is about to** start.* → Le film va commencer incessamment sous peu.

4. Le **présent en *be* + V-*ing*** est souvent utilisé pour exprimer le futur. Le plus souvent, la **date de l'événement est précisée**.
*We'**re meeting** the Mayor next week.*
Cette forme est employée soit pour évoquer des **événements projetés, quasi sûrs** : *She'**s having** a baby.* → Elle est enceinte, selon toute logique elle va accoucher ; soit pour exprimer une **volonté forte** : *I don't care how hard life can be, **I am** never **leaving** Glasgow.* → Je ne le veux pas.

5. Le **présent simple** avec un **repère temporel** précis peut servir à évoquer le futur.
*My plane **arrives** at 2 pm.* → C'est prévu ainsi.

Les temps de la narration

1. Le prétérit simple permet de raconter une **suite d'événements.**
*He **picked up** his sword and then he **slayed** the dragon.*

2. Avec le *past perfect* on peut évoquer un **événement antérieur à un autre événement passé.**
*He suddenly realised that he **had forgotten** to warn them of the danger.*

3. Le **modal *would*** (le passé de *will*) suivi d'une base verbale (BV) peut avoir plusieurs fonctions :
- Il permet d'évoquer le **futur dans le passé**.
  *They **would go** to the King to ask for his help.*
- Il peut aussi servir à évoquer un **événement passé qui est répété.**
  *Every evening the magician **would cast** the same spell on the village.*

4. Le prétérit en *be* + V-*ing* permet de décrire **une situation, un environnement ou une action en cours à un moment précis dans le passé.**
*The snow **was falling** and the birds **were flying** south when they finally approached their destination.*

5. Comme le *present perfect*, le *past perfect* permet de **faire le bilan**, mais **dans le passé.**
*By 5 o'clock they **had walked** ten miles. They **had been waiting** for this moment for months.*

Le prétérit vs le *present perfect*

1. Avec le **prétérit**, **l'événement est coupé du présent**. Ce qui intéresse l'énonciateur (la personne qui parle) est l'événement passé et non pas la situation présente.
*Back then she **was** a good worker who **did** her job well before discovering she **was** paid less than her male colleagues.*

2. Avec le ***present perfect***, l'énonciateur fait le **lien entre un événement situé dans le passé et la situation présente** pour en faire le bilan, évoquer les effets et / ou les conséquences aujourd'hui.
*The fight isn't over but women **have won** many rights in recent years.*

3. En plus du contexte général de la phrase, certains mots et expressions peuvent vous aider à faire le bon choix : pour le ***present perfect***, des expressions qui montrent un **lien avec le présent** : *so far, until now, recently, up to now*… ; pour le **prétérit**, des expressions qui indiquent que **l'événement est coupé du présent** : *last month, two hours ago, in 1989*…
*I **have visited** ten countries **so far** in my life.*
*I **went** to Wales **last year**.*

> **Attention !** Pour distinguer les deux temps, on ne peut pas se fier à la traduction en français car, le plus souvent, le *present perfect* et le prétérit simple se traduisent tous les deux par le passé composé.
> - *I **saw** the film.* → J'ai vu le film.
> - *I **have seen** the film.* → J'ai vu le film.

Le prétérit modal et le *past perfect* modal

1. Le prétérit modal n'évoque pas le passé mais un **événement irréel présent.** On l'emploie pour exprimer une **supposition**, un **regret**, un **souhait**.
*If I **were** you, I'd learn how to speak Spanish.* → Si j'étais toi, j'apprendrais l'espagnol. (Je ne suis pas toi, mais j'imagine ce que je ferais à ta place aujourd'hui.)

> **Attention !** On utilise *were* à toutes les personnes.

2. Le *past perfect* modal évoque un **événement irréel passé.**
*If he **had stayed** in his own country, he would have been killed.* → S'il était resté dans son pays, il aurait été tué. (Mais ce n'est pas le cas.)

3. Le prétérit modal et le *past perfect* modal s'emploient souvent **après *if (only)***, mais aussi **après *suppose, as if / as though, wish***.
*He talked about the revolution **as though** he **had been** there. He **wished** he **had learnt** English before arriving.*

4. Quand ***wish*** **est suivi d'un prétérit**, il exprime un **souhait.** On peut traduire en français par « si seulement ».
*I wish I **were** rich.* → Si seulement j'étais riche.
Lorsque ***wish*** **est suivi d'un *past perfect***, il exprime un **regret**.
*I **wish** I **had seen** him.* → Si seulement je l'avais vu. (Je regrette de ne pas l'avoir vu.)

Les expressions de temps

1. Les expressions de temps indiquent un **moment précis** ou la **fréquence d'une action.**
*She **hardly ever** goes but she helps out at the centre **now and again**.*

2. **Rappel :** Pour introduire les **mois, saisons, années**, on emploie ***in*** : *in May / in winter / in 2014* ; mais pour indiquer la **date**, on emploie : ***on*** : *on Monday(s)* ; *on February 14th* (à l'écrit) ; *on February the 14th* (à l'oral) ; on emploie également ***at*** : *at night / at weekends / at Christmas*.

3. On peut préciser le **nombre de fois qu'une action est faite** (par jour, par semaine, par mois…) : *once a week, twice a month*, mais attention : *three times a year*.

Pour dire « il y a… » (valeur temporelle), on utilise ***ago*** placé à la fin d'un complément de temps.
*She went to Glasgow two years **ago**.*

Les connecteurs temporels

1. Les connecteurs temporels servent à **structurer le récit.** Pour évoquer une succession d'événements, on utilise *first, then, finally*…

2. **Attention !** ***Before*** et ***after*** s'utilisent avec un **nom**, un **pronom** ou un **verbe en *-ing*** (*after that / the party / going to the party*).

3. Pensez à varier les connecteurs en fonction des besoins du récit (*all of a sudden* : « tout à coup », *meanwhile* : « pendant ce temps-là », *as soon as* : « dès que »).

Exprimer la durée : *since, for* et *during*

Pour exprimer la durée, il y a trois possibilités en anglais : *since, for* et *during*.

1. ***Since*** fait référence à un **point de départ.**
*I have been playing football **since 2012**.* → Depuis 2012 jusqu'à aujourd'hui.

2. ***For*** fait référence à **la durée d'une activité.**
*I went to London **for two weeks**.*

3. ***During***, qui peut se traduire en français par « au cours de », indique une **période pendant laquelle une action s'est produite.**
*He scored a goal **during** the match.*

Attention ! Si la phrase est au *present perfect*, on traduit par « depuis », et non par « pendant ».
I have lived here for three months. → J'habite ici depuis trois mois.

Les adverbes en *-ly*

1. Les adverbes servent à donner des **précisions sur un verbe** : *The witch shouted* ***loudly*** ; un **adjectif** : *She was* ***extremely*** *frightening* ou une **phrase** : ***Surprisingly****, they won the battle.*
2. Le plus souvent, on ajoute **-*ly* à un adjectif** pour former un adverbe :
   loud → *loudly* ; *extreme* → *extremely.*
3. Si l'adjectif se termine par *-y*, *-l* ou encore *-e*, la transformation exigera un **changement d'orthographe** : *-y* devient *-i* (*happy* → *happily*), *-e* disparaît (*possible* → *possibly*) et *-l* est doublé (*principal* → *principally*).

Les verbes à particule (*phrasal verbs*)

1. Un même verbe peut être suivi d'une variété de **particules qui modifient le sens du verbe** : *drop* = faire tomber ; *drop off* = déposer ; *drop in* = passer.
2. Il faut toujours tenir compte des mots qui suivent le verbe et faire **attention au contexte** pour éviter des contresens.
   I'm sorry for ***letting down*** *my friend.* → Je suis désolé d'avoir déçu mon ami.
   If Jim rings, could you ***let*** *him* ***in****?* → Si Jim sonne, pourrais-tu le faire entrer ?
3. Lorsque ces verbes sont employés avec un pronom complément, ce dernier s'intercale entre le verbe et la particule (*find out* / *find* ***it*** *out*).

Quelques verbes à particule :

blow	***up***	*exploser*
break	***up***	*se séparer*
bring	***about***	*provoquer*
carry / keep / go	***on***	*continuer*
cut	***down***	*réduire*
fill	***in***	*compléter*
find	***out***	*découvrir*
get	***in / on***	*monter*
give	***up***	*abandonner*
hang	***up***	*raccrocher*
make	***out***	*comprendre*
put	***up***	*loger*
run	***out***	*épuiser*
speak	***up***	*parler plus fort*
switch	***on / off***	*allumer / éteindre*
take	***off***	*enlever / décoller*
turn	***down***	*refuser*
turn	***on / off***	*allumer / éteindre*
turn	***out***	*se révéler*

Les verbes prépositionnels

1. Un **verbe suivi d'une préposition** qui **introduit un complément** est un verbe prépositionnel.
   We love ***listening to*** *this Doors album. His music* ***focuses on*** *making us think about society.*
2. Toutes les prépositions peuvent être associées à un verbe pour **introduire un complément** : *at*, *down*, *from*, *out*, *on*, *over*, *to*, *under*, *up*, etc. Comme en français, le sens de la préposition peut aider à comprendre la phrase (*from* → idée de provenance, *to* → idée de visée, etc.).

Les auxiliaires modaux (sens 1) et leurs équivalents *(Voir tableau p. 254)*

1. Les auxiliaires modaux de sens 1 peuvent servir à exprimer une **capacité** (au présent : *can* ; au passé : *could*), une **obligation** (*must*), une **interdiction** (*mustn't / can't*), une **absence d'obligation** (*needn't*), une **permission** (au présent : *may / can* ; au passé : *might / could*), un **conseil** (*should*) ou encore un **reproche** (*should have* + participe passé).
2. Les modaux sont toujours **suivis d'une base verbale sans *to* ni *-ing*** et la marque de la négation suit directement le modal.
   He ***might go****. She* ***mustn't stay****.*
3. **Deux modaux ne peuvent jamais se suivre.** Par exemple, pour exprimer la permission au futur, on peut utiliser *will* suivi d'une forme non modale équivalente.
   He ***may come*** *with us.* → *He* ***will be allowed to come*** *with us.*
4. ***Should*** + **BV** sert à donner un **conseil** : *You* ***should go***; alors que ***should*** + ***have*** + participe passé exprime un **reproche**. On peut aussi utiliser ***might*** et ***could*** pour faire un **reproche**.
   He ***should*** */* ***might*** */* ***could*** *have called us.*
5. Lorsqu'un modal n'est utilisable qu'au présent (*must*, *can*, *may*), il faut alors avoir recours à des **expressions équivalentes**, qui sont possibles au passé, présent et au futur.
   She ***must pay*** *for her plane ticket.* → *She* ***had to pay*** *for her plane ticket.*

Les auxiliaires modaux (sens 2) et leurs équivalents

1. Les auxiliaires modaux de sens 2 permettent à l'énonciateur d'indiquer le **degré de probabilité d'un événement** présent, passé ou futur.
2. Au **présent** et au **futur**, les modaux sont toujours **suivis d'une base verbale** : *They* ***must know****. / She* ***may go****.*
   Pour un événement passé, on utilise la structure : **modal** + ***have*** (+ ***not***) + **participe passé** : *He* ***can't have invented*** *a flying car.*
3. Deux modaux ne peuvent **jamais se trouver l'un à côté de l'autre.** La marque de la négation (*not*) se trouve entre le modal et la base verbale.
   They may ***not*** *remember.*

À RETENIR

Notion	Modal	Équivalent
Capacité / Incapacité	*can / can't* *He **can** play the piano. / She **can't** swim.*	*be able to* *Cats **are able to** retract their claws.*
Permission	*can / may* *He **can** join us later. / You **may** go now.*	*be allowed to* *You **are not allowed to** park here.*
Obligation	*must* *You **must** be here at 8.*	*have to* *You **have to** ask your father first.*
Absence d'obligation	*need not / needn't* *You **needn't** tell me what to do.*	*don't have to / haven't got to / don't need to* *You **don't have to** / **haven't got to** / **don't need to** be operated on.*
Interdiction	*can't / mustn't* *You **can't** stay here. / You **mustn't** do this.*	*be forbidden to / be prohibited to* *It's **forbidden to** walk on the lawn.*
Conseil	*should* *You **should** listen to me.*	*ought to / had better* *I **ought to** read this. / You'**d better** go now.*
Reproche	*should* *You **should have listened** to me.*	
Volonté / Refus	*will / won't* ***Will** you pass me the salt? / I **won't** go to his party.*	*want / refuse* *I **want** you to listen. / I **refuse** to go.*
Habitude au passé	*would* *When he was a teenager, he **would** spend his days sleeping.*	prétérit simple + expression de temps *I **played** tennis with my sister **every Sunday** when we were young.*

▲ **Les auxiliaires modaux (sens 1) et leurs équivalents**

4. Dans une phrase interrogative, on **inverse le modal** (qui est auxiliaire) et le sujet.
*She **might** be listening. → **Might she** be listening?*

5. Certaines expressions et certains adverbes (*it's possible that, perhaps, maybe, probably*…) peuvent aussi exprimer la probabilité et remplacer le modal.
*She didn't answer when I called. **Maybe** she was asleep.*

À RETENIR

Modal + degré de probabilité	Équivalent
can't → 10% *It **can't** be his sister. He's an only child.*	***I think it's impossible that** it is his sister.*
might / could → 25% *I **might** be five minutes late, but I'll do my best to be on time.*	***It's possible that** I will be late, but **it's highly unlikely** in my opinion.*
may → 50% *I **may** come to your party, I haven't decided yet.*	***Maybe** I will come to your party, **maybe** I won't.*
must → 80% *You **must** be John! Ann told me about you.*	***I'm sure that** you are John.*

▲ **Les auxiliaires modaux (sens 2) et leurs équivalents**

La voix passive

1. La **voix passive** se forme à l'aide de l'**auxiliaire *be*** et du **verbe au participe passé.**

2. L'auxiliaire ***be* porte la marque du temps de la phrase** : il peut donc prendre les formes suivantes (exemples p. 255) :
- le présent simple (*am / is / are*) ;
- le présent *be* + V-*ing* (*am / is / are being*) ;
- le *present perfect* simple (*has / have been*) ;
- le prétérit simple (*was / were*) ;
- le prétérit *be* + V-*ing* (*was / were being*) ;
- le *past perfect* simple (*had been*) et la base verbale après un auxiliaire modal (*could / may / will + be*).

3. On utilise la voix passive quand on s'intéresse non pas à celui qui fait l'action (l'agent) mais à la **personne ou l'objet qui subit l'action.** Cet élément devient alors **sujet du verbe.**
*The organisers have called off the concert. → The concert **has been called off**.*

4. L'**agent** est donc **souvent omis.** On ne le mentionne que s'il a une importance particulière et il est alors introduit par la préposition *by*.
*The Indian engineer **was contacted** by Google.*

	Actif		Passif
Présent simple	*The teachers **tell** the students to prepare a project.*	→	*The students **are told** to prepare a project.*
Présent *be* + V-*ing*	*The librarian **is closing** the school library early today.*	→	*The school library **is being closed** early today.*
***Present perfect* simple**	*Specialists **have written** many books on the subject.*	→	*Many books **have been written** on the subject.*
Prétérit simple	*The other students **chose** me to lead our group.*	→	*I **was chosen** to lead our group.*
Prétérit en *be* + V-*ing*	*Technicians **were fixing** the computers when we went to the computer room.*	→	*The computers **were being fixed** when we went to the computer room.*
***Past perfect* simple**	*By the time lunch was over the technicians **had fixed** the computers.*	→	*By the time lunch was over the computers **had been fixed**.*
Auxiliaires modaux	*They **must choose** a winner. The students **will appreciate** our project.*	→	*A winner **must be chosen**. Our project **will be appreciated**.*

▲ **Les différentes formes verbales au passif**

5. Certains verbes (*give, grant, send, offer, write, show*…) peuvent avoir **deux compléments directs** : *They gave James Baldwin an award.* On peut construire une phrase au passif avec l'un ou l'autre des deux compléments **en fonction de ce sur quoi on veut attirer l'attention.** Si on met le deuxième complément en position sujet, il faut ajouter *to* devant le premier complément : *An award was given **to** James Baldwin.*

6. Il n'est pas toujours possible de traduire une phrase au passif en anglais par un passif en français.

Il faut éviter la traduction mot à mot et avoir recours à une autre structure, par exemple une phrase à la voix active avec « on ».

They were told to leave the restaurant. → On leur a dit de quitter le restaurant.

Le discours indirect

Quand on passe du discours direct au discours indirect, plusieurs changements sont nécessaires.

1. Les guillemets disparaissent.

2. Si le **verbe de la principale est au présent**, le temps de la subordonnée ne change pas.

*"She **is laughing**."* → *He **says** that she **is laughing**.*

3. Si le **verbe de la principale est au prétérit**, dans la subordonnée :

– le verbe au présent passe au prétérit :

*"She **is laughing**."* → *He **said** that she **was laughing**.*

– le verbe au prétérit passe au *past perfect* :

*"He **left** earlier."* → *I **said** that he **had left** earlier.*

Remarque : Les modaux prennent leur forme *-ed* (quand elle existe) : *will* → *would*.

4. Le **pronom sujet change** (*we* devient *they*, *I* devient *he / she*…) ainsi que l'**adjectif possessif** (*my* devient *his / her*…) et le **pronom complément** (*us* devient *them*, *me* devient *him / her*).

*"**I'm leaving**."* → *She said **she** was leaving.*

5. On modifie les **compléments de temps et de lieu** (*here* devient *there*, *now* devient *then*, *tomorrow* devient *the day after*, *today* devient *that day*, *yesterday* devient *the day before*, *last week* devient *the previous week*, *next week* devient *the following week*…).

*"I **will** leave **next week**."* → ***He said** that he **would leave the following week**.*

6. Attention ! Le verbe introducteur ***tell*** est toujours **suivi d'un complément** : *He **told her** to leave.* Pour utiliser le verbe ***say*** à la place de *tell*, il faut ajouter ***to*** : *He **said to me** that he was tired.*

7. Contrairement au discours direct, au discours indirect, on ne retrouve **pas d'inversion de sujet dans les questions** : *He asked her if / whether she was Amish.* Le point d'interrogation disparaît. Les questions fermées (*yes / no questions*) sont introduites par *if*.

À RETENIR

Paroles prononcées	Paroles rapportées
Présent simple *"I **love** your jacket."*	Prétérit simple *He said (that) he **loved** my jacket.*
Présent *be* + V-*ing* *"I'm **gardening** behind my house."*	Prétérit *be* + V-*ing* *Suzy explained (that) she **was gardening** behind her house.*
Prétérit simple *"I **wrote** you a letter."* *Present perfect* *"I **have written** you a letter."* *Past perfect* *"I **had written** you a letter."*	*Past perfect* *Paul insisted (that) he **had written** me a letter.*
Futur *"We **will come** to your party."*	Conditionnel *They declared (that) they **would come** to my party.*
Impératif *"**Don't forget** your glasses."*	Structure infinitive *My mother told me **not to forget** my glasses.* (*not* se place avant l'infinitif)

▲ **Passage du discours direct au discours indirect**

Remarque :

- Les modaux changent quand il existe une forme passée : *can* → *could* – *may* → *might* – *will* → *would*.
- Le passé de *have to* et de *must* a la même forme : *had to*.

Les verbes introducteurs de paroles

Il y a un choix très large de verbes introducteurs de paroles, ce qui permet de **nuancer son discours** et d'**enrichir sa production orale et écrite**. Évitez d'utiliser trop souvent les mêmes verbes, comme *ask*, *say* et *tell*.

Pensez plutôt à : *wonder, enquire, whisper, shout, explain, argue, exclaim*…

*"They must rebuild the school as it's part of our heritage," Simon **argued**.*

*"What's out there in the real world?" she **wondered**.*

*"The witch is always a bad character," the child **remarked**.*

Autour du nom

Les articles

1. Il y a **trois articles** en anglais : ***a / an***, ***the***, **Ø** (article zéro). Ils servent à déterminer un groupe nominal.

2. L'article ***a / an*** est un **article indéfini**, on l'utilise pour mentionner un élément sans le distinguer des autres :

*He owns **a** media company.* → Une entreprise, on ne précise pas laquelle.

3. L'article ***the*** est un **article défini** et s'utilise **devant un élément spécifique** : soit parce qu'il est connu de tous : ***The** earth revolves around **the** sun*, soit parce que le contexte apporte des précisions : *He published an **article**. The **article** was about **disinformation**.*

4. L'article **Ø** s'utilise quand on parle d'une **notion en général** ou d'un **groupe tout entier**.

Ø Disinformation is a widespread problem. Ø Journalists are generally honest.

L'article Ø ne peut pas être suivi d'un nom dénombrable au singulier. Dans ce cas, il faut mettre le nom au pluriel.

*This report is about Ø **current affairs**.*

5. Les **noms propres** sont toujours précédés de l'article Ø ainsi que les **noms de pays**, sauf les pays considérés comme un ensemble.

***the** United States, **the** United Kingdom mais **Ø** England, **Ø** Australia*

6. *Last* et *next* + unité de temps sont toujours précédés de l'article Ø.

Ø last month / Ø last week

Les pronoms et déterminants personnels

À RETENIR

Pronom sujet	Pronom objet	Pronom réfléchi	Pronom possessif	Déterminant possessif
I *I love sushis.*	*me* *Sushis make **me** happy.*	*myself* *I made the sushis **myself**.*	*mine* *These sushis are **mine**.*	*my* *Don't touch **my** sushis.*
you	*you*	*yourself*	*yours*	*your*
he / she / it	*him / her / it*	*himself / herself / itself*	*his / hers*	*its / his / her*
we	*us*	*ourselves*	*ours*	*our*
you	*you*	*yourselves*	*yours*	*your*
they	*them*	*themselves*	*theirs*	*their*

Les pronoms réfléchis

1. Lorsqu'un **verbe exprime une action qui a un effet sur le sujet lui-même**, on emploie un pronom réfléchi.

*The young street artist was pleased with **himself**.*

2. Les pronoms réfléchis peuvent servir à **mettre le sujet en relief**.

***The artist himself** wrote the biography.*

3. Les verbes pronominaux français (« se » + verbe) ne correspondent pas toujours à l'emploi d'un pronom réfléchi en anglais.

Je me concentre sur ce dessin. → ***I'm concentrating** on this drawing.*

Attention ! En français, un verbe comme « se regarder » est un verbe pronominal. Mais tous les verbes pronominaux à sens réfléchi n'entraînent pas l'utilisation d'un pronom réfléchi en anglais.

- se concentrer → *to concentrate*
- s'habiller → *to get dressed*
- s'échapper → *to escape*
- s'évanouir → *to faint*
- se sentir → *to feel*
- se lever → *to get up*
- se cacher → *to hide*
- s'agenouiller → *to kneel*
- se détendre → *to relax*
- se raser → *to shave*
- s'asseoir → *to sit down*
- se lever → *to stand up*
- se laver → *to wash*
- se demander → *to wonder*

Les pronoms réciproques (l'un l'autre)

La **relation de réciprocité** (= échange) s'exprime avec ***each other*** (deux personnes concernées) ou ***one another*** (plus de deux).

*Artists who belong to the same school can understand **one another** better.*

Attention ! Certains verbes pronominaux à sens réciproque en français se traduisent par des verbes qui n'emploient pas de pronom réciproque :

- se battre → *to fight*
- se disputer → *to quarrel / to argue*
- se réunir → *to meet / to gather*

Les noms dénombrables et indénombrables

On distingue les noms **dénombrables**, qu'**on peut compter** et mettre au pluriel (*one dog / two dogs*), et les noms **indénombrables**.

1. Les noms indénombrables sont **toujours au singulier** et ne sont jamais précédés de *a / an* ni d'un nombre : ***Advice** is always useful.*
2. Les noms qui appartiennent aux catégories suivantes sont le plus souvent indénombrables : des **notions abstraites** : *sadness, research, news, knowledge, information*… ; les **couleurs**, les **langues**, les **sports**, les **matériaux,** les **aliments** : *water, bread*…
3. Les noms ayant un **sens collectif** sont indénombrables : *furniture, information, news, luggage*…, mais on peut toutefois les dénombrer en employant *some* ou un dénombreur : ***some** news, **a piece** of news / paper / advice, **a slice of** cake.*

Les noms et les adjectifs de nationalité

1. Les adjectifs de nationalité sont **invariables**.
2. Les noms de nationalité qui se terminent par *-ese*, *-ish*, *-ch* ou *-sh* **ne prennent pas de -s** mais sont suivis d'un **verbe qui s'accorde au pluriel** : *The **Vietnamese** are*… Ceux qui se terminent en *-an*, *-i* **prennent la marque du pluriel** : *The **Americans** are*…
3. Les noms et les adjectifs de nationalité prennent **toujours une majuscule**.

   ***Chinese**, **Japanese** and **Vietnamese** immigrants live on the West Coast.*

   ***Spanish** music is popular on both coasts of the USA.*

   ***Pakistanis** and **Jamaicans** arrived in Britain after the Second World War.*

   *The **British** are fond of **Chinese** and **Italian** food.*

Les mots composés

1. En anglais, les **mots composés** sont formés à l'aide de **noms**, de **verbes**, d'**adverbes** ou d'**adjectifs**, avec ou sans **suffixes.**
2. Il n'y a **jamais de marque du pluriel** dans les adjectifs composés : *a **high-rise** flat*. Dans les noms composés, le **pluriel est à la fin du mot principal** : *car exhausts, snowflakes*.
3. Le mot principal est toujours le dernier, contrairement au français.
4. Pour traduire, il faut commencer par le mot principal : *a housing project* → un projet de logement.
5. Certains ont un **sens passif avec** participe passé (*food produced in a sustainable way* → ***sustainably-produced** food*), d'autres ont un **sens actif avec V-*ing*** (*a light bulb that saves energy* → *an **energy-saving** light bulb*).

Les composés en *-ever*

1. Les composés en *-ever* permettent d'exprimer un **large choix**, une **absence de restriction** (équivalents de « quel que soit », « quoi que », « où que », etc.). Ils se construisent avec un **pronom interrogatif combiné à *-ever***.

   ***Wherever** you go, you will meet great people.*

   ***Whoever** you are, you should knock before coming in.*
2. On peut les remplacer par l'**expression équivalente** : ***No matter*** + ***wh-*** *(why / what / where / when / who / how).*

   ***No matter what** you're good at, you can be useful.*

Attention ! *However* (« quelle que soit la manière ») est suivi d'un adjectif ou d'un adverbe : *However busy you are, you can always find some free time* ; à ne pas confondre avec le mot de liaison *however* (« néanmoins »).

Le gérondif

1. Le **gérondif (V + *-ing*)** fonctionne comme un groupe nominal (GN) : il prend la place d'un sujet ou d'un complément.

   ***Swimming** is a hobby of mine, but my favourite activity is **hand-gliding**.*
2. On le retrouve souvent **après des verbes de goût** (*hate, can't stand, don't mind, like, enjoy, recommend, prefer, love*…).

   *He **hates flying** but he **loves bungee jumping**!*

Les quantifieurs

Les nombres et les chiffres

Pour bien utiliser les nombres et les chiffres en anglais, vous devez respecter quelques règles.

1. Les **années** : 2016 se dit *twenty sixteen*. Les **numéros de téléphone** : 055 28741 se dit *"oh" double five two eight seven four one*.
2. Pour les **nombres longs** : à l'**écrit** : placer une virgule tous les trois chiffres en partant de la droite. À l'**oral** : lire de gauche à droite le groupe de trois nombres approprié en ajoutant *million / thousand*, etc., sans *s* : 6,451,252 se dit *6 million, 451 thousand, 252*.
3. Pour les **décimaux**, la virgule française est remplacée par un point. On dit *point* et les chiffres après le point sont lus individuellement : 6.782 se dit *six point seven eight two*.

À RETENIR

Quantifieurs	*little* peu (= pas beaucoup)	*a little* un peu	*few* peu (= pas beaucoup)	*a few* quelques-uns	*some* du / de la / des	*much* beaucoup	*many* beaucoup	*too much / too many* trop de	*plenty of* beaucoup	*a lot of / lots of* beaucoup	*most* la plupart	*all* tous
Avec des indénombrables	*This singer had **little time** to promote his album.*	*He had **a little time** before the concert.*			*He took **some** money.*	*There was **much confusion** at the concert.*		*There is **too much money** in football.*		*Singers need **a lot of energy** to prepare a concert.*		
Avec des dénombrables			*He loved this pop star and missed **few concerts**!*	***A few concerts** were cancelled.*	*She has **some** friends.*		***Many artists** support a charity.*	*There are **too many players** on the pitch.*	***Plenty of journalists** asked for an interview.*	***A lot of fans** waited for their star.*	***Most** singers like to relax before a concert.*	***All** the fans came to his concert.*

▲ **Les quantifieurs**

Un **zéro** devant un point se dit *nought* alors qu'un zéro après un point se dit *oh* : *0.07 = nought point oh seven.*

4. N'oubliez pas d'ajouter le **pluriel** quand nécessaire pour les **fractions** : *1/2 = one half* mais *2/10 = two tenths.*

5. *Hundred, thousand, million, billion* (= milliard) sont invariables lorsqu'ils sont précédés d'un nombre : *two hundred people*, mais s'emploient également au pluriel et sont suivis de ***of*** pour exprimer une quantité indéfinie : *hundreds **of** people, thousands **of** cars, millions **of** dollars, billions **of** atoms.*

Autres quantifieurs

On choisit le quantifieur en **fonction de son sens** (un peu, beaucoup, la plupart…) et du **fonctionnement du nom** (dénombrable / indénombrable, singulier / pluriel).

Comparer des quantités

On peut comparer des noms pour exprimer une quantité (plus de, moins de, autant de…).

- **Comparatif de supériorité : *more* + nom + *than***
  *These singers have **more enthusiasm than** any others I know.*
  *They organise **more concerts than** the others.*
- **Comparatif d'égalité : *as many*** + nom dénombrable + ***as*** ou ***as much*** + nom indénombrable + ***as***
  *I've seen **as many films as** you.*
  *My favourite actor had **as much success as** yours.*
- **Comparatif d'infériorité : *fewer*** + nom dénombrable ou ***less*** + nom indénombrable + ***than***
  *This star used to have **fewer fans than** she has now.*

Les adjectifs

Les adjectifs en *-ing* et en *-ed*

Le même mot-racine peut avoir deux formes adjectivales : *-ed* et *-ing*.

1. L'adjectif en ***-ed*** décrit une **émotion** / un **état**.
*When I watched the horror film I was really **frightened**.*

2. L'adjectif en ***-ing*** décrit la **cause d'une émotion / d'un état**.
The horror film I watched was really frightening.

Attention ! Il ne faut pas confondre ces paires :
- *exciting / excited*
- *fascinating / fascinated*
- *interesting / interested*
- *tiring / tired*
- *heartbreaking / heartbroken*
- *boring / bored*

I'm boring. → Je suis ennuyeux / -se. ≠ *I'm bored.* → Je m'ennuie.

L'ordre des adjectifs

1. Rappel : L'adjectif est toujours **invariable** en anglais.

2. Quand il y a plusieurs adjectifs devant un nom, on va du plus subjectif au plus objectif.
*He is **a handsome, tall, American** actor.*

3. Un moyen pour retenir l'ordre des adjectifs :
ATACOM : Avis, **T**aille (forme, dimension), **Â**ge, **C**ouleur, **O**rigine (géographique, politique, nationalité, religion), **M**atière : *an ugly* (A), *large* (T), *old* (A), *brown* (C), *Chinese* (O), *leather* (M) *case.*

Attention ! Les adjectifs de **nationalité** (*Australian, French*), de **religion** (*Muslim, Catholic*) ou liés à une **appartenance politique** (*Republican, Democratic*) prennent toujours une majuscule.

Le comparatif et le superlatif des adjectifs

Pour exprimer la comparaison, on peut utiliser le comparatif d'(in)égalité, le comparatif d'infériorité, le comparatif de supériorité et le superlatif qui sont formés selon des règles différentes.

1. Comparatif de supériorité et superlatif :

- **Pour les adjectifs à une syllabe et ceux à deux syllabes se terminant par *-y*, *-le*, *-ow* et *-er* (adjectifs courts) :** on ajoute à l'adjectif *-er* + *than* pour le **comparatif** : *Curry is **spicier than** cottage pie and sausages are **nicer than** bacon.* On a la construction *the* + adj. + *-est* pour **le superlatif** : *That is **the funniest** story I have ever heard.*
- **Pour les autres adjectifs à deux syllabes et les adjectifs à trois syllabes et plus (adjectifs longs) :** le **comparatif** se forme avec *more* + adj. + *than* : *Britain's favourite dishes are **more multicultural** and **more diverse** today **than** in the past.*

Le **superlatif** se construit avec *the most* + adjectif : *Chinese stir-fry is* ***the most popular*** *meal in the UK.*

2. Quelle que soit la longueur de l'adjectif : **comparatif d'égalité** : on utilise *as* + adj. + *as* ; **comparatif d'infériorité** : *less* + adj. + *than.*

Pizzas are ***as tasty as*** *hamburgers. Honey is* ***less sweet than*** *sugar.*

3. Attention aux **adjectifs irréguliers** :
good – better – the best ; bad – worse – the worst ; far – further – the furthest.

À RETENIR

	Adjectifs courts	Adjectifs longs	+ reste de la phrase
Supériorité *This artist…*	adjectif ***-er*** *… is older…*	***more*** + adjectif *… is* ***more*** *gifted…*	***than*** + groupe nominal / pronom + proposition *…* ***than*** *M. Jackson / him.* *…* ***than*** *I thought.*
Infériorité *This artist…*	***less*** + adjectif *… is* ***less*** *old…*	***less*** + adjectif *… is* ***less*** *gifted…*	
Égalité *This artist…*	***as*** + adjectif *… is* ***as*** *famous…*		***as*** + groupe nominal / pronom + proposition *…* ***as*** *M. Jackson / him.* *…* ***as*** *M. Jackson does.*
Inégalité *This artist…*	***not as*** + adjectif *… is* ***not / isn't as*** *famous…*		

▲ **Le comparatif**

À RETENIR

	Adjectifs courts	Adjectifs longs	+ reste de la phrase
Supériorité *This artist…*	***the*** adjectif ***-est*** *… is* ***the*** *greatest…*	***the most*** + adjectif *… is* ***the most*** *gifted…*	***in / on*** ou ***of*** + groupe nominal ou nom *…* ***in*** *the country /* ***on*** *stage.* *…* ***of*** *the group.* ***ever*** + proposition *… I have* ***ever*** *heard.*
Inférioité *This artist…*	***the least*** + adjectif *… is* ***the least*** *popular…* (peu utilisé avec adjectifs courts)		

▲ **Le superlatif**

Les variations parallèles (*the more… the more*)

1. La variation parallèle permet de **montrer le lien entre deux propositions.**
The more *I read,* ***the more*** *I know.* → Plus je lis, plus je sais.

2. Les deux propositions, qui sont séparées par une virgule, commencent toujours par ***the*** **suivi d'un comparatif** (*more, less, -er*).

3. Lorsque la variation porte sur un adjectif ou un adverbe, les règles de base pour les comparatifs sont appliquées (voir p. 258).
The faster *he runs,* ***the more exhausted*** *he'll be.*

4. Il faut faire **attention à l'ordre des mots** lorsque la variation porte sur un **adjectif**, un **adverbe** ou un **nom**. Ces mots se retrouvent en tête de la proposition, contrairement au français.
The more waste *we generate,* ***the more polluted*** *the planet will become.* → Plus nous générons des déchets, plus la planète sera polluée.

5. La variation peut porter sur un **groupe verbal** et dans ce cas l'ordre des mots ressemble davantage au français.
The more *you listen,* ***the more*** *you learn.* → Plus tu écoutes, plus tu apprends.

6. Il est parfois possible d'**effacer le groupe verbal**, qui est sous-entendu dans l'énoncé.
The quicker *(he leaves),* ***the better*** *(it will be).*

Le génitif ('s) et le complément du nom

1. Pour relier deux noms (N1 et N2), l'anglais dispose de la forme génitive.

– **N1** peut désigner un **possesseur**.
[my mother]'s car
N1 N2

– **N1** peut aussi caractériser **N2.**
She went to a [girls'] school. → Elle est allée dans une école pour filles.
N1 N2

Le plus souvent, N1 désigne **un humain** (*mother / girls*).

Attention !
- Quand **N1 au pluriel** se termine par **-s**, on ne met que l'apostrophe pour indiquer le génitif : *the activists' work.*
- Pour les **noms propres** se terminant par **-s**, deux choix sont possibles : *Mr Jones' poster* ou *Mr Jones**'s*** (prononcé [ɪz]).
- Un **génitif incomplet** permet d'éviter une répétition ou de reprendre un élément comme *house* et *shop*.
*This leaflet is Paul**'s** (leaflet).*
*I'm at the butcher**'s** (shop).*
- Bien noter la différence entre :
*Paul**'s** and Peter**'s** parents* et *Paul and Peter**'s** parents.*
Dans le deuxième cas seulement, Paul et Peter ont les mêmes parents.

2. Si on ne peut pas utiliser un génitif *'s*, on emploie un **complément du nom**, souvent introduit par ***of*** : *the house **of** the woman sitting next to me* (pas de *s* car *woman* est suivi d'un long complément *sitting next to me*), *the door of the house* (*the house* n'est pas un humain, pas de *'s*).

Attention ! Disparition du ***the*** : quand on passe au génitif en *'s*, le complément vient prendre la place du déterminant *the* : *the house of my neighbour* → *my neighbour's house.*

La dérivation

1. La dérivation permet de **modifier le sens d'un mot** grâce à un préfixe et / ou un suffixe placé avant ou après le mot-racine : *fair* → ***un**fair* – *download* → *download**able**.*

2. On peut combiner plusieurs suffixes / préfixes : *It's **un**be-lievab**ly** expensive.*

3. L'ajout d'un suffixe peut **changer la catégorie grammaticale** du nouveau mot par rapport au mot-racine : *economic* (adj.) → *economically* (adv.).

4. La catégorie grammaticale du mot est en **fonction du suffixe** :
-ate, *-ify*, *-ise* = verbe ;
-tion, *-ism*, *-ity*, *-ing*, *-ness* = nom ;
-able, *-al*, *-ful*, *-ible*, *-ic*, *-less* = adjectif ;
-ly = adverbe.

Autour de la phrase

La forme interrogative

1. Il existe deux grands types de questions en anglais :
- les **questions fermées** : ***yes / no questions***, auxquelles on répond par oui ou non ;
- les **questions ouvertes** : ***Wh- questions***, qui commencent par un mot interrogatif.

2. L'ordre des mots est le même dans les deux types de question : **auxiliaire + sujet + verbe**.
Did you like the game? When did you win the match?

3. **Attention !** Si le **pronom interrogatif est à la place du sujet**, il n'y a pas d'inversion auxiliaire-sujet : **mot interrogatif (sujet) + verbe conjugué (+ complément)**.
***Who won** the match?*

4. **Si l'auxiliaire est *do* ou un modal** (*may*, *might*...), le verbe qui suit n'est pas conjugué.
***Did** you **watch** the match?*
*What **must** he **do**?*
Si l'auxiliaire est *have*, le verbe qui suit est un participe passé.
***Have** you **bought** the tickets?*
Et **si l'auxiliaire est *be***, le verbe qui suit est au participe passé (voix passive) ou en V-*ing*.
***Was** he **defeated**? **Were** you **running** in the race?*

5. Il existe de nombreux mots interrogatifs : ***who*** (« qui »), ***when*** (« quand »), ***where*** (« où »), ***why*** (« pourquoi »), ***which*** (« lequel »), ***whose*** (« à qui »), etc.
***Which** clothes will you take with you?*
***Whose** shoes are these?*
How peut se combiner à un adjectif ou un adverbe pour former un mot interrogatif : *how old* (« quel âge »), *how long* (« pendant combien de temps » / « depuis quand »), *how tall* (« quelle taille »)...
***How old** is his little brother?*
***How tall** is your mother?*

Attention ! Pour poser une question sur la quantité :
- ***how many*** + nom dénombrable au pluriel
***How many video games** do you have?*
- ***how much*** + nom indénombrable
***How much money** do astronauts earn?*

Les *question-tags*

1. Le *question-tag* sert à **confirmer une information**. Il est séparé du reste de la phrase par une virgule et prend la **structure d'une question** (auxiliaire + (*not*) + sujet). Il ne s'agit pas d'une véritable question.
*He likes Wonder Woman, **doesn't he**?* → Il l'aime bien, n'est-ce pas ?

2. Si la première partie de la **phrase est positive**, le ***tag*** **est négatif** et inversement.
*He left early, **didn't he**?*
*She isn't the first actress to play Snow White, **is she**?*

3. Dans le *tag*, l'**auxiliaire est à la forme pleine** et le **pronom reprend le sujet** de la phrase principale. La négation ***not*** est toujours **contractée**.
*Kevin has seen the film, has**n't he**?*

4. Les **pronoms** *everyone*, *everybody*, *anyone*, *someone*, *nobody* sont repris par le pronom ***they***.
*Someone wrote a book about it, didn't **they**?*

5. Avec ***let's***, on emploie toujours ***shall we?*** pour le *tag*.
*Let's go to the cinema, **shall we**?*

Les phrases exclamatives

1. **Avec *what* et *such***, l'exclamation porte sur un **groupe nominal**.
***What a surprise**! He is **such a clever man**!*

2. **Avec *how* et *so***, l'exclamation porte sur un **adjectif**.
***How sad**! It's **so heart-breaking**!*

Attention ! Ne pas confondre les **exclamatives en *how*** (*How clever he is!*) et les **questions** (*How clever is he?*).

La proposition infinitive

1. La proposition infinitive est une **subordonnée composée d'un sujet et de l'infinitif** (*to* + BV).

2. La fonction de cette proposition infinitive est **complément de la principale** (on peut la remplacer par *something* ou *this*).

*They want **Peter to work there**. / They want **something**.* → Ici, *Peter* est à la fois complément de la principale et sujet de la subordonnée. Il s'agit d'une phrase complexe.

3. Quand le sujet de la proposition infinitive est un **pronom**, c'est un **pronom personnel complément** qui est utilisé : *me – you – him / her / it – us – you – them.*

*They want **Peter / him** to work there.*

4. La proposition infinitive peut être utilisée **après des verbes exprimant une demande** (*ask*), une **pression sur autrui** (*order*), une **volonté,** un **désir** ou une **intention** (*want, would like, refuse, intend*), un **conseil** (*advise*) ainsi que des **verbes qui favorisent une action** (*allow, help, enable, teach…*).

*His parents **expect him to join** a volunteer programme.*

To V ou V-*ing*

1. Certains **verbes sont suivis de V-*ing*** : *avoid, continue, carry on, deny, like, love, prefer, enjoy, dislike, hate, mind, fancy…*

look forward to → avoir hâte de
be / get used to → avoir / prendre l'habitude de
be reduced to → en être réduit à
limit oneself to → se limiter à
object to → ne pas être d'accord avec

2. D'autres **verbes sont suivis de *to* + V** : *want, ask, allow, order, cause, encourage, incite, urge, force, oblige, get, order, persuade…*

3. Parfois le passage d'une forme à l'autre change le sens d'un verbe.

He stopped reading. → Il ne lit plus.
He stopped to read. → Il a commencé à lire (il a arrêté de faire autre chose pour se mettre à lire).

> Attention ! « Vouloir » peut être suivi d'un verbe conjugué, alors que *want* est suivi d'un verbe à l'infinitif.
> *I want you to come.* → Je veux que tu viennes.

La proposition relative

1. Dans une phrase complexe, la **proposition relative** apporte une **information supplémentaire sur l'antécédent**. Elle est introduite par un pronom relatif (*which, who, that, Ø…*) qui reprend l'antécédent et le suit immédiatement.

*The <u>man</u> **who came was my friend**.*

2. Le choix du pronom relatif est déterminé par la **nature de l'antécédent** (humain ou non-humain) et par la **fonction du pronom dans la relative** (sujet ou complément).

Antécédent	Humain	Non-humain
Pronom relatif sujet	*who*	*which / that*
Pronom relatif complément	*who(m) / that / Ø*	*which / that / Ø*

3. Attention ! Le relatif Ø ne peut être utilisé qu'en position de complément.

Many young people Ø I interviewed felt angry with society.
*The economic problems **which / that** hit Britain, caused high unemployment.*

4. On dit qu'une **proposition relative est déterminative** si elle apporte une **précision** qui est **essentielle** pour comprendre la phrase.

*The students **who** did their homework were given some sweets.* → <u>Seuls</u> les étudiants qui ont fait leurs devoirs ont eu des bonbons.

5. Lorsque la proposition relative ajoute une **information complémentaire** qui n'est pas essentielle à la compréhension, on dit qu'il s'agit d'une **proposition relative explicative.** Il faut dans ce cas mettre une **virgule avant et après** la proposition en question.

*The students, **who** did their homework, were given some sweets.* → Tous les étudiants ont eu des bonbons.

Dans ce type de proposition relative, on ne peut pas utiliser Ø ou *that*.

*The manager, **who** met the team last Thursday, said he thought the players were enthusiastic.*

La proposition relative et « dont »

1. Le « dont » français correspond à **différentes structures** en anglais :

*The author, **whose** book sold well, became quite famous.*
*The authors, **many of whom** were American, moved to Canada.*
*The book **Ø** I'm talking about sold well.*

2. En français, on utilise « dont », que l'antécédent désigne ou non un être humain. En anglais, on utilise l'**antécédent (humain) + *whose* + nom** : *The author, **whose** book sold well, became quite famous* ou l'**antécédent (non humain) + déterminant + nom + *of which*** : ***This book, the author of which** died in Canada, was published in 2001.*

> Attention ! Pas de déterminant *the* après *whose*.

3. Quand le **verbe** de la subordonnée relative fonctionne **avec une préposition**, on va :

– soit **commencer par la préposition** (il faut alors utiliser un pronom relatif) :

*Canada, **about which** young Americans knew very little in the 70s, was a very welcoming country.*

– soit **finir par la préposition** (on a alors souvent recours au pronom **Ø**) :

*Canada is the country Ø I have always dreamed **of**.*

Les structures causatives : faire faire quelque chose à quelqu'un

1. Dans les structures causatives, **le sujet est à l'origine d'une action mais ne l'accomplit pas lui-même.**
Painting makes me feel good. → C'est la peinture qui est la cause / l'origine de cette sensation agréable.

2. Certains verbes causatifs sont **suivis de la base verbale d'un deuxième verbe.**
Street art ***makes people appreciate*** *their town more.*
The authorities will ***have them rebuild*** *the gallery.*
D'autres sont **suivis d'un verbe à l'infinitif avec *to*.**
He was hesitant at first but I ***got him to try*** *some street food.*
The government ***forced the native Americans to leave*** *their homes.*

3. Attention ! L'ordre des mots est différent en français et en anglais.
Dondi made people react. → Dondi a fait réagir les gens.

4. *Quand le sujet du deuxième verbe est un pronom, il est pronom complément (me / you / him…) et non pronom sujet (I / you / he…). He made* ***us*** *realise how important art was.*

Les hypothèses en *if* et la projection

1. Il existe **trois types d'hypothèses** dont la forme change **selon le degré de certitude** que l'événement a de se produire.
- **Type 1** : *If* + présent simple, modal (*will, can, may*) + BV exprime une **hypothèse sur un avenir possible.**
  If I go to London, I will visit Downing Street.
- **Type 2** : *If* + prétérit modal, modal au passé (*would, might, could, should*) + BV exprime une **hypothèse moins probable, voire impossible** (irréel du présent).
  If he were richer, he would buy a house there. If I were you, I would go to Singapore.
- **Type 3** : *If* + *past perfect* modal, modal au passé + *have* + participe passé exprime une **hypothèse dans le passé**, dont on sait qu'elle ne s'est pas réalisée (irréel du passé).
  If you had trained harder, you would have won the race.

2. Pour **projeter une action dans le futur**, il est possible d'employer *when* avec un verbe au présent et non au futur.
When I am *older, I'll use public transport instead of driving a car.* → Quand je serai plus âgé(e), j'utiliserai les transports publics au lieu de conduire une voiture.

Attention ! *Be* devient *were* à toutes les personnes après *if* + prétérit modal : *If I* ***were*** *a politician, I would develop public transport.*

Enrichir son expression

Les mots de liaison

Le paradoxe

1. Certains mots de liaison permettent de **relier deux faits** (actions ou situations). **La relation entre ces deux faits est paradoxale.**
It's very cold in Canada. + He never wears a coat. → *Although it's very cold in Canada, he never wears a coat.*

2. *Although, (even) though, however* et *nevertheless* **introduisent des phrases** (comme « bien que » en français).
The Pentagon continued to request more troops ***even though*** *the death rate in Vietnam was the highest of any American war.*
Tandis que *despite* et *in spite of* **introduisent des noms** (comme « malgré » en français).
Despite *the vision most Americans had of Canada in the 70s, the country was in fact quite civilized and welcoming.*

La condition

Pour exprimer la **condition**, on peut utiliser : *provided, providing that* (« à condition que »), *as long as* (« tant que »), *unless* (« à moins que »), etc.
Brain stimulation is acceptable ***provided*** *the person receiving it is a consenting adult.*
We will keep using vaccinations ***as long as*** *the disease is not completely wiped out.*
The USA will have serious environmental problems ***unless*** *it does something now.*

Le but

1. En anglais, le **but** peut être introduit par les mots de liaison *(not) to / so as (not) to / in order (not) to* + BV, ou par *so that* + sujet + groupe verbal.
We left early ***so as not to*** *miss the bus.*

2. Pour **poser une question sur le but**, on utilise *what… for?*
What *did the artist paint this story* ***for? To*** *define his identity as Aboriginal. Many Aborigines sell their artworks* ***in order to earn*** *a living.*

3. Si la phrase a deux sujets, on utilise *for somebody to do something.*
He marched ***for people to have more rights.***

La cause et la conséquence

1. Pour exprimer la cause, on peut employer : *because, because of, due to, since, as, for* + V-*ing*.
He couldn't come ***because of*** *the rain.*

2. Pour marquer un **lien de conséquence entre deux propositions**, on peut employer : *consequently, as a consequence, so, that's why, therefore.*
Many people like Agatha Christie. ***As a consequence****, her novels have become bestsellers.*

3. Attention ! Certaines **expressions sont suivies d'un groupe nominal** : *I couldn't leave* ***because of*** *the rain*, alors que d'autres sont **suivies de propositions complètes** : *As it was raining, I couldn't leave.*

L'opposition

1. *Whereas* et *while* permettent d'**exprimer une idée contraire**.
   *I like this artist **whereas** my best friend hates him.* → J'aime cet artiste alors que mon / ma meilleur(e) ami(e) le déteste.
   *I'm into shopping **while** she thinks it's a waste of time.*
2. *Whereas* et *while* ne sont **pas interchangeables** quand on exprime une simultanéité et que la phrase commence par la conjonction. Dans ce cas, seul *while* est possible.
   ***While** he was drawing, she was painting.*

Similarités et différences

1. Pour **comparer et structurer son expression**, on peut utiliser des mots qui expriment la **similarité** (*similar to, like, both (of them), neither, all (of them), none (of them)...*) : ***Like** many other Olympians, Jessica Ennis has decided to remain loyal to her home city* ; ou la **différence** (*different from, unlike, contrary to...*) : *Muhammad Ali was **different from** his rivals. **Unlike them**, he was more than just a boxer.*
2. Les **mots qui sont accompagnés d'une préposition** (*similar to / different from*) peuvent être suivis d'un nom ou d'un groupe nominal, d'un pronom complément ou d'un V-*ing*.
   *He was **different from them** but **similar to us**.*
   Il en va de même pour ***like*** et ***unlike***.
   ***Like his idol / him**, he is very fierce and determined.*
   *It's **like watching** a football match on a screen.*
3. ***Both*** peut être suivi d'un nom, d'un groupe nominal ou d'un groupe verbal.
   ***Both cities** look interesting.*
   Mais, lorsqu'il est suivi d'un pronom, il faut ajouter ***of***.
   ***Both of them** like tennis.*

Ajout d'informations

Certains mots de liaison servent à **ajouter des informations** : *what's more, moreover, furthermore…*

*The living conditions were dreadful. **Moreover**, the food was inadequate.*

*She is very smart. **What's more** she works hard, so I'm sure she'll do well.*

L'accord et le désaccord

Pour mener à bien une discussion, il faut savoir **nuancer son opinion, préciser sa pensée**. En anglais, il existe de nombreuses expressions pour **nuancer l'accord ou le désaccord**. Il faut varier vos choix lexicaux et dans la mesure du possible éviter la répétition.

***You can say that again!** I can see we are **on the same wavelength** as I **fully agree** with you.*

*I **cannot adhere** to what he says at all. In fact, I'd say **the exact opposite is true**.*

*That's **going a bit too far**, don't you think? I think he may **have a point**. I mean, he **may not be right** but he **may not be entirely wrong** either.*

Attention ! La construction en anglais pour exprimer son accord n'est pas la même qu'en français : *I agree* / *I don't agree.* → Je suis d'accord / je ne suis pas d'accord.

Les expressions idiomatiques

En anglais, les **expressions idiomatiques**, qui **s'appuient sur des images**, sont nombreuses et souvent employées.

Si la traduction littérale peut être amusante, elle ne donne pas forcément le sens de l'expression. Il faut se servir du contexte général, de l'image véhiculée par l'expression. En cas de doute, consultez un dictionnaire en ligne.

*"Well, he **isn't the brightest light on the Christmas tree** (→ isn't very clever), even when he **pulls his weight** (→ works hard), and he was so **work-shy** (→ lazy) when it came to writing this play. **What takes the biscuit** (→ what is really annoying) is that he didn't **pull his finger out** (→ get to work) when I specifically told him to. He just asked me to **get off his back** (→ leave him alone). So I'm not surprised that watching the awful performance today was **like watching paint dry** (→ boring). He **drives me up the wall** (→ annoys me)!"*

Les faux amis

On appelle « **faux amis** » les **mots anglais qui ressemblent à des mots français mais dont le sens diffère** légèrement ou complètement. Seule une bonne analyse du contexte permet d'éviter des erreurs d'interprétation. Il est recommandé de lister les faux amis rencontrés lors de vos lectures pour les apprendre par cœur.

*It shouldn't be an **issue** (→ problem) any more.*

*After ten years he was **eventually** (→ finally) allowed back into the country.*

*Had they any idea who she **actually** (→ really) was…?*

Base verbale	Prétérit (V-*ed*)	Participe passé (V-*en*)	Traduction
Les verbes irréguliers dont les trois formes à l'écrit sont identiques.			
bet	bet	bet	*parier*
broadcast	broadcast	broadcast	*diffuser, émettre*
burst	burst	burst	*éclater*
cost	cost	cost	*coûter*
cut	cut	cut	*couper*
hit	hit	hit	*frapper*
hurt	hurt	hurt	*blesser*
let	let	let	*permettre*
put	put	put	*mettre*
read	read	read	*lire*
shut	shut	shut	*fermer*
spread	spread	spread	*étaler, étendre, se répandre*
Les verbes irréguliers dont le prétérit et le participe passé sont identiques.			
bend	bent	bent	*se courber, se pencher*
bleed	bled	bled	*saigner*
bring	brought	brought	*apporter*
build	built	built	*construire*
burn	burnt	burnt	*brûler*
buy	bought	bought	*acheter*
catch	caught	caught	*attraper*
deal	dealt	dealt	*s'occuper de, distribuer*
dig	dug	dug	*creuser*
dream	dreamt	dreamt	*rêver*
feed	fed	fed	*nourrir*
feel	felt	felt	*sentir, ressentir*
fight	fought	fought	*se battre*
find	found	found	*trouver*
get	got	got	*obtenir*
hang	hung	hung	*pendre, accrocher*
hear	heard	heard	*entendre*
hold	held	held	*tenir*
keep	kept	kept	*garder*
kneel	knelt	knelt	*s'agenouiller*
lay	laid	laid	*poser à plat*
lead	led	led	*mener, diriger*
learn	learnt	learnt	*apprendre*
leave	left	left	*laisser, quitter*
lend	lent	lent	*prêter*
light	lit	lit	*allumer*
lose	lost	lost	*perdre*
make	made	made	*faire, fabriquer*
mean	meant	meant	*vouloir dire, signifier*
meet	met	met	*rencontrer*
say	said	said	*dire*
sell	sold	sold	*vendre*
send	sent	sent	*envoyer*
shoot	shot	shot	*tirer*
sit	sat	sat	*être assis*
sleep	slept	slept	*dormir*
smell	smelt	smelt	*sentir*
spend	spent	spent	*passer, dépenser*

Base verbale	Prétérit (V-*ed*)	Participe passé (V-*en*)	Traduction
Les verbes irréguliers dont le prétérit et le participe passé sont identiques.			
stand	stood	stood	*être debout*
strike	struck	struck	*frapper*
teach	taught	taught	*enseigner, apprendre*
tell	told	told	*dire, raconter*
think	thought	thought	*penser*
understand	understood	understood	*comprendre*
win	won	won	*gagner*
Les verbes irréguliers dont la base verbale et le participe passé sont identiques.			
become	became	become	*devenir*
come	came	come	*venir*
overcome	overcame	overcome	*surmonter*
run	ran	run	*courir*
Le verbe irrégulier dont la base verbale et le prétérit sont identiques.			
beat	beat	beaten	*battre*
Les verbes irréguliers dont les trois formes sont différentes.			
be	was/were	been	*être*
bear	bore	borne	*supporter*
begin	began	begun	*commencer*
bite	bit	bitten	*mordre*
blow	blew	blown	*souffler*
break	broke	broken	*casser*
choose	chose	chosen	*choisir*
do	did	done	*faire*
draw	drew	drawn	*dessiner, tirer un trait*
drink	drank	drunk	*boire*
drive	drove	driven	*conduire*
eat	ate	eaten	*manger*
fall	fell	fallen	*tomber*
fly	flew	flown	*voyager en avion, voler*
forbid	forbade	forbidden	*interdire*
forget	forgot	forgotten	*oublier*
forgive	forgave	forgiven	*pardonner*
give	gave	given	*donner*
go	went	gone	*aller*
grow	grew	grown	*grandir, faire pousser*
hide	hid	hidden	*cacher*
know	knew	known	*savoir, connaitre*
lie	lay	lain	*être allongé*
ring	rang	rung	*sonner*
rise	rose	risen	*se lever (soleil), s'élever*
see	saw	seen	*voir*
shake	shook	shaken	*secouer*
show	showed	shown	*montrer*
sing	sang	sung	*chanter*
speak	spoke	spoken	*parler*
steal	stole	stolen	*voler*
swear	swore	sworn	*jurer*
take	took	taken	*prendre*
throw	threw	thrown	*jeter*
wake	woke	woken	*réveiller*
wear	wore	worn	*porter un vêtement*
write	wrote	written	*écrire*

La forme interrogative

1. Mettez les mots dans le bon ordre pour former une question.

people – these – are – Australia – from – ?
→ *Are these people from Australia?*

a. playing – had – the – when – Ray Charles – died – how long – ? – been – for – he – piano
b. understand – English – Texan – ? – can – accent – you – the
c. meeting – ? – attend – how many – will – the – attend – people
d. ? – haven't – any – got – politicians – solutions
e. does – who(m) – for – Paula – vote – to – know – ?
f. times – Steven – ? – question – has – that – how many – asked
g. didn't – Paris – ? – know – coming – you – to – that – the president – was
h. the – about – what – cinema – going – ? – to

2. Posez une question pour avoir l'information qui manque.

Sheila met (?) last week.
→ *Who did Sheila meet last week?*

a. My parents' plane will land at (?).
b. Kate's train is due in (?), the capital, tomorrow.
c. The people who are going to demonstrate this afternoon are from (?).
d. I'm thinking about (?), which is the best solution.
e. There will be (?) guests at the wedding dinner, that's a lot!
f. Brian feels (?) because he lost his job.
g. It is (?) outside, it's winter!
h. My sister takes piano lessons every (?).

3. Voici des réponses. Quelles étaient les questions ?

Andrea is going to (?) tomorrow.
→ *What is Andrea going to do tomorrow?*

a. The capital city? It is Washington D.C.
b. Tomorrow? I think that I am going to work.
c. 15? No, I don't think she is.
d. The reason I oppose cloning is because I think biotechnology is going too far.
e. Yes, I did. In fact I saw her yesterday evening.
f. Let me think, we invite Sam and his wife every other year for New Year's Eve.

Les *question-tags*

4. Trouvez le *question-tag* qui correspond.

Paul knew that singer very well. → *Didn't he?*

a. Leila and Sue often play together.
b. You and I must both apologize to our parents for what happened.
c. Your friends weren't invited to Kevin's birthday party.
d. Let's talk about it to find a solution.
e. I think I'm a little late.
f. You can't tell Robert the truth about the robbery.
g. Sheila works as a teaching assistant in New Zealand.
h. We shouldn't tell Peter that his friends are coming for his birthday.

L'expression du futur

5. Réécrivez les phrases avec *will*, *be going to* ou *be about to*.

One day, when I have more money, I (?) give some to the Heart Foundation.
→ *One day, when I have more money, I will give some to the Heart Foundation.*

a. Hurry up! We need to get on that train, it (?) leave!
b. When he is older Thomas (?) become a famous chef.
c. Stan has just finished his mid-term exams and he thinks that he (?) pass.
d. We don't have any time to buy popcorn, the movie (?) start.
e. Our garage sale is very successful. We (?) make a lot of money!
f. Wait! Don't close the door, my father (?) come in.
g. Lisa says that she is not feeling very well. I think that she (?) be sick.
h. When I get home, I (?) call her back.

6. Complétez les phrases. Faites les changements nécessaires.

My family (*move*) to New York next month for professional reasons. It's now mid-June and so I (*take*) my final exams. The first test (*begin*) at 8am on Monday morning. Once all the exams are over, I (*join*) them in New York. I (*not / know*) my exam results until August.

Le présent simple et le présent en *be* + V-*ing*

7. Complétez les phrases suivantes en mettant le verbe à la forme qui convient : présent simple ou présent en *be* + V-*ing*.

When you go to Sydney you (*usually – stay*) at the Four Seasons. But in which hotel (*you – stay*) now?
→ *When you go to Sydney you usually stay at the Four Seasons. But in which hotel are you staying now?*

a. Each time my friends (*go*) to Kenya they (*come back*) with wonderful pictures. Have a look at them: the animals (*walk*) so close to their jeep!
b. In this painting, I (*love*) the old man who (*sit*) on a bench. He (*seem*) to be contemplating the reflection of the branches on the surface of the water. I (*appreciate*) these naturalistic paintings.
c. Right now, I (*wonder*) whether I (*go – to see*) her tonight or tomorrow because she (*prefer*) relaxing in the evening when she (*come*) home from work.

d. At this time of the year birds (*usually – migrate*) to the African continent, (*you – agree*)? Well, they (*still – fly*) all over London.

e. (*you – know*) when Andrew (*come*)? He is supposed to be here already.

f. Brenda (*be*) funny. She (*be*) afraid of flying and (*not – trust*) the pilots. But look, she (*still – get*) on that plane!

g. My grandmother (*wear*) a thick pullover because it (*get*) cold.

h. I (*go*) to the cinema tonight. (*you – want*) to come with me? I (*know*) you (*not – like*) horror movies.

8. Voici les réponses. Utilisez l'information entre parenthèses pour retrouver les questions.

John and Sheila are trying to help her to find an apartment. → (*What – John and Sheila – try to do?*).
→ *What are John and Sheila trying to do?*

a. Not always. (*Thomas – usually do – his English homework?*)

b. The Bakers are seeing her tomorrow. (*When – the Bakers – plan – on seeing her?*)

c. The citizens are going to the city hall to vote for their new mayor. (*Why – all these people – go – to the city hall?*)

d. No, my mother is not working these days. (*Your mother – work – right now?*)

e. It is not a good idea, I have caught a cold (*What – you – think – about going ice-skating this afternoon?*)

f. They play only when they have some spare time. (*When – they – usually play – tennis?*)

g. Quite often. I like the atmosphere of pop music bands. (*How often – you – go – to pop music concerts?*)

h. Yes, we are going by car. (*We – go – by car – to the party tonight?*)

Le *present perfect* simple

9. Faites des phrases au *present perfect* simple.

The firemen are trying to fight the flames. (A fire – just – break out)
→ *A fire has just broken out.*

a. Look! I am buying a new car. (*Where – you – find – the money to buy a car?*)

b. Jane can't find her passport. (*You – see – it anywhere?*)

c. You are dreaming. (*You – already – finish – your exercises?*)

d. I'm not sure that our client is really interested. (*She – not – accept – our offer yet.*)

e. We have no news from our neighbour Angela. (*She – call – you?*)

f. Have you listened to the radio? I can't believe it. (*Lisa – be accused of murder!*)

g. Congratulations! (*You – pass – your final exams.*)

h. Do you know Paul Auster's latest novel? Well, no, (*I – not read – it yet.*)

Le prétérit simple

10. Réécrivez les phrases suivantes en mettant le verbe au prétérit simple.

When you (buy) your car?
→ *When did you buy your car?*

a. Steve (*meet*) Jane five years ago.

b. My grandfather (*not – go*) to war because he (*have*) five children to take care of.

c. At what time he (*say*) that he (*will*) arrive?

d. M. Donald Trump (*be*) elected President of the USA in November 2016.

e. Arthur's parents (*forbid*) him to go out because he (*cause*) some trouble.

f. You (*know*) that the US population (*be*) 325.7 million in 2017?

g. Neil Armstrong and Buzz Aldrin (*become*) the first human beings to walk on the moon on July 20, 1969.

h. I (*not – know*) that you (*get*) married last year.

Le prétérit en *be* + V-*ing*

11. Réécrivez les phrases suivantes en mettant le verbe au prétérit en *be* + V-*ing*.

Sylvia (watch) television all night.
→ *Sylvia was watching television all night.*

a. My brother (*not – drive*) at that time.

b. You (*listen*) to the manager when he (*speak*)?

c. Susan (*not – shop*) while you were at the gas station?

d. The Irish (*not – fight*) against the British Empire, they (*just – strive*) for independence.

e. When I (*talk*) to you, you could at least have made some effort to listen to me.

f. Barbara (*mow*) the lawn while you (*sleep*).

g. Your little brother (*scream*) last night?

h. Kathryn and Paul (*drive*) all night to reach their destination very early in the morning.

Le prétérit simple et le prétérit en *be* + V-*ing*

12. Mettez les verbes entre parenthèses à la forme qui convient (prétérit simple ou prétérit en *be* + V-*ing*).

Sarah (read) when she (hear) footsteps outside.
→ *Sarah was reading when she heard footsteps outside.*

a. Jonathan (*cook*) when he (*break*) the salad bowl?

b. Sebastian (*repair*) his car while I (*talk*) to him about my problem.

c. Last week I (*work*) on my computer when it suddenly (*crash*). I (*be*) furious because I (*lose*) all my data!

d. My little sister (*play*) peacefully on the sidewalk when suddenly a motorbike (*come*) out of nowhere and (*frighten*) her.

e. I (*have*) dinner with my family when the phone (*ring*).

f. Karen and Steve (*not – argue*), they (*just – share*) different opinions.

g. Kevin (*play*) the fool when he (*knock*) his forehead against that tree?

h. I think that the demonstrators (*not – realize*) what they (*do*) at that time.

13. Complétez les phrases. Faites les changements nécessaires.

My friends (*always – tell*) me to come and visit them in Scotland. So, I (*take*) that terrible afternoon flight to Edinburgh, and while we (*fly*) across the English Channel, some birds (*hit*) the left engine. We (*hear*) a terrifying crack. People (*scream*) but the pilot (*reassure*) all the passengers saying that we (*can*) still fly with the right engine!

Le *past perfect* simple

14. Pour chaque phrase, dessinez une frise chronologique sur laquelle vous indiquerez l'ordre dans lequel les actions se déroulent.

Emma came home (A) and she started cooking (B) the fish that she had bought (C) at the market earlier.

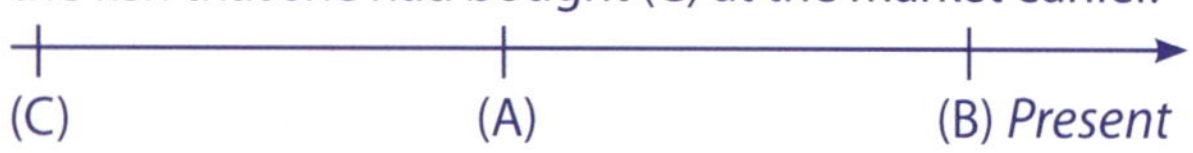

a. The car I saw (A) had already been sold (B) when I decided to buy (C) it.

b. Julia realized (A) that she had taken (B) the wrong road, so she drove (C) back.

c. When we met Johanna (A) we suggested that she pays us a visit (B) because we hadn't seen (C) her for a while.

d. I bought (A) Paul another gift because I realized that he had already bought (B) a red pullover last time when he came (C) to see us.

Le *present perfect* et le prétérit simple

15. Choisissez entre le prétérit simple et le *present perfect* pour compléter les phrases.

(*you – ever – organized*) a birthday party for so many people?

→ *Have you ever organized a birthday party for so many people?*

a. Aunt Suzan (*come*) to see us last week because her brother Rob (*die*) recently.

b. Look at these children, they (*just – cross*) the road without even checking if a car was coming up!

c. Leila (*meet*) her husband at university and they (*get*) married shortly after.

d. Well, we (*spend*) a wonderful afternoon together, I'm glad. Let's do that again next week!

e. I (*never – have*) the opportunity to live abroad when I was a child.

f. Can I borrow your pencil? – But of course, I (*just – finish*) my drawing.

g. Ken is very sick, he (*change*) a lot over the past weeks, don't you think so?

h. When (*you – realize*) that I (*want*) to meet her?

16. Mettez les verbes entre parenthèses aux temps adéquats pour compléter le texte.

My wife and I (*go*) to Canada last November. Despite the cold, we (*spend*) wonderful moments there. Our friends Jim and Kate (*join*) us in Vancouver. Now that we are back, I would like to go to an even colder place. I (*never – be*) to Alaska. Jim (*just – tell*) me over the phone this morning that he and his wife are ready to come with us.

Le *past perfect* et le prétérit simple

17. Choisissez entre le prétérit simple et le *past perfect* pour compléter les phrases.

Mina (*just – return*) home when Tim (*knock*) at her door.

→ *Mina had just returned home when Tim knocked at her door.*

a. Paul (*never – be*) to the USA before his trip last winter.

b. One month before Fiona (*go back*) to Australia to work, she (*be*) there for a two-week holiday.

c. Before my sister (*go*) to the cinema she (*pay*) a visit to my mother who lives close by.

d. Sean (*not – use*) his keys simply because he (*lose*) them.

e. His sons (*go*) out to play in the garden as soon as they (*have lunch*).

f. We (*never – think*) about it until yesterday when Tom (*tell*) us about it.

g. When they (*arrive*) at the station, the plane (*already – depart*).

h. Fortunately enough, Sarah (*buy*) her Christmas presents before the shops (*close*).

18. Mettez les verbes entre parenthèses aux temps adéquats pour compléter le texte.

When I (*meet*) Deirdre she (*already – move*) to Scotland. I (*go*) there as a tourist and (*enter*) a shop in which, the day before, I (*see*) a lovely cookery book on how to prepare some haggis. I (*see*) her immediately when she (*come*) in. I (*fall*) in love with her straight away.

Les temps du passé

19. Mettez les verbes entre parenthèses aux temps adéquats pour compléter le texte. Choisissez entre le prétérit simple, le prétérit en *be* + V-*ing* ou le *past perfect* simple.

When my father (*come*) in, I (*watch*) television with my little sister. We immediately (*know*) that something terrible (*happen*).

→ *When my father came in, I was watching television with my little sister. We immediately knew that something terrible had happened.*

a. The tourists (*wander*) along the pyramids when they (*hear*) their guide yelling at them. He (*warn*) them from the beginning not to get too close.

b. My stepmother (*move*) into our home last month after she (*sell*) her flat. I remember that when she (*unpack*) her belongings, she (*break*) that beautiful mirror.

c. My best friend (*argue*) with me yesterday. He (*tell*) me that I (*not – call*) him before stopping at his place. Apparently he (*flirt*) with his new girlfriend and (*not – want*) to be bothered.

d. Michael (*ice-skate*) when he (*fall*) on the ice-skating rink and (*break*) his ankle. I (*warn*) him so many times to be careful!

e. Fortunately Pamela (*wear*) her seatbelt when the car accident (*happen*). The driver in front of her (*not – notice*) that she (*be*) just behind him.

f. The sea liner (*peacefully – cruise*) when it (*hit*) an unexpected iceberg. Although the staff (*be warned*) that this part of the globe (*be*) icy, the captain (*keep*) his route.

g. If Martin (*know*) the truth, he would never have yelled at me as he (*do*). He (*scream*) and (*fulminate*).

h. Kathleen (*buy*) a lovely little puppy for her 5-year-old daughter Laetitia and she (*take*) care of it very well. But the little dog (*escape*) from the house because she (*not – close*) the door.

La voix passive

20. Réécrivez ces phrases à la voix passive en prenant comme sujet les éléments en gras.

A storm destroyed half of the city last week.
→ *Half of the city was destroyed by a storm last week.*

a. My parents had allowed **my little sister** to spend the night at her friend's.

b. Thousands of people will attend **the band's last concert.**

c. Look! The cleaning lady hasn't cleaned **your bedroom** for at least two weeks!

d. I think that you must tell **your best friend** the truth.

e. The local authorities are investigating **the origin of the disaster.**

f. Nothing can alter **his determination.**

g. My cousin regularly invites **my grandfather** for his birthday.

h. The mechanic is repairing **the motorbike**, I can't come to see you.

21. Réécrivez ces phrases à la voix passive en omettant l'agent.

They welcome the President for the first time.
→ *The President is welcomed for the first time.*

a. They have put up the exhibition ticket prices.

b. Someone stole my wedding ring!

c. Doctors are examining my mother.

d. The committee will award him the first prize.

e. You should repair the roof of your house.

Le comparatif

22. Remplacez les adjectifs entre parenthèses par des comparatifs (infériorité – / égalité = / supériorité +).

Antonia is (*tall* +) you.
→ *Antonia is taller than you.*

a. The house I bought in the countryside is (*comfortable* +) the previous one I had.

b. Big Ben? Well, I think it is approximately (*high* =) Notre Dame.

c. I really need to buy some new trousers, they are getting (*short* +) and (*short* +).

d. What an artist! He is (*talented* –) most of those I have seen.

e. The streets in Paris are (*narrow* +) those in London.

f. This English exercise is (*simple* +) the previous one.

g. Can you tell me why your car is always (*dirty* +) mine?

h. Bunny is (*smart* =) all the dogs I had before.

23. Complétez les phrases. Faites les changements nécessaires.

I visited California last summer and I find San Francisco much (*beautiful* +) Los Angeles. It is (*polluted* –) and (*friendly* +) in terms of human relationships. It is also (*hilly* +) and the inhabitants of Nob Hill seem to be (*wealthy* =) those who live in Beverly Hills. I have to come back!

Les auxiliaires modaux (sens 1)

24. Complétez cette conversation avec l'auxiliaire de modalité adéquat : *should – shouldn't – can – can't – must.*

Kevin: Hello Sam, (?) you tell me what time it is?
→ *Hello Sam, can you tell me what time it is?*

Sam: Hello Kevin, (?) you come to play soccer with me this afternoon?

Kevin: No, I'm sorry, I (?). I (?) help my father to mow the lawn.

Sam: But it is going to rain!

Kevin: Well, I know, but I (?) do my English homework as well. I will try to join you later but you (?) wait for me because there is no guarantee I (?) make it.

Sam: You (?) try to come because Peter will be there too, he is the best goalkeeper, as you know.

Kevin: OK, I'll do my best, but you (?) start playing without me.

Sam: You know that we (?) start without 11 players in the team.

Kevin: Sam, you (?) stop insisting, you are annoying me!

25. Complétez les phrases suivantes avec le modal adéquat : *could – must – mustn't – can't – shall – may – can – should.*

When my brother was younger, he (?) sprint for 100 meters five times in a row.
→ *When my brother was younger, he could sprint for 100 meters five times in a row.*

a. It is really hot in here, (?) I open the window, please?
b. I feel like going out tonight, (?) we go dancing?
c. Moving into my new apartment yesterday was very tiring, you (?) have helped me!
d. Lydia, you are going to spend a week at your grandma, you (?) behave badly with her, OK?
e. You are coughing too much, you (?) really stop smoking!
f. I just (?) stand up, I'm too tired!
g. Sorry to disturb you, (?) I come in?
h. It is too difficult for me to hide that from you, I (?) tell you the truth.

Les auxiliaires modaux (sens 2)

26. Complétez les phrases avec une des formes modales suivantes : *may – must – can't – should – shouldn't.*

You (?) be tired after the long journey.
→ *You must be tired after the long journey.*

a. Jacqueline's plane landed two hours ago, she (?) be home by now.
b. Firemen, ambulances and police cars are present on the site, there (?) have been a serious accident.
c. Arthur will lend you some money, it (?) be a problem for him, he is quite well-off.
d. Your father (?) not even know that his best friend is not coming to his 50th birthday party.
e. It's incredible, my brother Sam told me that he is going to leave his job, he (?) be serious!
f. I hear footsteps in the staircase, it (?) be John who is coming back from his meeting.
g. I am not really sure but I (?) have heard that there were at least five people killed in the accident.

27. Traduisez les phrases suivantes avec l'auxiliaire de modalité approprié : *may – may not – could – might – might not – can – can't – must.*

Peut-être qu'ils viendront. → *They may come.*

a. Il se pourrait que Kate ne vienne pas à mon mariage.
b. Si nous lui disons quelque chose la situation pourrait empirer.
c. Il se peut que les magasins ferment à 17 heures aujourd'hui.
d. Madame Stevens se comporte de manière très étrange ces jours-ci. Peut-elle être notre suspecte ?
e. Ces enfants pourraient être ceux de mes voisins.
f. Angela ne peut pas être la personne que j'ai vue hier. Autant que je sache, elle a quitté le pays.
g. Il est possible que les Martin ne soient pas à la maison aujourd'hui.

Les auxiliaires modaux et leurs équivalents

28. Remplacez l'auxiliaire de modalité entre parenthèses par son équivalent au temps adéquat : *(don't) have to – (not) be allowed to – be (un)able to – be forbidden to.*

You have just passed your driver's licence, now you (*can*) drive.
→ *You have just passed your driver's licence, now you are allowed to drive.*

a. Sullivan broke my precious vase. He (*must*) reimburse it.
b. Laura (*can't*) come today because she isn't here. What about tomorrow?
c. My grandmother says that we (*must*) be home at 7:00 p.m.
d. Of course, you (*can't – mustn't*) enter the stadium without buying a ticket.
e. Carol (*needn't*) take the bus, I will drive her to school.
f. Dad said that I (*could*) go out tonight until midnight.
g. My door key got stuck in the keyhole and I (*couldn't*) open it.
h. Yesterday I was at Beyoncé's concert, I managed to get backstage and (*could*) ask her for an autograph.

29. Remplacez l'expression entre parenthèses par son auxiliaire de modalité équivalent.

Look! That dog (*is able to*) dance on his back legs.
→ *Look! That dog can dance on his back legs.*

a. The poor man (*wasn't able to*) swim so he drowned.
b. You (*don't have to*) do your homework for tomorrow, there's no class.
c. Next month Andrea (*will be allowed to*) take two days off to go and see her uncle in Boston.
d. My mother asked my father for an explanation because she (*was unable to*) understand his reaction.
e. Ray doesn't feel very well, he (*have to*) see a doctor.
f. The fire alarm is still ringing, we (*are not allowed to / we are forbidden to*) go back into the building.
g. These bags are too heavy. Please help me, I (*am not able to*) carry them.

Les articles

30. Complétez les phrases avec l'article *a / an*, *the* ou l'article *Ø*.

(?) government declared (?) state of emergency in (?) USA after (?) heatwave struck (?) south of (?) country.
→ *The government declared a state of emergency in the USA after a heatwave struck the south of the country.*

a. (?) Queen Elizabeth is very popular in (?) United Kingdom.
b. Can Sue travel to New Zealand without (?) passport?

c. (?) influence of (?) Internet on (?) teenagers' lives is huge.
d. As (?) actor, Peter had to adapt to (?) very different and interesting roles.
e. (?) most of (?) people think that (?) government's new measures will reduce (?) unemployment.
f. Ethan works ten hours (?) day and just takes (?) few days off three times (?) year.
g. On (?) tropical markets you usually find (?) fruit, (?) vegetables and (?) spices.
h. Charles is (?) teacher and his wife Mary is (?) dentist.

31. Complétez le texte suivant à l'aide des articles appropriés (*a / an, the, Ø*).
I really like (1) South Africa. It is (2) vast country with (3) wide range of (4) varying landscapes and (5) equally diverse population. It has (6) strongest economy in (7) Africa and is (8) influential player in (9) African politics. In 2010, (10) South Africa hosted (11) first Football World Cup to be held on (12) African continent.

Les dénombrables et les indénombrables

32. Utilisez l'article ou le quantifieur approprié : *the – a piece of – a – some – the – a slice of – Ø*.
Can you please carry a (?) luggage to my hotel room, please?
→ *Can you please carry a piece of luggage to my hotel room, please?*
a. This is (?) very difficult job, but you can do it!
b. (?) information that you gave me was wrong.
c. Do you have (?) news about your job interview?
d. What (?) pity that Jonathan was not able to come with us to Ireland.
e. Could you please pass me (?) bread?
f. (?) advice my lawyer gave me was very useful.
g. What Paul did required (?) courage.
h. (?) furniture that you bought for my dining room fits perfectly.

33. Traduisez les phrases suivantes.
Le meuble est vraiment encombrant.
→ *The piece of furniture is really cumbersome.*
a. As-tu entendu les nouvelles à la radio aujourd'hui ?
b. Le morceau de pain que tu m'as donné est dur !
c. Je te donne deux conseils : travaille dur et crois en toi.
d. As-tu de l'argent sur toi ?
e. Je m'inquiète de plus en plus car je ne peux pas trouver de solution à mon problème.

Les quantifieurs

34. Utilisez le quantifieur approprié : *some – any – no*.
I'm curious. Give me (?) details.
→ *I'm curious. Give me some details.*
a. I have just seen (?) signs: they all say "(?) parking here".
b. (?) people have already arrived to attend your conference.
c. I'm sorry, I can't help you, I haven't got (?) time today.
d. You look very thirsty. Would you like (?) water?
e. There is absolutely (?) excuse for what Sheila did.
f. James never got (?) answers to the questions he asked him.
g. My sister's new corporation hasn't hired (?) employees yet.
h. Has your father had (?) problem with the second-hand car he bought from me?

35. Utilisez le quantifieur approprié : *much – many – little – few – a lot of*.
I'm afraid that for my English essay I've got (?) ideas.
→ *I'm afraid that for my English essay I've got few ideas.*
a. Unfortunately, Andrew's success story got (?) attention from the media.
b. When I moved into my new house, I didn't get (?) help from my neighbours.
c. There were (?) students in my class today due to the strike.
d. Not (?) birds were saved from the oil slick.
e. After our employee resigned there was (?) trouble in the delivery service.

La proposition relative

36. Complétez les phrases avec le pronom relatif *which / that* ou *Ø* lorsque c'est possible.
He arrived early, (?) was a surprise to us all.
→ *He arrived early, which was a surprise to us all.*
a. I give you the last document (?) was missing, you can add it into my file.
b. Karen never called me back, (?) upset me.
c. All (?) Thomas said was (?) he didn't make that mistake on purpose.
d. My sister Eileen started yelling at me, (?) reminded me of my mother.
e. The floods (?) hit the town last year were devastating.
f. The information (?) I have will not make you happy.
g. Teresa is the most educated person (?) I have ever met.

37. Complétez ce texte avec les pronoms relatifs *which, that, Ø* ou *who*.
The artist (1) was given the award of "actor of the year" is someone (2) I like very much. The film (3) he last played in was an adventure movie (4) was entirely shot in Jamaïca. His female partner was a young beginner (5) was very talented too. I can't remember her name, it is a name (6), I'm sure, is going to be well-known very soon.

Crédits photographiques

couverture Richard James Taylor/4 Corners Images **11** Hero Images/Getty Images **13** Andy Smith/www.agefotostock.com **14 h** PHOTO12.COM / ALAMY **14 bd** SIPA PRESS **15 h** Tatiana Bralnina/GETTY IMAGES France **15 h** SHUTTERSTOCK **15 bg** © Paul - stock.adobe.com **15 bd** Benjamin Rondel/PLAINPICTURE **16 h** Maxime BRAULT/REA **16 bg** ADOBE STOCK PHOTO / FOTOLIA **16 bd** Dean Drobot/SHUTTERSTOCK **17 h** DR **17 bd** SHUTTERSTOCK **18 h** SHUTTERSTOCK **18 bg** Pacificstock/HEMIS **18 b** Westend 61/HEMIS **18 m** SHUTTERSTOCK **19** Tomas del Amo/Getty Images **20-21** Shutterstock/Halfpoint **22-23** Photo12/Alamy **24** Andre D. Wagner **25 h** Jerry McBride : Durango Herald **25 b** theyesloiteringproject.com **26 h** Michael Galinsky **26 b** Joo/Caters/sipa **27** Non Sequitur © 2010 Wiley Ink, Inc. Dist. by Andrews Mcmeel Syndication. Reprinted with permission. All rights reserved. **30** Shutterstock/Monkey Business Images **31** Alamy/Photo12 **32** Alamy/Photo12 **33** Alamy/Hemis **34 h** Ernest Cole/Magnum Photos **34 bg** Ian Berry/Magnum Photos **34 bd** Gallo Images/Getty Images **35** Alet Pretorius/Gallo Images/Getty Images **36 h** Bongani Mnguni/City Press/Gallo Images/Getty Images **36 b** Nardus Engelbrecht/Gallo Images/Getty Images **37** Gallo Images/Getty Images **40** Hill Street Studio/Getty Images **41** Louise Gubb/Corbis/Getty Images **42-43** Klaus Vedfelt/Getty Images **44 h** Naoise Jo **44 b** Sean Byrne **45 h** KiwiCutz Men's Hairstylist Education/Ciaran O'Sullivan **45 b** Alan Place **46** Alamy/Photo12 **47** Conor McCabe **48** Rick McKee/Cagle Cartoon **52** Getty Images/iStockphoto **53** learning.gaa.ie/DR **54-55** Jim West/agefotostock **56 h** thehappyorg.org **56 b** DR **57** from the TED video, ©TED Conferences, LLC **58** TEDxRenfrewCollingwood et Andrew Federman **59** Gallo Images Editorial/Getty Images **62** Shutterstock/Nenad Aksic **63** Alamy/Photo12 **64 h** Naoise Jo, Sean Byrne, KiwiCutz Men's Hairstylist Education/Ciaran O'Sullivan, Alan Place **64 b** Jim West/agefotostock **66-67** Megapolis, 2008, Nelson Cardoso/nelsoncardosofilho.comb, ph© Bridgeman images **68 hg** Bernhard Richter/Shutterstock **68 hd** Tinnaporn Sathapornnanont/Shutterstock **68 m** Keep Smiling Photography/Shutterstock **68 bg** lspi138/stock.adobe.com **68 bd** nito/Shutterstock **69 h** S.Borisov/Shutterstock **69 mh** Ttstudio/Shutterstock **69 mb** Btos/stock.adobe.com **69 b** Jon Chica/Shutterstock **70 hg** Corbis via Getty Images **70 hd** Leonard Nadel/National Museum of American History **70 mg** PixHound/stock.adobe.com **70 md** Joshua Resnick/stock.adobe.com **70 b** Pixelbliss/stock.adobe.com **71 hg** Lewis Hine, Costa/Leemage **71 hd** Bridgeman images **71 bg** iuliia_n/stock.adobe.com **71 bm** bigacis/stock.adobe.com **71 bd** Jennifer Woodard Maderazo **72 h** David McNew/Reuters **72 b** Dorothea Lange/National Archives and Records Administration **73** Stanley Kubrick for Look magazine/Museum of the City of New York. X2011.4.10303.2 ©SK Film Archives **74 h** *La La land*, 2017, réalisation Damien Chazelle, collection Christophel © Black Label Media/Gilbert films/Impostor Pictures/Marc Platt Productions/Summit Entertainment **74 b** *How I met your mother*, collection Christophel © CBS Broadcasting **75 hd** *The Get down*, collection Christophel © Bazmark films/Sony pictures television **75 md** *Mr Robot*, collection Christophel © Universal cable productions **75 mg** *Jessica Jones*, collection Christophel © ABC Studios/Marvel Studios/Tall girls productions **75 bg** *Friends*, collection Christophel © Warner Bros TV/DR **75 bd** *Brooklyn 99*, collection Christophel © 2016 Fox Broadcasting **76 h** Jim Morrison Mural in Venice Beach © Rip Cronk, photo Justin Meyers **76 b** Audoin Desforges/Pasco **77 h** DR **77b** Al Pereira/Getty Images/AFP **82** Steve Debenport/Getty Images/iStock **83** Stefano Politi Markovina/AWL Images RM/Getty Images **84-85** Martin Roemers/Panos-Rea **85 d** Shutterstock/andriano.cz **86 h** Taxi Fabric/Barcroft India/Getty Images **86 b** Taxi Fabric **87** Rafiq Maqbool/AP/SIPA **88** Ableton.com. DR **89 h** Shutterstock/Emmanuel Nalli **89 b** Shutterstock/arun sambhu mishra **92** Getty Images/iStockphoto **93** Marji Lang/LightRocket/Getty Images **94-95** Hello World!, 2008, by Christopher Baker Victoria Jones/PA Photos/ABACA **96-97** Martin Parr/Magnum Photos **97** DR **98 hg** Scott Griessel/stock.adobe.com **98 hm** MStudioImages/Getty Images **98 hd** Marco Piunt/Getty Images **98 bm** PhotoAlto/Sigrid Olsson/Getty Images **99 g** Cavan Images/plainpicture **99 m** Onnie A. Koski/Shutters/Sipa **99 d** Electra K. Vasileiadou/Getty Images **100 g** John Springer/Corbis/Getty Images **100 d** collection christophel **101** Roger-Viollet **102** *Sweatshop Deadly Fashion*, réalisation Joakim Kleven **103** *Sweatshop Deadly Fashion*, réalisation Joakim Kleven **104** DR **105 h** DR **105 b** DR **107** Shutterstock/101images **110** Shutterstock/wavebreakmedia **111** Casey Kelbaugh/The New York Times-REDUX-REA **112** Byron Company/Museum of the City of New York/Getty Images **113** © The Andy Warhol Foundation for the Visual Arts, Inc./Licensed by ADAGP, Paris 2019, photo FineArtImages/Leemage **114** Walker Art Gallery, National Museums Liverpool/Bridgeman images **115** *Le portrait de Dorian Gray*, réalisation Oliver Parker, 2009, collection Christophel©Ealing Studios **116 hg** Jacqueline Salmon/Artedia/Leemage **116 hd** ©The estate of Jean-Michel Basquiat/Adagp, Paris 2019, photo collection privée/Bridgeman Images **116 mg** Courtesy of the artist and Metro Pictures, New York **116 bg** Dmitri Kasterine **116 bd** © 2019 Calder Foundation, New York Calder, ADAGP, Paris, photo Art Resource, NY **117 hg** © The Easton Foundation/Adagp, Paris 2019, photo Christie's/Artothek/La Collection **117 hm** Erik Olson **117 hd** Krista Kennell Patrick McMullan/Getty Image **117 mh** Bridgeman Images **117 md** Erik Olson **117 bg** © The Estate of Francis Bacon /All rights reserved/Adagp, Paris and DACS, London 2019, photo AKG images **117 mb** Chalkie Davies/Getty Images **118** © copyright and courtesy of Mohau Modisakeng, photo Willis Ryder Arnold /St Louis Public Radio **119** © Estate of Vivian Maier, Courtesy Maloof Collection and Howard Greenberg Gallery, New York **120 h** Selfie pris par le singe Naruto avec l'appareil du photographe David Slater **120 md** Petri Artturi Asikainen/Getty Images **120 mg** Alicia Parreau **120 b** Aurora Petra/stock.adobe.com **121 h** Saul Loeb/AFP **121 b** Self-Portrait, de Charlotte Colbert, 2017 ; photo Victoria Jones/PA Photos/Abaca **123** DR **126** Shutterstock/George Muresan **127** hoozone/Getty Images **130-131** Getty Images/iStockphoto **132-133** Nigel Millard **134** Cameron Spencer/Getty Images/AFP **135** Heinz Kluetmeier/Sports Illustrated/Getty Images **136** Cameron Spencer/Getty Images South America **137** collection particulière **140** Monkey Business/stock.adobe.com **141** ImageSource/REA **142-143** Stuart Roy Clarke/Alamy/Photo12 **144 h** Bridgeman Images **144 b** Graham Twyford **145** Alamy/Photo12 **146** Collection Christophel/DR **147** © Courtesy of SportBible **148 h** Topical Press Agency/Hulton Archive/Getty Images **148 b** Shaun Bloodworth/Vision Sports Publishing **149** Lidia Crisafulli **150** Keystone France **151 h** Shutterstock/Aby Gail **151 b** Alamy/Photo12 **156** Andy Smith/www.agefotostock.com **157** Jason Henry/The New York Times-REDUX-REA **158-159** Henrik Sorensen/Getty Images France **160-161** Alamy/Photo12 **162 g** Maurice Rougemont/Gamma **162 d** Jeremy Sutton-Hibbert/Alamy Live News/Hemis **163** Jeff J Mitchell/Getty Images/AFP **163 m** finwal89/stock.adobe.com **163 b** tverdohlib/stock.adobe.com **164** Nick Hedges **165** Lesley Smith **168** Shutterstock/PT Images **169** omursin/stock.adobe.com **171** Nigel Howard/Evening Standard/eyevine/Abaca **172** Gian Ehrenzeller/Epa/Maxppp **173** Gary Doak/eyevine/Abaca **174** Ruth Israel **175** Tim Rooke/Shutterstock/Sipa **178** Riverside Museum **179** umich-edu **182-183** Carl Warner **184** iStock **185** Erin Schaff/The New York Times/Rea **186** Daniel Cronin ourchildrenstrust.org **187** Earth Guardians.org/DR **188** Alamy/Photo12 **189** Tom Stromme/AP/Sipa **192** Shutterstock/SpeedKingz **193** WWF **195** Maze runner The scorch trials, réalisation Wes Ball © Gotham group/Temple Hill Entertainment, photo collection Christophel **196** Lightlife Foods, Inc. **197 h** The Toronto Star/Zuma/Rea **197 b** Toby Melville/Reuters **198 h** Alamy/Photo12 **198 b** Ugly Produce Is Beautiful. **199** James Oatway/Royal Academy for Engineering **202** Shutterstock/Africa Studio **203** Shutterstock/Monkey Business Images **204-205** Shutterstock/Pajor Pawel **206-207** David Levene/eyevine /Abaca **208** Alamy/Photo12 **209 h** Stuart Nicol/Evening Standard/Getty Images **209 b** Alamy/Photo12 **210 h** In Pictures Ltd./Corbis/Getty Images **210 b** Private Collection/Look and Learn/Ohana Collection/Bridgeman Images **211** Alamy/Photo12 **214** Hero Images/Getty Images **215** Sunshine International Arts **217** Collection Christophel © ABC Studios **218 h** Transcendental Graphics/Getty Images **218 m** Archivist/stock.adobe.com **218 b** Granger NYC/Rue des Archives **219 g** *Favourite Fairy Tales* by Sarah Hayes, illustration P.J. Lynch, Walker Books Limited **219 d** Bridgeman Images **220** BIS/Ph. Sally Chappell © Archives Larbor/DR **221** Illustrations, by Lane Smith, copyright © 1992 by Lane Smith **222** The Roald Dahl Story Company Limited. DR **223** Calvin and Hobbes © 1990 Watterson. Reprinted with permission of Andrews Mcmeel Syndication. All rights reserved. **224 h** Maleficient, réalisation Robert Stromberg © Moving Picture Company/Roth Films/Walt Disney Pictures, photo collection Christophel **224 b** Liam Walsh/Condé Nast Publications Inc **225** Matthew Land **230** Shutterstock/PT Images **231** Su Blackwell **232** Andy Smith/www.agefotostock.com – Hero Images/Getty Images **233** DGLimages/Getty Images France **236** Radius Images / Photononstop **237** KOUNADEAS IOANNHS/Shutterstock **238** ScottTalent/Getty Images France **239** WWW.CARTOONSTOCK.COM **240** Photo12/Alamy **241** Photo12/Alamy

Pour toutes les images en filigrane du manuel : © Freepik.

Crédits textes

19 Alan Brennert, *Molokaï*, St Martin's Press, 2013. DR **24** © *Britta Lockting*, Curbed and Vox Media Inc., https://ny.curbed.com/, 20.07.2018. **27** Jean M. Twenge, *Why teens aren't partying anymore*, www.wired.com, 12.27.2017. DR **35** Hlumelo Siphe Williams, *Mandela's Legacy Lives on in South Africa Through Its Young People*, 2018. DR **36** Musa Ndlangamandla, *The youth of 1976 vs the 'born frees'*, The Young Independents, 15.06.2018. DR **47** © Sheila Wayman, *The Irish Times*. **48** © Sheila Wayman, *The Irish Times*. **48** © Ita O'Kelly, *The Irish Times*. **49** © Brian Manning, *Pros and cons of transition year*, spunout.ie **57** © 2013 National Public Radio, Inc. Excerpt from news report "A Kenyan Teen's Discovery: Let There Be Lights To Save Lions" by Nina Gregory as originally published on npr.org on March 1, 2013, and is used with the permission of NPR. Any unauthorized duplication is strictly prohibited. **59** © Scientific American **73** From *The Pursuit Of Happiness* by Douglas Kennedy. Published by Hutchinson. Reprinted by permission of The Random House Group Limited. © 2001 **76** *Experience The Doors in Los Angeles*, Discover Los Angeles, Updated on January 4th, 2018. DR **76** © "Kung Fu Kenny, King Kunta, K-Dot. Whatever you call him, Kendrick Lamar is a Pulitzer Prize winner," written by Randall Roberts, published April 16, 2018, LA Times. **86** © Eva Recinos, *Taxi Fabric Turns Cabs into Traveling Art*. Originally published in VICE: Creators, January 31, 2016 **87** Sridevi Nambiar, *The Most Iconic Street Art In Mumbai*, 26 September 2016, Culture trip. DR **88** © Andrew, *Searching for Sound: Listening to Bombay with Sandunes*, Ableton **89** Gregory David Roberts, *Shantaram*, St. Martin's Press, 2004. DR **100-101** Magazine *Movie Classic*, Mar.-Jul. 1933. DR **102** © Sasha Haines-Stiles, *Money Fashion Power*, fashionrevolution.org, 2017 **103** A Harvest of Thorns, Corban Addison © Regulus Books, LLC, Reproduced by permission of Quercus Editions Limited **134** Usain Bolt, *Faster than Lightning: My Autobiography*, HarperSport, 2003. DR **135** *A Triumph for Women*, Alaska Sport Hall of Fame. DR **136** *Doomed Expedition to the South Pole*, 1912, Eye Witness to History. DR **145** Excerpt(s) from FEVER PITCH by Nick Hornby, copyright © 1992 by Nick Hornby. Used by permission of Riverhead, an imprint of Penguin Publishing Group, a division of Penguin Random House LLC. All rights reserved. **146** © *Clement Barker's letter during WWI*, 1914. **146** James Rush, *A football was kicked out of our trenches and we played the Germans': Poignant letter recounting famous 1914 Christmas Day truce rediscovered nearly 100 years on*, 23 December 2012, Daily mail. DR **147** © *The Street Football Tournament Attracting Premier League Stars*, Courtesy of Sport Bible **149** © Sabrina Mahfouz and Hollie McNish 2017, 'Offside', Methuen Drama, an imprint of Bloomsbury Publishing Plc. **150** © Telegraph Media Group Limited 2014 **150** © Copyright Guardian News & Media Ltd 2019 **151** © Daniel Draper, Farleys **162** Sean Murray, *It was more than a building. It represented Glasgow's creative soul': my memories of the School of Art*, 17 June 2018, www.thedrum.com. DR **163** © Copyright Guardian News & Media Ltd 2018 **164** © *Scotland's Housing Crisis*, Shelter Scotland, 2015, www.scotlandhousingcrisis.org.uk. **165** *Red Road Stories Volume 1*, Mar 22, 2010, www.issuu.com. DR **172** © Copyright Guardian News & Media Ltd 2019 **173** *"There's space for everything"*: interview with Hollie McNish, By Chloe Scaling, 15.06.2018, Palatinate. DR **174** © "Strawberry Yoghurt" written by Hollie McNish © Hollie McNish and published on her YouTube channel **180** Excerpt(s) from THE SWEET REVENGE OF CELIA DOOR by Karen Finneyfrock, copyright © 2013 by Karen Finneyfrock. Used by permission of Viking Children's Books, an imprint of Penguin Young Readers Group, a division of Penguin Random House LLC. All rights reserved. **175** George the Poet, 2013. **186** https://fr-fr.facebook.com/youthvgov/ DR **187** Excerpt(s) from WE RISE: THE EARTH GUARDIANS GUIDE TO BUILDING A MOVEMENT THAT RESTORES THE PLANET by Xiuhtezcatl Martinez, copyright © 2017 by Xiuhtezcatl Martinez. Used by permission of Rodale Books, an imprint of the Crown Publishing Group, a division of Penguin Random House LLC. All rights reserved. **188** © Title: Standing Rock: The Protectors, Author: Madeline Cottingham, Publisher: Madeline Cottingham **189** *Stand Up*, Taboo, 2016. D.R. **196** © Copyright Guardian News & Media Ltd 2019 **199** © Copyright Guardian News & Media Ltd 2019 **208** © *Too Black, Too Strong* (Bloodaxe Books, 2001) Reproduced with permission of Bloodaxe Books. www.bloodaxebooks.com **209** © Marika Sherwood, *Claudia Jones, a life in exil*, Lawrence and Wishart Limited **210** *Notting Hill carnival 2018: Why the Caribbean origins of Europe's biggest street party are so important*, Georgia Chambers, The Evening Standard, 24.08.218. DR **211** © Copyright Guardian News & Media Ltd 2019 **221** *The Princess and the Bowling Ball* from THE STINKY CHEESE MAN: AND OTHER FAIRLY STUPID TALES by Jon Scieszka, text copyright © 1992 by Jon Scieszka. Used by permission of Viking Children's Books, an imprint of Penguin Young Readers Group, a division of Penguin Random House LLC. All rights reserved. **222** ©The Roald Dahl Story Company Limited **225** Copyright © 2016 Timbuktu Labs, Inc. from the book GOOD NIGHT STORIES FOR REBEL GIRLS by Elena Favilli and Francesca Cavallo published by Timbuktu. Printed by permission.

Crédits sonores

25 *Municipal Equation: episode 17*, Tony Hawk Foundation. DR **32** *The born free generation: 20-year-olds in South Africa prepare for first vote*, The Guardian. D.R. **37** *The Fall* at the State Theatre, DR **48** *Level Up: How Important Is Transition Year?* TODAY FM. DR **59** *Google science fair winner talks innovation and why girls' education is so personal, CNBC Africa*. DR **64** ©2017 National Public Radio, Inc. Excerpts from news report titled "All-Girls Teen Engineering Team Creates A Solar-Powered Tent For Homeless People" were originally broadcast on NPR's Morning Edition on June 22, 2017, and is used with the permission of NPR. Any unauthorized duplication is strictly prohibited. **72** *Hispanics in California now outnumber whites – BBC News*, BBC. DR **72** © *Thomas Steinbeck Speaks: California's Rich Diversity*, Thomas Steinbeck. **76** *Ray Manzarek in Venice*. DR **88** *Searching for Sound: Listening to Bombay with Sandunes, Ableton.com*. DR **118** *For South African artist, self-portraits reflect life, history*, St. Louis Public Radio. DR **128** ©2015 National Public Radio, Inc. Excerpts from news report titled "Narcissistic, Maybe. But Is There More To The Art Of The Selfie?" were originally broadcast on NPR's All Things Considered on July 27, 2015, and is used with the permission of NPR. Any unauthorized duplication is strictly prohibited. **135** *Libby Riddles' Iditarod Victory*, Alaska Sports Hall of Fame. DR **144** *Football's loyal fans*, BBC. DR **148** *Playing with The Boys*, BBC. DR **164** *Were they asuccessful?* BBC. DR **172** *From a whisper to a roar, Youth Speaks empowers young people worldwide*, KALW RADIO. DR **174** © "Strawberry Yoghurt" written by Hollie McNish © Hollie McNish and published on her YouTube channel **186** *Why Nearly Two Dozen Young People Are Suing the Federal Government Over Climate Change*, WBUR. DR **187** *Xiuhtezcatl Roske-Martinez, Earth Guardians speaks at UN Climate Reception, United Nations Non-Governmental Liaison Service (UN-NGLS)*. DR **188** *Native Americans Refuse Oil Pipeline, Wochit News*. DR **198** © *Food waste is the world's dumbest problem*, VOX. **198** *Anthony Bourdain Wants You to Stop Wasting So Much Food*, WBUR. DR **209** *History of Notting Hill Carnival, 1 Heart TV Channel*. DR **210** *Notting Hill Carnival: Artistic Traditions – Carnival and The Performance of Heritage (3/5), OpenLearn from The Open University*. DR **224** *100 Women 2016: UK author says updating fairy tales is important*, BBC. DR

Nous avons cherché en vain les éditeurs et les ayants droit de certains textes et photos reproduits dans ce manuel ainsi que certains audios. Leurs droits sont réservés aux Éditions Bordas (DR).

N° de projet: 10244255 - Dépôt légal: avril 2019
Achevé d'imprimer en Italie par Grafica Veneta - Trebaseleghe en avril 2019